FYNBOS: SOUTH AFRICA'S UNIQUE FLORAL KINGDOM

EDITED BY LENI MARTIN
DESIGNED BY WILLEM JORDAAN, CAPE TOWN
PRODUCTION CONTROL BY ABDUL LATIEF (BUNNY) GALLIE
DUSTJACKET DESIGN BY WILLEM JORDAAN, CAPE TOWN
MAP PAGE 10 BY ANGUS CARR; PAGE 31 BY WILLEM JORDAAN
TYPESETTING BY DIATYPE SETTING CC, CAPE TOWN
REPRODUCTION BY UNIFOTO (PTY) LTD, CAPE TOWN
PRINTED AND BOUND BY
TIEN WAH PRESS (PTE) LTD, SINGAPORE
FIRST PUBLISHED 1995
REPRINTED 1995

TEXT © UNIVERSITY OF CAPE TOWN 1995
PHOTOGRAPHS © COLIN PATERSON-JONES 1995, EXCEPT
FOR PHOTOGRAPHS SUPPLIED BY: RODNEY BORLAND
(108/5);ANTHONY BOUGHER (PAGE 37/3); CAPE NATURE
CONSERVATION (PAGES 103/3, 117/4); ATHERTON DE VILLIERS
(PAGES 72, 132/3); ADRIAN DENEYS (PAGE 48/3); JOHN
HOFFMANN (PAGE 128/3); MICHAEL MORCOMBE (PAGE 37/5);
DAVE RICHARDSON (PAGES 46/2, 128/4); PETER STEYN
(PAGES 98/6, 116/2); ZELDA WAHL (PAGES 97/4, 101/2).
COPYRIGHT FOR THESE PHOTOGRAPHS REMAINS WITH
THE OWNERS.

ISBN 1-874950-10-5

INSTITUTE FOR PLANT CONSERVATION

FERNWOOD PRESS

PUBLISHED IN ASSOCIATION WITH THE
INSTITUTE FOR PLANT CONSERVATION

P O BOX 15344 8018 VLAEBERG
REGISTRATION NO. 90/04463/07

FYNBOS

SOUTH AFRICA'S UNIQUE FLORAL KINGDOM . RICHARD COWLING . DAVE RICHARDSON . PHOTOGRAPHY BY COLIN PATERSON-JONES

THIS BOOK IS DEDICATED TO THE FRIENDS OF
THE FYNBOS, PAST, PRESENT AND FUTURE.

THE PUBLICATION OF THIS BOOK WAS SUPPORTED BY A GRANT
FROM THE PEW CHARITABLE TRUSTS. THE PUBLISHER ACKNOWLEDGES
WITH GRATITUDE THIS GRANT, TOGETHER WITH THE GENEROUS
SUPPORT OF SOUTH AFRICAN BREWERIES.

CONTENTS :

Orange *Pillansia templemannii* with a *Berkheya* species.

1, 2, 3

4, 5, 6

1 *Leucadendron sessile*
2 *Erica patersonia*
3 *Chondropetalum tectorum*
4 *Protea cynaroides*
5 *Satyrium coriifolium*
6 *Brunia stokoei*

FOREWORD The Cape fynbos is a wonder of the world. It makes up four-fifths of the Cape Floral Kingdom which covers an area of less than 90 000 square kilometres – comparable with Malawi or Portugal – and hosts 8 600 plant species, 5 800 of which are endemic. To put this in perspective, the British Isles, three and a half times larger, have only 1 500 plants, fewer than 20 of which are endemic. The whole of tropical Africa harbours 30 000 plant species in almost 20 million square kilometres – or only 3.5 times as many species in an area 235 times as large. Still more remarkable is the Cape Peninsula with its 2 285 plant species in an expanse smaller than that of London. Table Mountain alone has almost 1 500 species in 57 square kilometres. So super-special is the Cape Floral Kingdom that it has been designated one of the earth's six plant kingdoms, putting it on a par with the Boreal Forest Kingdom which covers 50 million square kilometres.

Yet this extravagance of life's diversity is little known outside South Africa (and not always within it). I lived for 24 years in Kenya, but I never enjoyed Africa's wild nature in its superlative abundance and variety until I visited Cape Town. While Serengeti contains four million wildebeest and other herbivores, and Lakes Nakuru and Naivasha each have 400 bird species, the Cape is in a league of its own. Not even the richest parts of Amazonia come close. Yet few people appreciate the wonder that is the Cape – even though many Cape plants, such as geraniums, have become household adornments worldwide. The Cape Floral Kingdom contains 526 of the world's 740 erica species, with their glorious flowers; 96 gladiolus species out of the world's 160; and 69 proteas out of 112 on earth. The Cape is indeed a global epicentre of biodiversity.

Let us celebrate, then, the principal vegetation of the Kingdom, fynbos. Trees are very rare in natural fynbos. Regrettably, though understandably, settlers of whatever sort have wanted wood for construction and fuel, so they have introduced tree species such as pines and wattles, many of which have 'escaped' from plantations and encroached into fynbos habitats. Given the present rate of tree spread, forests could take over as much as half of fynbos habitats by the end of this decade. Because the plant material of forests is much greater than that of fynbos, forests release only half as much water from upland catchments, to the detriment of the fast-expanding human communities in the naturally thirsty Cape lowlands.

Alas, the fynbos and the rest of the Cape Kingdom's vegetation are being backed into a corner, both figuratively and literally. More than 1 400 plants feature in the Red Data list as being critically rare, endangered or vulnerable – almost as many as the entire flora of the British Isles. An appalling 29 of these are known to have already become extinct. One-third of the original fynbos has already been lost to agriculture, among other forms of development, or to invasion by alien plants (mainly those darned trees), and most of the rest suffers accelerating attrition. Much wilderness habitat is already broken up into a patchwork of relicts dispersed among farmlands and urban areas. Some plant species hold out in localities of just a single square kilometre, and feature fewer than the 500 individuals often regarded as a minimum for genetic viability. One area of a mere one-twelfth of a square kilometre contains three endemic species. Another area, in the middle of a racecourse, features four endemics. Yet these areas are 'needed' for a cricket pitch, a housing site and a bus depot.

1 Angulate tortoise
2 Black eagle
3 Rock dassie
4 Ground woodpecker
5 *Felicia amoena*
6 *Watsonia angusta*, Franschhoek Pass

Of all the earth's 'hot spots' (areas with exceptional biodiversity and exceptional habitat threat) the Cape Floral Kingdom ranks among the very hottest.

Fortunately there could be better times ahead. A host of organisations, both official and private, are actively exploring the international scope for 'getting something done'. Both scientists and economists are trying to demonstrate the economic value of fynbos vegetation. The watershed values are sizeable, even if little heeded thus far. Cape Town and nearby urban communities depend for 90 per cent of their water on a 1750-square kilometre catchment. After losing much of its natural vegetation to alien invaders, the catchment produces 400 million cubic metres less water per year than it used to – an amount one-third greater than the present community consumes.

Still more important is the prospect of exploiting the flora for additional ornamental plants to meet the growing demand in export markets far afield. The Cape flora contains 1400 bulb species, only a small number of which have been used for horticulture. Just think of more than 100 pelargonium species, plus numerous gladioli and freesias, waiting to make their international appearance. Then there is the potential to harvest plant materials for pharmaceuticals and medicines. The world market in plant-based drugs, while little explored, is already worth $45 billion per year.

Most promising of all could be ecotourism. South Africa has lions and elephants aplenty, drawing half a million tourists a year. What if more of these visitors could be persuaded to extend their safaris to the Cape? Their tourist spending could eventually make plant conservation a highly competitive form of land use. Moreover, ecotourism worldwide is worth well over $100 billion a year, a total roughly the same as South Africa's gross national product. This strategy could do most of all to safeguard the floristic glories of this 0.02 per cent of the earth's land surface. Could South Africa's Rand belt, with its mineral output worth $14 billion a year, eventually be matched by the commercial muscle of the Cape Floral Kingdom?

What counts meanwhile is to publicise the splendours of the Cape and its vegetation. There can hardly be a better way to do so than through a book such as this. Sumptuous and informative, it is one of the best books I have encountered in all my quarter century as a conservationist. Reader, if you want to play your part in the conservation campaign to save a true wonder of our world, enjoy it to the full, then show it to your friends, your political representative, and anybody else who would surely want to know about one of South Africa's greatest glories.

NORMAN MYERS

VISITING FELLOW, GREEN COLLEGE, OXFORD UNIVERSITY
MARCH 1995

6

ACKNOWLEDGEMENTS Knowledge of the biology of fynbos has accumulated over many centuries. The veldlore of the San and Khoi-khoi was assimilated by the Dutch settlers and recorded in the diaries of the early travellers, collectors and field biologists. Until the middle of this century most research on fynbos was aimed at taxonomic studies of the flora and fauna. The past few decades have witnessed a massive expansion in research on the history, ecology and management of fynbos ecosystems. Indeed, more is known about fynbos than about any other centre of biodiversity in the world.

Much of the material in this book is based on the research and insights of our contemporaries: friends, colleagues and mentors. They have, over the years, generously shared their ideas and experiences with us and we would like to express our gratitude.

Firstly, we thank the following colleagues in various departments at the University of Cape Town: Nicky Allsopp, Esteban Azorin, Jaana Ball, Anne Bean, William Bond, Bruce Campbell (now at the University of Zimbabwe), Karen Esler, Elsie Esterhuysen (now retired), Tony Hall, John Hoffmann, Pat Holmes, Jenny Jarvis, Steve Johnson, Owen Lewis, Peter Linder, Mandy Lombard, Pat Lorber, Barry Lovegrove (now at the University of Natal, Pietermaritzburg), Ian Macdonald (now with WWF South Africa), Mike Meadows, Jeremy Midgley, Tony Milewski (currently working in East Africa), Eugene Moll (now exiled in Australia), Cliff Moran, Penny Mustart, John Parkington, Mike Picker, Shirley Pierce, Mike Richards, Peter Ryan, Roy Siegfried, Willy Stock, Terry Trinder-Smith, and Ed Witkowski (now at the University of the Witwatersrand).

At the National Botanical Institute we are grateful to: Neville Brown, George Davis, John Donaldson, Anthony Hitchcock, Timm Hoffman, Brian Huntley, Barrie Low, John Manning, Dave McDonald, Ingrid Nanni, Ted Oliver, Tony Rebelo, John Rourke, Mike Rutherford, Kim Steiner, Dee Snijman, Hugh Taylor and Ernst van Jaarsveld.

The following people were also generous with their information and assistance: Jan Bosch, Johan Breytenbach, Greg Forsyth, Coert Geldenhuys, Fred Kruger, Dave le Maitre, Pat Manders and Brian van Wilgen at the Division of Forest Science and Technology of the Council for Scientific and Industrial Research (CSIR); Ernst Baard, Chris Burgers (especially for providing unpublished data on cost-effective catchment management), Peter Lloyd, Christo Marais, Greville Ruddock, Mike and Ann Scott, 'S W' van der Merwe and Jan Vlok at Western Cape Nature Conservation; Charlie Boucher, Hilary Deacon, Freddie Ellis, Jan Giliomee, Jan Lamprechts, Rob Martin, Le Fras Mouton and Berty van Hensbergen at the University of Stellenbosch; Bruce McKenzie and Cornelius Ruiters at the University of the Western Cape; Gert Brits, Kobus Coetzee, Gerhard Malan and Mark Wright at the Agricultural Research Council (Elsenburg); and Di Donnelly, Tony Gordon, Rob Kluge, Mike Morris and Stefan Neser at the Plant Protection Research Institute.

From time to time overseas researchers have visited the fynbos region and provided us with a new context for assessing our vegetation, leaving behind them many novel insights. In particular, we are grateful to Martin Cody (of the University of California, Los Angeles), Peter Grubb (of Cambridge University), Jon Keeley (of the Occidental College, Los Angeles), Byron Lamont (of Curtin University, Perth), Norman Myers (independent researcher,

NAMAQUALAND

• Nieuwoudtville

• Vanrhynsdorp

GIFBERG

The fynbos region

MAJOR CONSERVATION AREAS

Olifants

• Clanwilliam
•
• Leipoldtville

CEDERBERG

KOUE BOKKEVELD

KAROO

• Piketberg

ATLANTIC OCEAN

• Saldanha Bay
• Hopefield
Langebaan Lagoon • Langebaan

Berg

West Coast National Park

SWARTLAND

GROOT WINTERHOEK
• Tulbagh
• Ceres

WITTEBERG

KLEIN SWARTBERG

SWARTBERG

BAVIAANSKLOOF

• Darling

ANYSBERG

TOUWSBERG

• Ladismith

• Oudtshoorn KAMMANASSIE

KOUGA

• Malmesbury

• Wellington

• Worcester

DU TOIT'S KLOOF

ROOIBERG

GAMKABERG
* Gamka Mountain Nature Reserve

LANGKLOOF

Gamtoos

• Paarl
BOLAND
KLEIN DRAKENSTEIN Robertson

LITTLE KAROO

OUTENIQUA

• Joubertina

JONKERSHOEK
Stellenbosch *

FRANSCHHOEK * Jonaskop
RIVIERSONDEREND

LANGEBERG

LANGEBERG

• George

TSITSIKAMMA

• Humansdorp

CAPE TOWN
• Table Mountain
CAPE FLATS

Swellendam •

Bontebok National Park

Knysna

Plettenberg Bay

Nature's Valley

• Villiersdorp
• Greyton

Breede

• Heidelberg

• Riversdale

Goukamma Nature Reserve

CAPE PENINSULA

False
Bay

Grabouw
• Caledon

OVERBERG

• Albertinia

Gouritz

• Mossel Bay

Tsitsikamma National Park

Cape St Francis

Cape of Good Hope Nature Reserve

Kogelberg *

KLEIN RIVER

• Stanford

Potberg
*

Cape Point

Cape Hangklip
Betty's Bay

Hermanus

AGULHAS
• Elim
PLAIN

• Bredasdorp

De Hoop Nature Reserve

HOTTENTOTS HOLLAND

Gansbaai

Pearly Beach

Cape Agulhas

INDIAN OCEAN

Oxford), Phil Rundel (of the University of California, Los Angeles) and Ray Specht (of the University of Queensland). We would also like to thank Norman Myers for writing the Fore-word to the book.

We have benefitted from interactions with many governmental and non-governmental organisations, exchanging information with them and, in particular, learning from them a great deal about the realities of the struggle for conserving fynbos. In this respect we are grateful to Daphne Barends, Kay Berg, Barry Heydenrych, Philip Ivey, Doug Jeffreys and Farieda Khan of the Botanical Society of South Africa; Andy Gubb and Di Wilson of the Wildlife Society of Southern Africa; Liz Ashton, Paul Britton and James Jackleman of the Cape Town City Council; and Roy Ernstzen, Howard Langley and Adam Mecinski of the Western Cape Regional Services Council. We have always enjoyed the enthusiastic support of the South African Protea Exporters' Association and wish to thank, especially, Maryke Middel-mann for her help.

The Fynbos Biome Project, a cooperative research programme started by the CSIR, ran from 1976 to 1986. This remarkably successful programme stimulated much of the excel-lent research that is summarised in this book, and the fact that it achieved so much was due in no small measure to the excellent coordination provided by Brian Huntley's team, namely Marie Breitenbach, Tisha Greyling, Margie Jarman, Diane Stafford and Pam van Helsdingen. Today, the project continues in a much-altered format as the Fynbos Forum, coordinated by the Foundation for Research Development's Danny Walmsley and chaired by Christo Marais.

There are many other people with no official affiliations who have greatly enriched our experience and knowledge of fynbos. Many of these are landowners who have welcomed us on their farms and private reserves. Others form the spirited corps of amateur naturalists and self-employed enthusiasts who have contributed so much to our knowledge of fynbos. We thank in particular Johan and Margaret Albertyn, John and Janice Albertyn, Ian and Avanol Bell, the late Irma Booysen, Jeremy and Alida Croudace, Dianna and the late Bob Durrant, Mike Fraser, Roger and Gael Gray, Ivan Harris, Liz McMahon, Walter and Ruth Middelmann, Wally Petersen, Peter Salter, Peter Slingsby, Peter Steyn, Muriel and the late Michael van Breda, and Marie Vogts.

We appreciate the assistance of a number of people who have helped us to transform our manuscript into printed pages. Shirley Pierce's perceptive editing of our first drafts greatly improved our submitted text. Our secretary at the Institute for Plant Conservation, Wendy Paisley, provided invaluable assistance in many ways during the project, as did Corlia Richardson. The production team at Fernwood Press provided excellent support: Pieter Struik advised us how to develop a marketable commodity from our wildly ambitious ideas and our editor, Leni Martin, quietly but firmly helped us to produce an accessible, accurate and logically consistent text. We are also grateful to Peter Borchert for helping us to define the book's direction at an early stage.

Financial assistance for the production of this publication came from a grant from The Pew Charitable Trusts, and generous donations by Leslie Hill and the South African Breweries.

SUURBERG

Sundays

Uitenhage

Algoa Bay
PORT ELIZABETH

Cape Recife

1

1 *Disa uniflora*
2 *Amaryllis belladonna*   2

A final word by way of preamble. This book is by no means comprehensive and there are bound to be flaws in some of our interpretations. It is the nature of scientific reasoning that knowledge accumulates by the refutation of theories about how the world works. We would welcome any observations which confirm or refute statements in this book. Please direct them to us at the Institute for Plant Conservation, University of Cape Town. And above all, have fun in the fynbos!

RICHARD COWLING & DAVE RICHARDSON

INSTITUTE FOR PLANT CONSERVATION
CAPE TOWN, MARCH 1995

PHOTOGRAPHER'S ACKNOWLEDGEMENTS My photographs in this book represent just part of an experience of the fynbos which has entranced me for most of my adult life. That experience has been shared over the years with a host of people which has included my family; other fynbos plant enthusiasts such as Gerhard Kirsten; and those working in and with the fynbos such as Mike Viviers, John Manning, John Winter, Greville and Louie Ruddock, Mark Johns, Adam Nel, Rory Allardice, Willie Julies, Tom Barry, 'S W' van der Merwe, Jaco van Deventer, Dave Osborne, Dave McDonald, Ivan Donian, Mike Brett and Phil Hockey. These people and many others have variously made free their time, expertise, companionship and hospitality. I am also grateful for the help I received from Ernita van Wyk and Berty van Hensbergen, and Jenny Jarvis in photographing a striped mouse and a Cape dune molerat respectively.

My special thanks go to Marie Vogts – doyenne of research on the fynbos who first had the idea of producing a book like this – and to Peter Borchert who kept faith with the project and, in addition, gave me support and encouragement in my mid-life career change from research scientist to nature photographer and writer.

John Rourke and Jan Vlok are longstanding and good friends who, over many years, have been unstinting in sharing with me their extraordinary conceptual and practical knowledge of the fynbos and its plants. My wife Dee has gently combined the roles of botanical consultant, companion and critic with patience and love. I am deeply grateful. Between them, these three have tempered my passion with a bit of knowledge – never a bad thing.

COLIN PATERSON-JONES

CAPE TOWN, MARCH 1995

1

1. DISCOVERING FYNBOS

What does fynbos mean to most people? To some it is the drab green that clothes the mountain slopes; to others it is the obstacle they must step on or over to reach a distant peak; and to others still it is a nuisance – vegetation which must be eradicated to reduce the fire hazard, or cleared to make way for pastures. Sadly, for most people, fynbos means absolutely nothing at all – they have simply never heard of it.

In many ways, the lack of appreciation for fynbos is understandable. At a distance it does seem uninspiring and uninviting – an expanse of hard and leathery bushes and tough, spiky grasses lashed by relentless winds in summer and blustery storms in winter. But there is beauty in fynbos, and to experience it you have to get in close, to browse among the bushes and discover the rich variety of exquisite flowers. For it is the diversity of its plants that is the most intriguing feature of fynbos. With more than 7000 species crammed into 46 000 square kilometres, the potential for discovery is endless, and there is a special excitement in knowing that you may find hundreds of unfamiliar species in a landscape that is new to you, and even, perhaps, a species as yet unknown to science.

Much of the formidable diversity in fynbos is the result of high numbers of species within the major genera. There are, for example, 526 species in the *Erica* genus, 245 in *Aspalathus*, and 138 in *Phylica*. It is little wonder that even the experts are often puzzled, with the result that taxonomic uncertainty is the hallmark of experienced fynbos botanists. Although there are those who specialise in particular groups of fynbos plants and in particular areas, no one, either now or in the past, can claim to have a working knowledge of the entire fynbos flora.

1 It is a harsh, desolate landscape that greets the half million or so tourists who each year enter the Cape of Good Hope Nature Reserve at the southern tip of the Cape Peninsula. Drab bushes line the road, large tracts of land have been recently burnt, and blackened plant skeletons among white sand and stark rocks create an uneasy impression of scorched earth in what is supposed to be a nature reserve. Somewhere along the route to Cape Point, the destination of most of the tourists, visitors may catch sight of a flash of colour: a mass of ericas in a distant vlei; a crimson watsonia at the roadside; or the post-fire flowering of *sewejaartjies*, seen here on a bleak spring day. But, in all likelihood they will be unaware that they are passing through terrain that with more than 1000 different plant species in a mere 77 square kilometres represents one of the richest concentrations of plant diversity on earth.

But don't let this diversity put you off – it is comparatively easy to learn to recognise the fynbos genera and at least the common species in your area. And besides simply identifying plants, there is a wealth of biology and ecology to observe. Many of the most interesting discoveries in fynbos natural history have been made by amateurs. All that is needed to get you started on your own journey of discovery is some basic background knowledge, and that is what this book aims to provide.

THE EARLY PLANT HUNTERS

There is a long tradition of discovering fynbos. The original inhabitants of the region, the San and the Khoi-khoi, depended on the vegetation for food and medicine, and also used it as housing material and to make weapons and prepare poisons. Their knowledge must have been extensive

to distinguish and exploit the many plants they used, and it is not unlikely that certain events in the fynbos year, such as the bulb flowering season, were important in religious and cultural ceremonies. Sadly, almost all this aboriginal knowledge on the use and appreciation of fynbos plants has been lost, and what could have been a long and unbroken chain representing the cultural importance of fynbos has been severed.

The arrival of Europeans at the Cape of Good Hope heralded the period of written, and thus widespread, appreciation of Cape plants. Indeed, such was the fascination for the area that it became the first destination outside Europe to be systematically explored by European botanists. The first illustration of a fynbos plant, depicting a dried flowerhead of *Protea neriifolia*, appeared in a book

of unusual plants written by Carolus Clusius, Professor of Botany at Leiden University, and published in Antwerp in 1605. Thus it is likely that *P. neriifolia* bears the distinction of having been the first botanical item to reach Europe from southern Africa. The Cape very quickly became renowned as a treasure chest of interesting and beautiful species, particularly among the enthusiastic plant lovers of the Low Countries, and sailors were encouraged to collect plants at what Clusius described as 'that extreme and celebrated Promontory of Aethiopia commonly called the Cape of Good Hope'.

The establishment of a permanent settlement at the Cape by the Dutch in 1652 was to initiate a new era in the scientific exploration of the Cape flora. Expeditions were mounted to explore the countryside, first in the vicinity of

2 The sixteenth century Dutch botanist Clusius referred to the cone of *Protea neriifolia* as an 'elegant thistle' and reported that it had been collected on the northeast coast of Madagascar! In fact, the specimen may well have been collected from the low sandstone hills near Mossel Bay, where *P. neriifolia* still grows.

In the early part of the seventeenth century many Cape plants, but especially bulbs, were illustrated in botanical works published in the Low Countries. Bulbs were particularly popular not only because the Dutch were passionately interested in them, but also because they were able to survive the long sea voyage to Europe. Cape Peninsula species which undoubtedly attracted the attention of Old World plant hunters were *Agapanthus africanus* (**3**) and *Gladiolus bonaespei* (**4**).

The early plant hunters at the Cape of Good Hope were astonished by the rarity of many fynbos species growing there. These two members of the protea family, *Serruria decumbens* (**1**) and *Leucadendron floridum* (**2**), are confined entirely to the southern Cape Peninsula where they grow in a few small populations.

The fynbos continues to yield species that are new to science, and always exciting to find. One recently discovered treasure that has only just been described is *Brachysiphon microphyllus* (**3**) from the Touwsberg, a remote fynbos inselberg in the Little Karoo. The genus *Vexatorella*, a colourful member of the protea family illustrated here by *V. latebrosa* (**4**), was described by Dr John Rourke as recently as 1984.

5

6

the settlement and later, under the governorship of Simon van der Stel and his son and successor, Willem Adriaan, much further afield. Simon van der Stel himself led an expedition to Namaqualand in 1685, during which he narrowly missed death after being charged by a large rhinoceros in the renosterveld near the Piketberg. Three years later a team of explorers travelled eastwards across the Overberg, Outeniqualand and the Little Karoo, eventually turning back in the Camdeboo, about 30 kilometres northwest of present-day Aberdeen. Intrepid travellers such as these brought back with them reports of plants and specimens which increasingly filled the pages of botanical books published in Europe.

The eighteenth century witnessed the expansion of the colony at the Cape, as Khoi-khoi society collapsed as a result of intrigue, war and disease. By 1752 the colonial

frontier had extended to present-day Humansdorp, virtually on the eastern boundary of the fynbos region. The early European pastoralists learnt their veldlore from the Khoi-khoi, using many fynbos plants for food and medicine and, like the Khoi-khoi, moving their stock in search of good grazing from the foothills to the coast according to the season. This connection between Khoi-khoi and settler culture, based on their common need to survive in a species-rich but infertile environment, is a fascinating but largely untold story. White nomadic farmers, known as *trekboere*, who made use of *veldkos* (food from the veld) and indigenous herbal remedies survived on the fringes of the fynbos region until as late as the 1940s. These pioneer folk, like the Khoi-khoi, must have had a deep appreciation for fynbos plants that was born out of the need to survive rather than out of scientific curiosity.

In the meantime, exploration of the Cape flora thrived under the governorship of Rijk Tulbagh who, during his term of office from 1751 to 1771, was responsible for organising several expeditions within the colony and beyond its borders, and regularly sent consignments of plants to the botanic gardens at Amsterdam and Leiden. In 1772, a year after Tulbagh's death, the appearance at the Cape of three extraordinary botanical collectors – Francis Masson (a Scot), and Anders Sparrman and Carl Peter Thunberg (both Swedes) – was to provide another major boost for the exploration of the Cape flora. All three travelled extensively in the fynbos region, carefully observing and collecting indigenous flora and fauna. They also published accounts of their travels which did much to stimulate the interest of other adventurers and natural historians, encouraging them to visit the Cape. Thunberg, who is recognised as the

The Khoi-khoi, and after them the nomadic farmers or *trekboere*, used decoctions from aromatic species such as *Eriocephalus africanus* (5) to cure chest ailments. The farmers also made the nectar from *Protea repens* (6) into a syrup which was used as a sweetener as well as a medicine to treat coughs.

1

2

3

4

'father of Cape botany', published the first comprehensive treatment of the Cape flora, *Flora Capensis*, which appeared in three parts between 1807 and 1820.

The last decades of the eighteenth and early part of the nineteenth centuries saw a massive increase in the scientific understanding of the Cape flora. Some of the great professional collectors of this period include William Paterson (who collected in the Cape from 1777 to 1779), William Burchell (1811-1815), C.L.P. Zeyher (1825-1842), J.F. Drège (1826-1834), C.F. Ecklon (1829-1832) and W.H. Harvey (1835-1842). Between 1860 and 1865 Harvey, a businessman turned professor of botany at the University of Dublin, published in collaboration with O.W. Sonder, a German apothecary and botanist, the first three volumes of *Flora Capensis: being a systematic description of the plants of the Cape Colony, Caffraria and Port Natal.*

This monumental work of seven volumes, which provided the taxonomic skeleton essential for the later scientific study of fynbos flora, was finally completed under the editorship of W.T. Thistleton-Dyer in 1933. Its compilation was made possible only through the labour of the early plant hunters, whose zeal was stimulated by boundless curiosity as well as by the financial support of benefactors (who, incidentally, paid handsomely to procure specimens for their private herbaria).

FYNBOS RESEARCH IN SOUTH AFRICA

Under British rule, after 1806, the Cape Colony expanded rapidly, as did local educational institutions which fostered an indigenous culture of botanical study. From the mid-1800s local collectors, botanists and herbaria were taking over the tasks of botanical exploration and taxonomy

that were previously the sphere of their European counterparts. Amateur botanists still played a crucial role alongside their professional colleagues, and foremost among them was Harry Bolus, a businessman with a passionate interest in orchids and ericas. He did much for the advancement of botanical education in South Africa, founding in 1902 a chair in botany at the South African College (later the University of Cape Town) which, in 1917, became the Harry Bolus Chair of Botany. He also bequeathed to the university his herbarium (now the Bolus Herbarium) and library, together with a part of his fortune for their maintenance. His niece, Louisa Bolus, became the first curator of the Bolus Herbarium where she conducted pioneering research on the Mesembryanthemaceae, or *vygies*, an unwieldy Cape family comprising more than 2000 species.

The pioneering work of the great plant collectors is commemorated in the names of certain genera and species such as *Erica thunbergii* (**1**), *E. fourcadei* (**2**), *Gladiolus pillansii* (**3**) and *Tritoniopsis burchellii* (**4**). Neville Pillans worked at the Bolus Herbarium from 1918 until 1964 and collected many thousands of specimens. William Burchell, one of the foremost collectors at the Cape Colony, had a collection of plant and animal specimens which amounted to 60 000 items, the largest natural history collection to have ever left Africa.

5

6

7

Other notable amateur botanists active in the Cape in the late 1800s and early decades of this century were Peter Macowan (a teacher), E.E. Galpin (a banker), John Muir (a doctor), Henri Fourcade (a forest surveyor) and Rudolf Marloth (a chemist). Fourcade, who was based in the Tsitsikamma where he collected intensively, had a private herbarium and an excellent library. He left all his possessions to the University of Cape Town, and the Fourcade Bequest has provided a valuable source of funds for the publication of scientific works. Rudolf Marloth was a botanist extraordinaire whose skills lay not only in taxonomy (as was the case for most botanists of his time), but also in plant geography, ecology, anatomy, economic botany and botanical education. Credited with the first scientific observations in the fynbos of seed dispersal by ants (myrmecochory), flower imitation (mimicry) and many other phenomena, he has been acclaimed as the father of fynbos natural history.

The establishment of a university botany department and a botanic garden in Cape Town in the early part of this century resulted in the recruitment of several botanists from Great Britain who were to lay the foundations of a strong tradition in the formal study of Cape plants and their ecology. Harold Pearson arrived in Cape Town from the Royal Botanic Gardens, Kew, in 1903 as the first incumbent of Harry Bolus's chair of botany at the South African College. Over a period of less than 13 years this remarkable man made great strides for Cape botany. In addition to being an active researcher and an inspiration to his students, he was the major force behind the founding of the Botanical Society of South Africa and the National Botanic Gardens at Kirstenbosch in 1913. He became honorary director of the garden and was responsible for its planning and layout, creating what has become a major international showpiece for Cape flora. The epitaph on his tomb in the cycad amphitheatre at Kirstenbosch is appropriate: 'If ye seek his monument, look around.'

Another welcome import was R. H. Compton, who arrived in Cape Town in 1919 to become the director of the National Botanic Gardens at Kirstenbosch and Harold Pearson Professor of Botany at the University of Cape Town, posts which he held for 34 years. Under his directorship Kirstenbosch achieved acclaim as a botanic garden of international importance. Compton was also responsible for initiating the *Journal of South African Botany* in 1935, the first local journal to publish scientific papers dealing exclusively with the plant life of South Africa.

Kirstenbosch, the brainchild of Harold Pearson, is a magnificent national asset and a splendid tribute to southern Africa's superb flora. A garden home to nearly 7000 species, most from the fynbos, it provides a wonderful outdoor laboratory (**5**) and a beautiful environment for the sheer appreciation of plants (**6**), as well as promoting the horticulture of fynbos species such as *Ixia viridiflora* (**7**).

In 1923 R. S. Adamson came to Cape Town from Manchester University to occupy the Harry Bolus Chair of Botany at the University of Cape Town, which he did most productively until his retirement in 1950. He was responsible for the first research undertaken on the effects of fire in fynbos, a study which no doubt influenced the development of fire management policy at the time. Adamson's best known taxonomic work is the *Flora of the Cape Peninsula*, published in 1950, which he co-edited with Captain T.M. Salter, a retired Royal Navy officer and amateur botanist.

A special word must be reserved for Margaret Levyns. Born and bred in Cape Town, she was encouraged by Professor Pearson to study botany and in 1916 took up a lecturing post at the South African College. She remained there many years, long after she was due to retire in 1945,

and in her quiet and dignified way she made an enormous contribution to our knowledge of the Cape flora, publishing numerous scientific papers on taxonomy, anatomy, plant geography and ecology. In 1929 she published a *Guide to the flora of the Cape Peninsula* and was one of the principle contributors to Adamson & Salter's *Flora of the Cape Peninsula*. Mention should be made too of the role played by Elsie Esterhuysen, a latterday collector in the old tradition who amassed more than 36 000 fynbos specimens, many of which were taken from the most remote mountain peaks.

The years since World War II have been a very active period for Cape botany. Taxonomic research has continued, and by 1984 it was possible for Pauline Bond and Peter Goldblatt to publish their remarkably comprehensive *Plants of the Cape flora: a descriptive catalogue*.

Most of this taxonomic research has been undertaken by professional botanists employed by universities and by the National Botanic Gardens and the Botanical Research Institute (which merged in 1991 to become the National Botanical Institute). Yet amateurs have continued to play an important role in the study of the Cape flora. One thinks of the late Peter Jackson (a physician, enthusiastic conservationist and author/photographer of *Wild flowers of Table Mountain*), Ion Williams (an engineer who revised *Leucadendron* and many genera in the Rutaceae), the numerous volunteer workers in the Botanical Society, and the many photographers, artists and writers who have popularised the Cape flora in a magnificent series of floral guides and illustrated monographs.

The greatest strides in our knowledge of Cape botany have been the advances over the past two decades in

1 The high peaks of the Cape mountains have yielded many hundreds of new plant species over the past few decades, largely as a result of the zeal of Elsie Esterhuysen who collected most of her 36 000 plant specimens in these habitats. Many more species may still be discovered in out-of-the-way localities such as the upper peaks of the Elandskloof Mountains near Villiersdorp, where *Erica pinea* grows.

2

3

our understanding of the ecology of fynbos. Much of this research was done under the auspices of the Fynbos Biome Project, a collaborative research venture which, in a structured way, brought together researchers from state departments and universities. Operational from 1976 to 1985, the programme also fostered amateur naturalists, conservationists, farmers and others with an interest in fynbos by encouraging them to attend research meetings and co-opting them onto specialist committees. This extraordinarily productive phase led to many new insights into the ecology of fynbos, some of which have been rapidly incorporated into policies for the wise management of the biome.

The results of the Fynbos Biome Project's research and subsequent findings have been summarised in *The ecology of fynbos: nutrients, fire and diversity* (1992), a technical book with chapters written by leading fynbos ecologists. However, although public awareness of the beauty, fascination and economic importance of fynbos has increased markedly in the past few decades, so too have the threats to fynbos, and there was an urgent need for a more popular text that, by conveying the latest scientific findings to amateur botanists and natural historians, will increase public awareness even further.

Building on a long and admirable tradition of fynbos discovery, this book is part of a larger programme of the University of Cape Town's Institute for Plant Conservation to improve awareness of the Cape flora and its component vegetation, fynbos. We have attempted, through written word and photographic image, to convey the excitement of fynbos, one of the world's most remarkable botanic wonders.

2 A recent and exciting find in the remote Gamkaberg in the Little Karoo was a new species of *Mimetes*, *M. chrysanthus*.

3 Ion Williams, an amateur botanist, revised the genus *Leucadendron* (Proteaceae), producing a monograph in 1972 with descriptions and notes on the biology and ecology of 80 species, many of which had not yet been described. One of the genus is *L. eucalyptifolium*, a handsome shrub which is found on the lower slopes and coastal flats of the southern Cape.

2

2. WHAT IS FYNBOS?

What is this vegetation that warrants so much attention? Fynbos is neither a type of protea nor any single kind of bush, but is the term given to a collection of plants (a vegetation type) that is dominated by shrubs and comprises species peculiar to South Africa's southwestern and southern Cape. Although many city dwellers have little familiarity with it, rural folk have long known fynbos for its poor grazing quality and its soils that have little agricultural value. Indeed, the vegetation's apparent worthlessness may explain the origin of the term 'fynbos'.

When the Dutch arrived at the Cape in the mid-seventeenth century they required timber for building. Table Mountain and its environs offered little in the way of exploitable forest, although there were a few small patches on the mountain's eastern slopes near Kirstenbosch and a larger area was discovered at Hout Bay. Remnants of these forests can still be seen today. The predominant vegetation on the Cape Peninsula had timber too slender or fine for harvesting, and was thus apparently given the name 'fijnbosch'. It has also been suggested that the name referred to the dominance of small- or fine-leaved shrubs. Whatever its origin, the term 'fynbos' is now firmly entrenched in popular and scientific literature, and has been enthusiastically assimilated into the cultural heritage of South Africa.

DEFINING FYNBOS

A shrubland with an unusual mixture of plant types of different shapes and sizes that botanists term growth forms, fynbos is characterised by four of these growth forms: tall protea shrubs with large leaves (proteoids); heath-like

---

1 Once widespread throughout the western and southern Cape between Clanwilliam and Port Elizabeth, today fynbos is restricted mainly to the more mountainous and inaccessible parts of the region. It comprises three main growth forms – proteoid, ericoid and restioid – all of which can be seen here on Jonaskop, in the Riviersonderend range. A fourth growth form, geophytes, is less visible as the leaves of most species die back in the dry summer months.

2 Of all fynbos groups, the proteoids have been most extensively studied as they are showy, usually conspicuous and, as cut flowers, have economic potential. Most proteoid species are killed by fire and therefore rely on seed for regeneration. Seeds are either released after ripening and dispersed by ants, or stored on the plant in woody cones and released after fire, when they are dispersed by wind. *Aulax cancellata* is one of only three species in this genus.

1

shrubs (ericoids); wiry, reed-like plants (restioids); and bulbous herbs (geophytes). The growth forms may occur in varying abundance across fynbos landscapes, and their relative proportions within an area are used to define the different types of fynbos. Whereas proteoids and ericoids may be scarce in certain fynbos types and most geophytes appear only in the wetter months, restioids are always present. Thus, the presence of restioids is the unique distinguishing feature of fynbos.

The tallest shrubs in fynbos are the proteoids, all of which belong to the family Proteaceae. They are mostly 1 to 3 metres in height, have large, leathery leaves, and include all the taller species of *Aulax*, *Leucadendron*, *Leucospermum*, *Mimetes*, *Orothamnus*, *Paranomus*, *Protea* and *Vexatorella*.

The ericoid, or heath-like, growth form comprises about 3000 species, including the 627 species of the family Ericaceae (termed ericaceous ericoids) and many of the largest fynbos genera such as *Aspalathus* (245 species), *Agathosma* (130 species), *Cliffortia* (106 species), *Muraltia* (106 species) and *Phylica* (133 species). The leaves of ericoids are small and mostly hard, with the edges rolled under.

Restioids comprise all 310 species in the Restionaceae, a family closely related to the grasses. Large genera in the Restionaceae include *Elegia* (32 species), *Ischyrolepis* (46 species), *Restio* (83 species) and *Thamnochortus* (31 species).

The final group is the geophytes and, with about 1400 species, fynbos has the richest geophyte flora in the world. Some of the larger genera are the irid *Gladiolus* (96 species), the lily *Lachenalia* (54 species) and the orchid *Disa* (53 species). The geophytes are less visible than other growth forms, however, as most die back during the dry summer months. Only after fire are nearly all the species most conspicuous, when their mass flowering displays enliven the dreary blackened landscape.

FYNBOS PLANT COMMUNITIES

Fynbos vegetation can be subdivided into a number of different categories or, to use botanical parlance, plant communities. Such communities are usually determined on the basis of their component species, but the many thousands of species in fynbos would make this a daunting task. An alternative system has been devised to classify fynbos communities according to the relative proportions of their growth forms, in particular of proteoids, restioids and ericoids. The last-mentioned growth form is

---

Proteoids encompass a wide range of shrub shapes and floral forms, as exemplified by *Protea punctata* (**1**), *Leucadendron daphnoides* (**2**), *Mimetes splendidus* (**3**) and *Protea eximia* (**4**).

With more than 3000 species, the ericoids comprise the richest growth form in fynbos, but compared with the proteoids their biology is poorly known. With one or two exceptions, the ericoids store their seeds in the soil. Examples of this growth form are *Acrostemon eriocephalus* (Ericaceae) (**5**), *Phylica plumosa* (Rhamnaceae) (**6**), *Erica cerinthoides* (Ericaceae) (**7**) and *Nebelia sphaerocephala* (Bruniaceae) (**8**).

subdivided into species belonging to the Ericaceae, termed ericaceous ericoids, and the remainder. Using this simple system, it is possible to recognise five major fynbos plant communities.

Proteoid fynbos

Easily identified by the high cover of proteoid shrubs, proteoid fynbos is a 'bushy' type of fynbos that is always taller than about 1.5 metres and can be very colourful in winter when the proteas are in flower. It occurs at low altitudes (mostly lower than 1000 metres above sea level) in the mountains and is widespread on the coastal plains, but is most common at the base of mountains where deep soils, known as colluvium, have accumulated under the influence of gravity. This soil in which proteoid fynbos thrives tends to be deep, well-drained and yellow to red in colour, and is usually more fertile than the soils in which other fynbos communities grow. The rainfall that supports proteoid fynbos is relatively low, ranging from 400 to 1000 millimetres a year.

Proteoid fynbos can be further divided into different types depending on the dominant proteoid shrubs. These are well represented in floral guides to the fynbos region and are reasonably easy to identify. In addition, most forms of proteoid fynbos are easily accessible, making this particular community an ideal starting ground for understanding different species' preferences for different environments in fynbos. Convenient areas for viewing the variations that occur in proteoid fynbos include the coastal strip between Pearly Beach and Cape Agulhas; the De Hoop Nature Reserve, including the Potberg area; Robinson's Pass in the western part of the Outeniqua Mountains; and the Swartberg Pass north of Oudtshoorn.

Restioids, all members of the southern hemisphere family Restionaceae and ancient precursors of the true grasses, comprise the growth form which uniquely characterises fynbos. Very little is known about their biology, they are very difficult to identify and are poorly described in floral guides. All members of the Restionaceae have separate male and female plants and many have ant-dispersed seeds. Some that may be seen in the Cape flora are *Rhodocoma gigantea* (**9**), *Askidiosperma nitidum* (**10**), *Thamnochortus cinereus* (**11**), and the marsh-loving species *Anthochortus crinalis* (foreground) and *Chondropetalum tectorum* (**12**).

Not only does fynbos have the world's richest flora of bulbous plants or geophytes, but also some of the most beautiful. Most geophytes belong to the lilioid families Amaryllidaceae, Iridaceae, Liliaceae and Orchidaceae, but there are also many fynbos geophytes in the daisy, geranium and oxalis families. Fynbos geophytes include *Oxalis polyphylla* (Oxalidaceae) (**13**), *Gladiolus hyalinus* (Iridaceae) (**14**), *Babiana klaverensis* (Iridaceae) (**15**) and a newly described species, *Cyrtanthus flammosus* (Amaryllidaceae) from the Baviaanskloof (**16**).

Ericaceous fynbos

Named thus because of its high cover of ericoids or heaths belonging to the family Ericaceae, ericaceous fynbos, of all fynbos types, most closely resembles the temperate heathlands of Europe. Other characteristics of this plant community are an abundance of broad-leaved sedges belonging to the genus *Tetraria* and a high cover of species belonging to the endemic families Bruniaceae, Grubbiaceae and Penaeaceae. Restioids are common but never dominant, and Proteaceae are usually shorter than 1 metre and include many *Leucadendron*, *Mimetes* and *Spatalla* species.

Ericaceous fynbos is found in permanently moist and cool environments on the seaward-facing slopes and upper peaks of the coastal mountains between Stellenbosch and Humansdorp. Many of the middle to upper slopes of the Langeberg, Outeniqua and Tsitsikamma mountains are clothed in ericaceous fynbos and at times are brightly coloured from the mass flowering of ericas. Annual rainfall for most of these areas averages about 1500 millimetres, much of which falls in summer. Relatively mild conditions are enjoyed throughout the year, although freezing night-time temperatures are regular and occasionally the higher peaks are blanketed with snow in winter. The soil comprises black, fine-grained, organic-rich sands which are very acid – not unlike the peaty soils of European heathlands.

Dry fynbos

Where soil conditions in fynbos are so dry that there is insufficient moisture to sustain shallow-rooted and drought-vulnerable restioids, the vegetation is dominated by small-leaved ericoid shrubs that are able to extract soil moisture from deep underground. Thus the driest sites support a plant community known as dry fynbos and typified by a sparse cover of almost exclusively ericoid shrubs. Although dry fynbos bears a superficial resemblance to ericaceous fynbos, its cover of ericaceous ericoids and restioids is meagre, and proteoids are also rare.

This community is most widespread in the drier, inland mountains, particularly in the northwest where, for example, it covers much of the lower slopes of the Cederberg. It is also widespread on coastal dunes, occurring even under conditions of moderately high rainfall because the young, sandy soils are poorly consolidated and they retain little moisture. On the lowlands dry fynbos merges into renosterveld and succulent karoo, and includes many species and growth forms that are typical of these non-fynbos vegetation types.

1 Proteoid fynbos is easily recognised by the high cover of tall and bushy proteoid shrubs, and different types are described according to the dominant shrubs. Shrubland dominated by *Protea laurifolia*, such as this in Michell's Pass near Ceres, extends throughout the lower slopes and plains of the western mountains to the very northern edge of fynbos at Nieuwoudtville. The waboomveld in the background is a distinctive form of proteoid fynbos characterised by the waboom and always associated with relatively fertile and deep rocky soils on drier aspects of the lower mountain slopes between the Gifberg in the northwest and Uitenhage in the southeast.

Restioid fynbos

Not all fynbos soils are suitable for the growth of woody plants such as proteoids and ericoids. In some areas, where rainfall is low but predictable, shallow-rooted herbaceous plants absorb all the moisture entering the soil, leaving nothing for deeper-rooted shrubs. In other areas, where drainage is blocked by a water-impermeable layer, too much water is the problem, and the ground remains saturated for large parts of the year. Again, these conditions are unsuitable for most woody plants, with the result that herbs predominate.

These two sets of conditions define the habitats of restioid fynbos, a community characterised by the predominance of restioids and the poor cover or total absence of shrubs, particularly tall ones. Restioid fynbos on well-drained soils is very widespread in the drier parts of the fynbos region, except in the eastern areas where the restioids are replaced by grasses. In the mountains it is most widespread on the shallow soils of the dry, north-facing slopes, and on the coastal lowlands it usually grows on deep, well-drained sands where the annual rainfall is less than 350 to 400 millimetres. Wet restioid fynbos may be found wherever water drainage is impeded for long periods, but is most common on level, low-lying areas which receive runoff from adjacent uplands.

Grassy fynbos

In the eastern part of the fynbos region – starting along the foothills of the Langeberg in a narrow band that widens eastwards to occupy much of the country from the Baviaanskloof-Kouga mountain complex to Port Elizabeth and then extends along the Suurberg to Grahamstown – a different type of fynbos exists. This is grassy fynbos, a

2 Ericaceous fynbos is a true heathland dominated by ericoids that are all members of the Ericaceae. It is impossible to generalise about the species composition of this community since it is the major habitat for the more than 500 species of fynbos ericas. Up to 12 different *Erica* species may cohabit in 50 square metres of ericaceous fynbos. It is well worth a trek to cool, moist and heathy mountains, such as the Riviersonderend range near Greyton where *Blaeria equisetifolia* flourishes, to witness this remarkable diversity first-hand.

3 The distinguishing feature of dry fynbos is its dominance by non-ericaceous ericoid shrubs. It is widespread throughout the more arid areas, especially in the northwest where species of *Elytropappus*, *Euryops*, *Diosma*, *Metalasia*, *Passerina* and *Phylica* clothe the lower slopes of the Cederberg. A relatively high cover of vygies (*Lampranthus* and *Ruschia* species) as well as annual daisies like these seen near Clanwilliam reflect the links between dry fynbos and succulent karoo.

4 Dry fynbos also grows on freely drained coastal dunes of the southern Cape like these at Goukamma, near Knysna. In these habitats ericoid shrubs such as *Metalasia muricata* (foreground) co-exist with a variety of subtropical thicket shrubs.

community in which restioids are by and large replaced by summer-growing subtropical grasses, subtropical thicket shrubs are relatively common, and proteoids are rare. It grows on the lower and northern mountain slopes and on coastal lowlands where conditions are relatively warm and dry, but is replaced by proteoid fynbos where the rainfall exceeds about 600 to 800 millimetres.

There are two possible reasons for grasses being more abundant in the east. Firstly, since the eastern region receives much of its rainfall in summer, periods of high soil moisture coincide with high temperatures in the lower-lying areas, resulting in conditions suitable for the growth of subtropical grasses. Secondly, in the more fertile soils in the east (see Chapter 3) subtropical grasses die back in the unfavourable winter season and regrow from dormant buds in spring. The cost to a plant of

investing scarce nutrients in a completely new set of leaves each year can be prohibitive in infertile soils. A lifestyle as extravagant as this can only be supported where soil nutrient levels are relatively high.

THE DRIVING FORCES

Why does fynbos grow where it does? The answer lies in the driving forces – the key physical and biological factors which govern its distribution. There are four major physical forces in fynbos: summer drought, low soil nutrients, recurring fire and wind, and their effects on shaping the appearance and lifestyles of fynbos plants and animals are discussed in detail in subsequent chapters. Biological forces are less important in fynbos and certainly less conspicuous than in other vegetation types; in savanna, for example, large mammals such as elephants can

transform a woodland landscape into a grassland one.

Summer drought and wind

Botanists have suggested that the mediterranean-type climate of cool season rain and warm season drought in the southwestern and southern Cape has been a major evolutionary force acting on fynbos plants and animals. This may well be true, but it should be borne in mind that, as the climatic patterns of the entire fynbos region show, summer drought is a variable feature, more intense in the west of the region than in the east.

The broad climatic patterns are quite simple. In the southwestern Cape, bounded by the Atlantic Ocean and the north-trending mountains from Cape Hangklip to the northern Cederberg, the winter weather is dominated by a succession of cold fronts which strike the west coast as blustery northwesterly winds bringing rain to much of the

1 Restioids predominate over woody plants in restioid fynbos, and are especially common where water drainage is impeded, resulting in waterlogged conditions throughout the wet winter months. Several species of restioids thrive in this patch of wet restioid fynbos on the Kliphuisvlakte in the Koue Bokkeveld.

area. As a front moves over the land, the wind changes to westerly and later a shower-bearing southwesterly. A southerly wind heralds the passing of the front and draws onto the land from the southern ocean a chilly stream of air that may cause snow to fall on the mountains. Then, as the front moves away, the skies clear and the southwestern Cape enjoys a few days of glorious winter sunshine before the approach of the next front, which is preceded by a warm northeasterly or 'berg' wind. This veers to the northwest, rain falls and another cycle begins. In the depths of winter, between June and August, cold fronts are a weekly occurrence, but in spring and autumn they materialise on average once a fortnight.

Summer conditions are very different, characterised by high pressure cells and southeasterly winds which carry little moisture. Resulting from the steep pressure

gradients associated with the juxtaposition of cold sea and warm land, these winds are strong and their speeds are accelerated wherever mountains or promontories extend into the ocean. Thus, some of the windiest areas in summer are Elands Bay, Cape Point and Cape Hangklip. Cape Point experiences more than a hundred days of gale-force winds a year!

The situation from the Overberg eastwards is less well defined in terms of winter rainfall and summer drought, owing to the influence of the north-south mountain chain and of the Agulhas Current. Presenting themselves as a barrier to the moisture-bearing winds, the mountains exert a profound influence on the climate of the fynbos region. In winter, when the northwesterlies are lashing rain along the west coast, it is sunny and dry in the Overberg. And in summer, when the southeasterly winds are carrying

onshore the moisture they have picked up from the warm Agulhas Current, the resultant drizzle seldom reaches the west coast. It falls on the coastal plains and the mountains between the Overberg and the eastern Cape, and gathers as cloud which hugs the higher peaks, including Table Mountain, of the north-south chain.

It is possible, therefore, to divide the fynbos region into two zones: one with a true mediterranean-type rainfall pattern of winter rain and summer drought, and one which receives rain throughout the year. The exact boundary is difficult to determine as the proportion of summer rain increases rapidly between Caledon and Swellendam, but thereafter remains fairly constant to Port Elizabeth. However, for the purposes of this book we will regard it as coinciding with the Breede River.

Where does this leave the role of summer drought

2 Ancient dunes and windblown sands along the western and southern coastlines provide an excellent habitat for tall restioids. Here the low but predictable availability of moisture enables the shallow-rooted and drought-sensitive restioids to soak up all the soil water, leaving nothing for deeper-rooted shrubs. *Willdenowia incurvata*, seen here near Langebaan, is the characteristic species of the dry restioid fynbos along the west coast from Milnerton to southern Namaqualand.

Grassy fynbos typifies eastern landscapes with their gently bevelled plateaux and rounded slopes. The combination of relatively fertile soils and summer rain promotes the growth of grasses belonging to genera such as *Diheteropogon*, *Eragrostis*, *Heteropogon*, *Themeda* and *Tristachya* which are widespread in the tropics of Africa and elsewhere. Grassy fynbos also includes many everlastings, orchids and other geophytes which thrive in the montane grasslands of the

Eastern Cape and Kwazulu-Natal. Restioids and proteoids are poorly represented, the latter comprising mainly wide-ranging species such as *Leucospermum cuneiforme*, seen here in the Baviaanskloof (**3**). Like all fynbos communities, grassy fynbos does have its share of endemic species, including the unusual daisy shrub *Oldenburgia grandis*, shown in its Suurberg stronghold (**4**).

as a determinant of fynbos distribution? It is quite clear that hot, dry summers are an important ecological factor in the true winter-rainfall zone, although their effects are tempered in the higher mountain regions which receive considerable moisture from southeast cloud. In the non-seasonal rainfall zone, midsummer is still the period of greatest stress for plants, despite the occurrence of rain. There are two explanations for this: firstly, for a number of reasons spring and autumn (and not high summer) are the periods of greatest post-frontal rain; and secondly, the hotter, windier conditions of midsummer reduce the effectiveness of rain. In conclusion, summer drought is an important factor in fynbos, but its intensity and duration vary across the landscape; only the extreme western part of the fynbos region experiences a true mediterranean-type climate. What is characteristic of

the entire fynbos region, however, is that most rain falls in the cooler months.

Nutrient-poor soils

It is remarkable that the tremendous diversity of plant life represented in fynbos should exist in soils which are notoriously deficient in all the nutrients essential for plant growth. Levels of nitrogen and phosphorus, for example, are a fraction of the amounts required to sustain agricultural crops. In a sense this has been a blessing since crop farmers shunned these barren soils, allowing fynbos to survive intact even in accessible areas. Only recently have technological advances resulted in the large-scale ploughing of fynbos-dominated land.

Fynbos soils are infertile mainly because the rocks from which they are derived are deficient in nutrients. The predominant rocks associated with these poor soils are

the quartzites and hard sandstones of the Table Mountain and Witteberg groups which form the impressive mountains of the Cape Folded Belt. The softer shales of the Bokkeveld Group, which occur on the lowland plateaux and valley bottoms, yield more fertile soils.

Most mountain soils are whitish, acid (having a low pH) sands which are both shallow and rocky. In high-rainfall areas and on steep slopes the percolating action of water leaches scarce nutrients from the soil, resulting in a bleached horizon which appears, on the cutface of a soil pit, as a whitish band about 30 centimetres deep. On the upper seaward slopes and high summits of the coastal mountains, where it is always cool and wet and where plant material decomposes very slowly, soils are black and peaty. At the base of mountains, where weathered soil material or colluvium accumulates, soils are deep,

1 The strictly winter-rainfall zone of the fynbos region is confined to its western areas, bordering on the cold Atlantic Ocean. During the midwinter months of June, July and August rain-bearing and often violent northwesterly fronts, like this one lashing the southern Cape Peninsula, occur almost every week.

yellow to red in colour and with a higher clay and nutrient content than on the upper slopes and plateaux.

On the coastal lowlands fynbos grows on a wide variety of surfaces, including the infertile and acid wind-blown sands of the west and south coasts, in soils derived from limestone, and on coastal dunes. The limestone-based and coastal dune soils are unusual in that they are alkaline rather than acid and, having been deposited by the sea, have high levels of calcium and phosphorus from the decomposition of shellfish and other marine animals. However, as is typical of alkaline soils, the high pH means that essential nutrients are bound up in forms unavailable to plants.

Fire

It is no exaggeration to say that without fire there would be no fynbos. Sweeping through the vegetation at recurring intervals and consuming everything in its path, fire can be likened to elephants in the savanna, hurricanes in the tropics and drought in the deserts. Like these elemental forces in their respective environments, it is a keystone factor in the long-term survival of fynbos and, as part of the cycle of destruction, regeneration, maturation and destruction again, is an integral part of its biology. Many of the features of fynbos plants and animals have evolved in response to fire.

Why does fynbos burn? Firstly, it is flammable; secondly, it experiences long periods when the weather is suitable for fires; and thirdly, there are numerous sources of ignition to start fires. As many hikers know, fynbos makes excellent kindling for campfires. Hot, windy conditions in summer dry out the vegetation and increase its flammability. However, fynbos may burn at any time of the year, provided that dry spells persist for a week or more. These may occur even in midwinter, when hot and dry berg winds sometimes blow for days on end.

Before humans invaded the fynbos region, fires were started by lightning or by rockfalls. Lightning-ignited fires are most frequent in autumn, when subtropical air and the thunderstorm weather associated with it penetrate the fynbos region from the northeast. Although a burgeoning human population over the last 300, and especially the last 50, years has resulted in a dramatic increase in the number of fires started by people, lightning still plays a role in initiating the fire cycle. This was demonstrated recently during a single sultry March night, when some 12 fires were ignited by lightning strikes on the slopes of the Kogelberg above False Bay.

It is not fire itself that influences fynbos but the more

2 The warm Agulhas Current which bathes the southern fynbos coast provides summer rain which allows for the penetration of tropical vegetation into the temperate fynbos region. This dune forest at Groenvlei near Knysna imparts an atmosphere reminiscent of the forests of Kwazulu-Natal's subtropical coast. Indeed, many of the forest plants, including the dominant white milkwood trees, range as far afield as the coast of Mozambique and Tanzania.

3 Limestone is an unusual substratum for fynbos since the derived sands are alkaline and not acid and have relatively high levels of phosphorus. However, the high alkalinity, the result of calcium-rich deposits from marine shellfish, ensures that most life-supporting nutrients are bound up in forms unavailable to plants. In order to colonise limestone certain fynbos plants have acquired physiological adaptations that cope with this unusual soil chemistry. The result has been the evolution of more than 100 species that are endemic to the limestones of the southern Cape coast. These include *Erica calcareophila*, which grows at Groot Hagelkraal on the Agulhas Plain.

The Cape Floral Kingdom owes its status to the very high numbers of species, genera and families which are endemic to it. Of the six endemic families, some examples are: Retziaceae (*Retzia capensis*) (**1**), Geissolomaceae (*Geissoloma marginatum*) (**2**), Stilbaceae (*Stilbe ericoides*) (**3**), Penaeaceae (*Saltera sarcocolla*) (**4**) and Roridulaceae (*Roridula gorgonias*) (**5**).

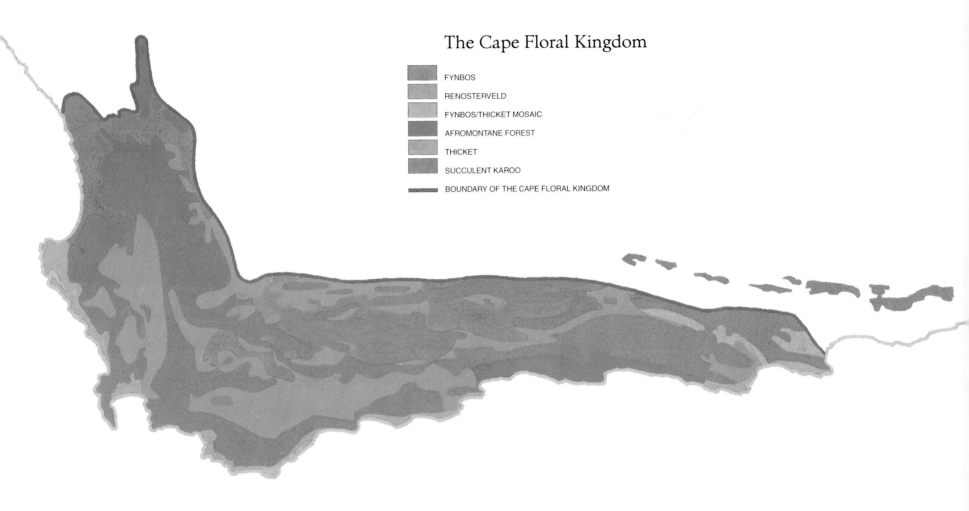

The Cape Floral Kingdom

- FYNBOS
- RENOSTERVELD
- FYNBOS/THICKET MOSAIC
- AFROMONTANE FOREST
- THICKET
- SUCCULENT KAROO
- BOUNDARY OF THE CAPE FLORAL KINGDOM

complex fire regime, an overall pattern which incorporates the frequency of fire, the season in which it burns, its intensity and the area it covers. Generally, fynbos burns at frequencies of between five and 40 years, with an average fire-free interval of about 12 to 15 years. Because most fires occur in summer and in mature vegetation with high fuel loads, they are hot or intense and, in general, they cover large areas, ranging from several hundred to many thousands of hectares.

FYNBOS, THE CAPE FLORAL KINGDOM AND THE FYNBOS BIOME

Considerable confusion has arisen over the years regarding the distinctions between fynbos, the Cape Floral Kingdom and the fynbos biome. Fynbos, as we have explained, is a type of vegetation uniquely characterised by restioids and confined to the nutrient-poor soils of the southwestern and southern Cape. The Cape Floral Kingdom is a floral province defined on the basis of the number of plant species, genera and families which grow there and nowhere else, i.e. are endemic to the area. Its extent is shown in the accompanying map. Although fynbos is the dominant vegetation type in the Cape Floral Kingdom, contributing more than 80 per cent of its species, the Kingdom also includes substantial areas of non-fynbos vegetation types. These are renosterveld, subtropical thicket, succulent karoo (in the Little Karoo) and afromontane forest (in the George and Knysna districts), and are described on pages 32 to 35. However, it does not include the isolated patches of fynbos in the Suurberg Mountains between Addo and Grahamstown.

This tiny region, covering less than 90 000 square kilometres, is home to about 8500 species of plants. What is unique for such a small area is the extraordinarily high number of endemic species, genera and families: approximately 68 per cent of the species, 20 per cent of the genera and six families. The endemic families are the Geissolomaceae, Grubbiaceae, Penaeaceae, Retziaceae, Roridulaceae and Stilbaceae. A seventh family, the Bruniaceae, is almost endemic, with only one of its 75 species not restricted to the Cape Floral Kingdom. These levels of endemism rank amongst the highest in the world and are more typical of certain islands than they are of continental areas.

The remarkable features of the Cape Floral Kingdom led botanists to classify it as one of six floral kingdoms in the world. The others, namely the Boreal, Palaeotropic, Neotropic, Australasian and Antarctic, all cover huge

areas, sometimes spanning two or more continents. Whereas the Boreal Kingdom occupies 40 per cent of the earth's surface, stretching across all the northern continents, the miniscule Cape Kingdom covers less than 0.04 per cent of the world's land surface!

What is the difference between fynbos and the fynbos biome? The highest category of plant community recognised in the world, a biome is defined in terms of climate and the dominant growth forms in the vegetation. Seven biomes (fynbos, savanna, succulent karoo, Nama-karoo, desert, grassland and forest) are recognised in South Africa. The savanna biome, for example, is recognised on the basis of moderate summer rain, dry winters and vegetation comprising a mixture of grasses and trees, whereas the succulent karoo is characterised by low rainfall in winter, very dry summers and vegetation in which dwarf

succulent shrubs predominate. The fynbos biome is defined by moderate to high amounts of winter rain and a predominance of low to medium-height shrubs, and as such includes three vegetation types: fynbos, renosterveld and subtropical thicket. It occupies an area of some 70 000 square kilometres between Port Elizabeth and Clanwilliam, with a few outlying patches to the east and north of these two towns respectively. Thus, fynbos is only one (albeit the most widespread) of the three shrubland vegetation types which are included in the fynbos biome.

WHAT ISN'T FYNBOS?

We have seen that not all vegetation types in the south-western and southern Cape are fynbos. In addition to renosterveld and subtropical thicket, which are components of the fynbos biome, succulent karoo and afromontane

forest grow alongside fynbos in the winter-wet areas of the Cape. All four of these other vegetation types grow in habitats with combinations of soil conditions, climates and fire regimes that are different from those in fynbos. Whereas renosterveld shows a strong resemblance to fynbos, afromontane forest, on the other hand, is unmistakably different. Since all who are interested in fynbos will encounter these vegetation types both in the field and elsewhere in this book, a brief overview of each is given.

Renosterveld

Although this fire-prone shrubland superficially resembles fynbos, there are three ways in which it can be distinguished: it lacks restioids; proteoids are extremely rare; and it grows in clay-rich soils that are always less sandy and more fertile than fynbos soils. Where the annual rainfall is greater than about 600 millimetres, renosterveld

1 As the landscape becomes drier fynbos gives way to succulent karoo, usually via a band of renosterveld. The flora of the succulent karoo biome is remarkably rich, comprising some 5500 species, and includes the world's richest concentration of succulents. The winter-rainfall part of the biome, centred on Namaqualand, is renowned for spectacular displays of spring annuals, such as may be seen near Vanrhynsdorp, at the northern margin of the fynbos region.

is replaced by fynbos, and where it is less than 250 to 300 millimetres succulent karoo takes over.

Renosterveld takes its name from the *renosterbos*, a member of the daisy family, or Asteraceae, which is the most abundant and conspicuous species in the vegetation type. The connection with the 'renoster', or rhinoceros, remains a mystery: perhaps the dull, grey appearance of the *renosterbos*-dominated vegetation resembled the hide of the black rhinoceros which once roamed the Cape; or perhaps these animals used to concentrate for browse and shelter in the subtropical thickets which lined the riverbanks of renosterveld landscapes. In times when rhinoceros did occur in the Cape, renosterveld was widespread on the lowlands of the west coast (Swartland) and the south coast (Overberg), but today more than 70 per cent of its extent has been replaced by agricultural lands.

Succulent karoo

The vegetation in the succulent karoo is sparse, and is dominated by dwarf shrubs, most of which have succulent leaves and are commonly known as *vygies*, or mesembs. The overwhelming abundance of succulents is one feature that distinguishes the succulent karoo from fynbos; others are a low cover of ericoids, and the absence of restioids and proteoids. Like renosterveld, succulent karoo vegetation grows mainly in nutrient-rich soils, but it is not fire-prone, its plant cover being too sparse and succulent to sustain a burn. It is restricted to areas which receive rainfall of less than 250 millimetres, predominantly in winter. The word 'karoo' is derived from the Khoi-khoi word meaning dry.

The flora of the succulent karoo matches that of the fynbos in terms of diversity, peculiarity and international

2 Renosterveld is not a particularly colourful vegetation type, being characterised by a uniform greyness imparted by the dominant ericoid shrub known as *renosterbos*. Botanists have suggested that this weedy and unpalatable plant has come to dominate renosterveld as a result of overgrazing in historical times and that in its original form, at least in the Overberg, renosterveld resembled a grassland rather than a shrubland. What is not widely appreciated is that renosterveld harbours an extremely rich geophyte flora, including this *Bulbinella latifolia* growing on the Rooiberg in the Little Karoo.
3 Subtropical thicket occurs throughout the warmer, drier parts of the eastern seaboard of subtropical Africa and a similar vegetation extends into the tropics. In the fynbos region it is most widespread in the river valleys of the east where it is known as valley bushveld. Along the south and west coasts thicket on coastal dunes, such as this near De Kelders on the shore of Walker Bay, is known as strandveld. The dominant shrubs are species of *Cassine*, *Euclea*, *Rhus* and *Olea*, and they all are of tropical rather than Cape affinity.

significance. In addition to having the highest number of plant species of any semi-arid area, the succulent karoo has the richest succulent flora in the world. It is the main home of the *vygies* which belong to the family Mesembryanthemaceae, a group of leaf succulent plants comprising more than 2000 species, and harbours many hundreds of other succulents, including crassulas, euphorbias, stapeliads, haworthias and aloes. Other special features of the succulent karoo are its rich geophyte flora and the spectacular displays of spring annuals in the Namaqualand area. Many succulent karoo plants have very restricted distributions and more than 1000 species are classified as rare and endangered.

Subtropical thicket

As its name implies, subtropical thicket is a dense, often impenetrable shrubland or low forest comprising species whose affinities lie with the subtropical areas to the east of the fynbos region. It cannot be confused with fynbos since it lacks completely the typical proteoid, ericoid and restioid growth forms, and it is generally resistant to fire. Moreover, it occurs in nutrient-rich soils, and in areas which are relatively well protected from fire, such as river valleys, rock screes and outcrops, termite mounds or '*heuweltjies*', and coastal dunes. At an annual rainfall of less than 300 millimetres subtropical thicket is replaced by succulent karoo, although it does extend into this vegetation along watercourses. Where the annual rainfall is higher than about 800 millimetres it gives way to afromontane forest.

Unlike fynbos and renosterveld plants, thicket species are not especially adapted to fire. Although many of the evergreen shrubs and low trees which dominate thicket can resprout, their foliage is not particularly flammable and the vegetation will burn only under exceptionally hot and dry conditions. They also differ from fynbos and renosterveld plants in that their seedlings establish from bird-dispersed fruits amongst mature vegetation during the intervals between fires. However, these seedlings are usually killed by fire before they grow large enough to become resistant. This explains the preference of thicket for nutrient-rich and fire-free sites: thicket seedlings grow faster where soils are richer and, in areas where fire intervals are long, seedlings can mature into fire-resistant plants. Subtropical thicket also differs from fynbos in having relatively nutritious foliage. Many of the larger mammals such as elephant and black rhinoceros that once inhabited the fynbos region would have spent much of their time browsing in this vegetation. By embodying an

The largest area of afromontane forest in southern Africa occurs in the southern Cape and is centred on Knysna, where it covers more than 60 000 hectares. These magnificent but relatively species-poor forests are either preserved or managed for the sustainable production of high-quality timber. Giant Outeniqua yellowwoods are a conspicuous feature of many afromontane forests.

ecosystem which is representative of the 'real Africa', sub-tropical thicket greatly enriches the fynbos region.

Afromontane forest

Best exemplified by the forests of Knysna and by small patches in protected gorges on Table Mountain, afromontane forest is of medium height to tall (15 to 30 metres) and evergreen. In the fynbos region it is confined to fire- and wind-protected sites with year-round moisture, growing in deep soils that are more fertile than fynbos soils. It requires an annual rainfall that is usually higher than 800 millimetres, and nearly always grows at an altitude lower than 1000 metres. Afromontane forest can be found in isolated pockets from Kirstenbosch on the Cape Peninsula, along the southern coastal mountains – such as at Grootvadersbosch – to the Knysna area of the southern Cape, where it covers more than 60 000 hectares. The forest flora is relatively small, comprising fewer than 450 species, of which about 40 per cent are trees or shrubs. Characteristic trees include the true and Outeniqua yellowwoods which often emerge above the forest canopy.

Like those of their subtropical thicket counterparts, the fruits of afromontane forest species are dispersed mostly by birds, and forest seedlings are continually establishing in adjacent fynbos and being destroyed by the next fire. However, in sites that are more fertile and better protected from fire, mature forest plants are able to develop. Because of the low flammability of forest foliage, most fires only singe the forest margin, resulting in an abrupt transition to fynbos.

As its name implies, afromontane forest is associated with the high mountains of Africa, occurring in an archipelago of small 'forest islands' from the Cape Peninsula to the Drakensberg, and thence along the east African uplands to the high plateaux of Ethiopia. It is a temperate forest type, requiring cool, moist conditions throughout the year. Since such conditions occur at lower altitudes in the more southerly latitudes at Africa's tip, the forest also occurs at lower altitudes here, growing almost to the seashore near Knysna. The major tree species are common to all forests across the continent, so that a traveller armed with a knowledge of the Knysna forest flora should be able to identify many trees on the slopes of, for example, Mount Kenya.

FYNBOS IN CONTEXT

Fynbos as an African vegetation type

Many South Africans who claim fynbos as their own would be surprised to learn that vegetation which is strikingly

There is a misconception that prior to colonial settlement afromontane forests covered vast areas along the foothills of the coastal mountains from Swellendam to Humansdorp, and that exploitation for timber substantially reduced their area. In fact, forest distribution is strongly limited by fire and only in suitable fire-free sites, like this one in the Tsitsikamma, does forest replace fynbos.

similar occurs throughout sub-Saharan Africa, Madagascar and the Mascarene Islands (Mauritius and Réunion) in cool, montane environments where rainfall is high and soils are leached, and often in association with afromontane forest. These fynbos-like shrublands include many 'typical' fynbos genera and growth forms. More than 40 per cent of the approximately 115 *Protea* species grow outside the fynbos region, and most are found in fynbos-like vegetation in subtropical and tropical Africa. Similarly, although fynbos harbours a staggering 71 per cent of the 740 described species of *Erica*, 194 occur elsewhere in Africa and on Madagascar, mostly in high-altitude heathy vegetation. Other large genera which are concentrated in the fynbos but have species which extend northwards include ericoids such as *Cliffortia*, *Muraltia* and *Phylica*, and many geophytes such as *Aristea*, *Disa*,

Gladiolus and *Hesperantha*. However, only about four species of Restionaceae grow in tropical Africa.

It is possible, therefore, to find landscapes in tropical Africa which bear a strong resemblance to those of the fynbos region. Patches of afromontane forest occur in a matrix of heathy shrubland, with proteas, ericas and other ericoid shrubs, and colourful bulbs growing alongside temperate grasses. Is this not fynbos? Not quite – the restioids are missing. But this does not deny the strong links between fynbos and similar vegetation in Africa. In a sense, the plant community grassy fynbos acts as a bridge between 'Cape' and 'African' fynbos. Indeed, it is appropriate to view fynbos as an African vegetation type which has its maximum expression, in terms of area covered and species density, in the southwestern Cape, at the southern extremity of the continent.

Fynbos as a mediterranean-type ecosystem

The fynbos region is often described as one of the five mediterranean-climate ecosystems of the world, the others being the Mediterranean Basin itself, coastal California, central Chile and southwestern Australia. Like fynbos, these areas are very rich in plant species and harbour numerous endemics. Their predominant vegetation is an evergreen, fire-prone shrubland that is termed *maquis* and *garrigue* in the Mediterranean Basin, chaparral in California, *matorral* in Chile, kwongan in Australia and, of course, fynbos in South Africa. The vegetation of these widely scattered areas is strikingly similar: a response to the comparable ecological conditions – winter rain, summer drought and periodic fire – experienced in them. It demonstrates the phenomenon known as convergent evolution, whereby unrelated plants and animals subject

---

1 An excellent example of rich extra-Cape fynbos with a large endemic flora can be found in the Chimanimani Mountains of eastern Zimbabwe. The soils there are infertile sands derived from ancient quartzites, providing a stronghold for numerous locally endemic species belonging to fynbos genera. *Leucospermum saxosum* is a typical fynbos species of Chimanimani.

2 Proteas are common throughout subtropical and tropical Africa, where they grow mainly on infertile and sandy soils similar to those which mantle the Cape mountains. *Protea dracomontana* is a colourful emergent in the subalpine grassland of the Natal Drakensberg.

to similar ecological conditions show a similarity in appearance and lifestyle.

On closer scrutiny, it is apparent that two of these mediterranean-climate ecosystems, namely fynbos and kwongan, show particularly strong similarities. Whereas the other shrublands usually comprise a single layer of large-leaved shrubs which form a dense canopy, fynbos and kwongan have an additional lower layer of ericoid shrubs and restioids. In fynbos the upper layer is dominated by proteoid shrubs, and in kwongan by a mixture of proteoids and *Eucalyptus* shrubs called mallees. Kwongan proteoids resemble very closely those in fynbos, but many belong to a subfamily of the Proteaceae, the Grevillioideae, which is represented by only one species in Africa: *Brabejum stellatifolium*, a tree of Cape afromontane forests known as wild almond. *Banksia*, *Dryandra*,

Grevillea and *Hakea* are all proteoid genera represented in kwongan. The ericoid layer is mainly made up of heath-like members of the eucalyptus family, but also include many species belonging to the Epacridaceae, a family closely related to the Ericaceae. As in fynbos, kwongan restioids are members of the Restionaceae, although no genera are shared between the shrublands of the two continents.

There are a number of additional similarities or convergences which set fynbos and kwongan apart from the other mediterranean-climate shrublands. Both boast a wealth of geophytes, but few annuals; in both there are few shrubs which establish seedlings from bird-dispersed fruits in the periods between fires; both have the highest incidence in the world of shrubs which store seeds in cones on the canopy (serotiny) and of shrubs with seeds

which are dispersed by ants (myrmecochory); both harbour a high number of shrub species which do not resprout, but are killed by fire; and both are home to large numbers of species which produce copious nectar and are pollinated by birds or mammals (rodents in fynbos and marsupials in kwongan).

Why do fynbos and kwongan show such strong convergent evolution and differ in so many respects from the other mediterranean-type shrublands? Although all five shrublands share winter rain and summer drought conditions, fynbos and kwongan have an additional common factor: they both grow in soils which are extremely poor in nutrients. This nutrient poverty results in similarly high flammability of the vegetation of both areas, and this in turn leads to more frequent fires in fynbos and kwongan than in the other mediterranean-type shrublands. Thus,

3 As a result of convergent evolution, the kwongan which grows on nutrient-poor soils in the winter-rainfall region of southwestern Australia is almost identical in appearance to the fynbos of South Africa's southwestern Cape which thrives under similar conditions. In the Barrens region, where the environment is almost identical to that of the Agulhas Plain, mallee shrubs of the eucalyptus family (foreground) grow alongside a *Banksia* species (Proteaceae).

Not only do kwongan and fynbos organisms look similar, but they also perform similar functions. On both continents the large proteoid shrubs produce copious nectar and are pollinated by birds: an orangebreasted sunbird on the fynbos species *Protea aurea* (**4**) and a New Holland honeyeater on the kwongan proteoid *Banksia menziesii* (**5**).

two powerful ecological selective forces interact and combine to produce similar evolutionary pathways.

FYNBOS BIODIVERSITY

With more than 7000 plant species crammed into 46 000 square kilometres, biodiversity at the species level in fynbos vegetation is the highest in the world. The Cape Peninsula alone hosts, at the latest count, 2285 plant species in an area less than a hundredth the size of the British Isles, in which only 1400 different plant species grow.

Yet fynbos landscapes are not uniformly rich in plant species. In the winter-rainfall areas (to the west of the Breede River) they support, on average, twice as many species as similar-sized landscapes in the eastern, non-seasonal rainfall zone. A patch of mountainside in the Kogelberg will have twice the number of species of an

equivalent area, sharing similar soils and rainfall, in the Outeniqua Mountains. Indeed, in terms of plant species richness, the Kogelberg may be regarded as the heart of the Cape flora, for a 240-square kilometre landscape there is home to 98 species of *Erica* alone. This figure is almost certainly the highest species density for any plant genus in the world. On the other hand, the entire George district, which is about ten times larger than the Kogelberg landscape and includes the extensive ericaceous fynbos of the wet Outeniqua Mountains, harbours some 63 *Erica* species. A similar pattern of decreasing species numbers away from the southwestern winter-rainfall region exists for all the larger fynbos genera and has intrigued botanists for decades. What explains it? In order to answer this question we must understand the ways in which species are packed into, or accommodated in, a landscape.

Biodiversity at the species level can be measured in three different ways. The first, termed alpha diversity, refers to the number of species in a community, usually measured as a sample plot of 1000 square metres. The second, beta diversity, reflects the amount of change in species composition in plant communities along a gradient, such as a mountain slope with changing conditions of soil or rainfall. Finally, gamma diversity reflects the change in species composition in the same environment but in different geographical locations. For example, measures are made of the change in the species composition in plots on two different mountain peaks with similar soils and climate. When all three measures of diversity are high – i.e. when species-rich communities (high alpha diversity) show large changes along environmental gradients (high beta diversity) and across geographical

1 The Kogelberg is the heart of the fynbos flora, where 1417 species are known to be crammed into a mere 240 square kilometres. This enormous diversity results largely from the rapid change in species composition along habitat gradients of changing chemical and moisture conditions in the soil (beta diversity) and a similarly rapid change between different locations of the same habitat, such as different mountain peaks (gamma diversity). These levels of diversity are amongst the highest recorded anywhere. *Mimetes hottentoticus* is confined to just two peaks of the Kogelberg's botanical treasure chest.

gradients (high gamma diversity) – the landscapes are exceptionally rich in species.

Alpha diversity in fynbos averages about 65 species in a 1000-square metre plot and, interestingly enough, this value shows little change across the fynbos region. This means that communities in the Kogelberg have, on average, the same number of species as communities in the Outeniqua Mountains. Where alpha diversity does vary from one community to the next within both areas, it does so in quite a complex way. The generalisation which emerges is that the most productive sites with the tallest vegetation, invariably some form of proteoid fynbos, support fewest species. This is because the tall, dense overstorey of proteoid shrubs suppresses the lower layer of restioids and ericoids.

The change in the complement of species along environmental gradients, or beta diversity, is exceptionally high in fynbos. In the winter-rainfall zone species composition may change completely from one community type to the next. Hikers will have noticed the remarkable change in conspicuous species of Proteaceae and Ericaceae as they ascend mountains in this region, and similar patterns occur for the less showy ericoids and the restioids. The pattern for the eastern zone of non-seasonal rainfall is different: here the change in species complement is lower, averaging about 50 per cent from one habitat to the next. Whereas a subtle shift in soil conditions will result in a massive change in species in the west, the corresponding change in the east will be far smaller.

The most remarkable feature of fynbos biodiversity, in the winter-rainfall zone at least, is the enormous variation in species in the same habitats in different geographical locations – a gamma diversity that is unparalleled elsewhere in the world. A good example is the comparison between the Kogelberg and the Cape Peninsula, two regions which have a similar array of coastal and mountain habitats, soil types and climates, are separated only by the sandy Cape Flats and the waters of False Bay, and yet have less than 50 per cent similarity in species. Thus a knowledge of the Peninsula flora is only partly useful in other fynbos landscapes. It is little wonder, therefore, that even fynbos botanists tend to learn only the names of genera and some of the more widespread species! Gamma diversity in eastern landscapes is much lower than in the west, varying between 20 and 30 per cent. This means that a knowledge of the centrally located floras of the Outeniqua and Swartberg ranges will hold good for much of the remaining eastern zone.

The most spectacular component of biodiversity in fynbos is the enormous variety in flower form and colour, as illustrated by the king protea (**2**), *Disa atricapilla* (**3**), *Erica perspicua* (**4**), *Disperis capensis* (**5**), *Nerine sarniensis* (**6**), *Dilatris pillansii* (**7**), *Pelargonium* sp. (**8**) and *Aloe plicatilis* (**9**).

We can now appreciate why the southwestern landscapes are so much richer in species than those in the east: both beta and gamma diversities are much higher in the west. The ultimate explanation lies in the different evolutionary histories of fynbos in the two regions, as is explained in the following chapter.

Another aspect of fynbos biodiversity which requires some mention is the low diversity of growth forms. Nearly all the thousands of species in fynbos are shared among only four: the proteoids, ericoids, restioids and geophytes. Moreover, an unusual – and to naturalists a highly exasperating – feature of fynbos is that within each growth form the stems and leaves of the different species and genera are very similar. Any attempt to identify an erica species without its flowers is a waste of time, and even to distinguish between different genera without either

flowers or fruits requires a great deal of experience. Indeed, it is ironic that, from afar, fynbos does not look at all diverse. One may travel great distances, covering enormous changes in climatic and soil conditions, and still see the same growth forms in slightly different mixtures. Yet each change in ecological conditions is associated with an astonishing change in species.

This uniformity in growth form is in striking contrast to other species-rich areas of the world. In tropical rainforests, for example, species richness is paralleled by a high richness of growth forms: giant trees festooned with an abundance of lianas and epiphytes of all shapes and sizes tower above many layers of shade-tolerant trees, shrubs and forest-floor herbs.

For fynbos, it is in the shape and size of its flowers that its great diversity lies. The large *Erica* genus in particular

exhibits considerable floral variation, as do *Disa*, *Gladiolus*, *Leucospermum*, *Pelargonium*, and many other fynbos genera. This diversity – and indeed most fynbos natural history – is best appreciated on hands and knees amidst a tangle of restios and small-leaved shrubbery, where it is possible to appreciate the beautiful variation in flower form, fragrance and colour.

The floral beauty in the fynbos is manifested in a wide variety of plant families, including the sedge family represented by *Ficinia radiata* (**1**), the sundew family represented by *Drosera pauciflora* (**2**), the pea family represented by *Podalyria tayloriana* (**3**) and the protea family represented by the silver tree (**4**).

3. ORIGINS

How and when did fynbos originate? Do the landscapes and ecosystems in this southern corner of Africa have a recent history or are they very ancient? It is to answer questions such as these that palaeoecologists, or researchers into prehistoric ecosystems, undertake their scientific detective work, piecing together shreds of evidence from many sources to form a narrative. New evidence is continually emerging to substantiate or challenge earlier narratives. The story changes. We are never quite sure . . .

In the fynbos region palaeoecologists have studied the structure of rocks from the very oldest to the most recent; have identified the remains of plants and animals left fossilised in primeval swamps and caves and in ancient outdoor kitchens and garbage heaps; and, with varying success, they have aged their evidence, both inanimate and organic, using a variety of sophisticated techniques. The evidence is, however, fragmentary and there are large slices of time for which there is no record of ancient ecologies. Because time relentlessly destroys the residues of life, we know much more about the past 10 000 years than about the past ten million years, and before that we know very little at all. Nonetheless, we know enough to tell a story about the physical and biological history of the fynbos region.

It is a long story, covering 1000 million years, and can be divided into three parts: the long beginning; the mild middle; and fynbos's fiery birth. The long beginning covers the 885 million years between the deposition of the oldest sediments in the fynbos region and the replacement of gymnosperms by flowering plants and dinosaurs by mammals, about 65 million years ago. Over much of

The Cape mountains, made of hard and durable quartzites of the ancient Table Mountain Group of sediments, have been slowly but steadily eroded since their dramatic birth some 250 million years ago. It is difficult to imagine that the impressive peaks of the Klein Drakenstein range near Paarl are merely worn-down stumps of much loftier mountains. These rocky and eroded slopes, with their nutrient-impoverished soils, formed the cradle in which the earliest progenitors of fynbos grew.

this period there was no life on the land, and when land plants and animals did evolve, they showed little resemblance to most contemporary life forms. Our story, therefore, concentrates on the development of fynbos landscapes which, by the end of this long beginning, resembled quite closely those which we see today.

The mild middle comprises the next 60 million years, when conditions in the fynbos region were generally warm, wet and tropical. Great rainforests covered wide expanses of the region, but here and there – in swamps, in shallow soils and in locally dry sites – was evidence of a proto-fynbos. Although to begin with, climatic conditions were generally favourable for luxuriant plant growth, they slowly changed, becoming drier and less tropical. By about five million years ago conditions were relatively dry and cool, and climatic patterns began to resemble those

of today. The forest began to retreat and there is evidence that, for the first time, fire had become an important ecological factor. A further worsening of the climate resulted in the virtual elimination of the forest, a greater incidence of fire, and, in response to the lower vegetation cover, the erosion of deep soils. It was in the impoverished soils of this bleak, treeless and fire-swept landscape that fynbos was born.

THE LONG BEGINNING

The story of the fynbos landscape begins 1000 million years ago, when Africa was part of a giant supercontinent called Gondwanaland. The landmasses now known as South America, Antarctica, Australia, India, Madagascar and New Zealand, and some of the Pacific Islands such as New Caledonia, all formed part of this supercontinent,

1 During most of the past 65 million years the predominant vegetation in the present-day fynbos region was luxuriant and leafy rainforest, not unlike this afromontane forest in the Knysna area.

2 The low granite hills of the west coast are the remnants of a subdued landscape dating back some 500 million years, before the evolution of land plants. Today these same granite koppies are home to a rich flora, epitomised by this exuberant *Bulbinella elata*.

Sequence of some important events in the history of the fynbos region

	GEOLOGICAL TIME-SCALES	TIME (MILLIONS OF YEARS)	SOME IMPORTANT EVENTS
The long beginning	PRECAMBRIAN	950	DEPOSITION OF THE OLDEST SEDIMENTS BEGINS
		600	INTRUSION OF THE CAPE GRANITES
	PALEOZOIC	500	
		450	DEPOSITION OF THE CAPE ROCKS
		340	
		280	FORMATION OF THE CAPE MOUNTAINS
		215	
		140	GONDWANALAND BREAKS UP; GYMNOSPERM FORESTS IN THE FYNBOS REGION
	MESOZOIC	113	FIRST FLOWERING PLANTS
		95	PROTEACEAE POLLEN
		80	FLOWERING PLANTS DOMINATE
The mild middle	PALEOGENE	65	EXTINCTION OF DINOSAURS; TROPICAL RAINFOREST IN THE FYNBOS REGION; MAMMALS RADIATE
		35	DRIER PHASE – A PROTO-FYNBOS EXPANDS
	MIOCENE	25	RETURN OF WARM, WET CLIMATES AND TROPICAL FORESTS
		16	GROWTH OF THE ANTARCTIC ICE SHEET
		13	DEVELOPMENT OF THE BENGUELA CURRENT
		6	MARKED EXPANSION OF ICE SHEETS IN ANTARCTICA
The fiery birth of fynbos	PLIOCENE	5	FYNBOS FORMS INCREASE AND FOREST DECLINES; FIRST EVIDENCE OF WIDESPREAD FIRE
		4	CONTINENTAL GLACIATION IN THE NORTHERN HEMISPHERE; INCEPTION OF MEDITERRANEAN-TYPE CLIMATE
		3	FYNBOS IS PREDOMINANT VEGETATION
	PLEISTOCENE	1.5	GLACIAL-INTERGLACIAL CYCLES WITH A PERIODICITY OF 100 000 YEARS AND WARM INTERGLACIALS OF ONLY 10 000 YEARS
		0.5	EARLY HUMANS INHABIT THE FYNBOS REGION
		0.075	LAST GLACIAL (COLD CLIMATE). GRASSY VEGETATION ON LOWLANDS WITH MANY GRAZING MAMMALS
		0.012	
	HOLOCENE	0	PRESENT INTERGLACIAL (WARM CLIMATE). SHRUBBY VEGETATION ON LOWLANDS WITH MANY BROWSING MAMMALS

and the area which is now the fynbos region was joined to the southeastern coast of Argentina.

The basic geological pattern during this period was a series of cycles of sediment deposition, mountain building and erosion. The present-day fynbos region lay at the fringe of a large basin inundated by an inland sea, and it was beneath the gentle waters at the margins of this basin that various sediments, forming the oldest known rocks in the fynbos region, began to accumulate about 950 million years ago. In time they became fine-grained shales, sandstones and limestones – known today as the Malmesbury, Kaaimans, Kango and Gamtoos groups – which are relatively rich in essential nutrients such as phosphorus. These sedimentary rocks were then deformed and folded in a period of mountain building during which, between 600 and 500 million years ago, the Cape granites were intruded through the earth's crust.

A long cycle of erosion followed, and this ancient mountainous landscape was reduced to a low, featureless plain, save for some rolling hills bordering a coastal plain between Piketberg and Worcester. In later times most of the rocks forming these hills were covered by younger sediments, but subsequent erosion and faulting has exposed them in places. Today they form important features in the fynbos landscape, including the wheat-covered plains of the Swartland (on Malmesbury shale), the Darling hills and Paarl Rock (on Cape granite), and the Cango Caves (on Kango limestone).

The relatively peaceful period of erosion was brought to an end about 450 million years ago by another cycle of mountain building, erosion and deposition of new rocks. These rocks were to become a crucial factor in the birth of fynbos: they were subsequently folded and warped into the mountains that typify the fynbos region we recognise today. Called the Cape Supergroup, they comprise a massive sandwich of sediments, hard sandstone alternating with softer shale, which were deposited over a period of 110 million years. The earliest group of sediments, called the Table Mountain Group, is made up largely of sandstone and includes a single sandstone layer more than 3000 metres thick in what amounts to the biggest pile of sand in the world. The fine-grained Bokkeveld Group shales were deposited on top of the Table Mountain sediments, and on top of them came the Witteberg Group, the youngest in the Cape sequence. Like the Table Mountain Group, these last sediments are made up largely of sandstones, although bands of softer shale also occur throughout the strata.

2

By about 340 million years ago the Cape sedimentary cycle had come to a halt. The rocks which dominate the fynbos landscapes of today were in place and a period of relative stability ensued. Then began the most dramatic period in fynbos history: the creation of the Cape Fold Mountains and, with them, the familiar mountainous fynbos landscapes. In the building of the Cape mountains, between 280 and 215 million years ago, the massive piles of sedimented sand, silt and clay were thrust upwards in almost vertical folds to heights many times those of the present peaks.

Millions of years of erosion have reduced the Cape Fold Mountains to worn-down stumps – a mere vestige of what they once were. Erosion-resistant sandstone covered with nutrient-poor sandy soils form the residual mountains, and the softer shales have been reduced to the more fertile valleys and gentle coastal plains. In the southeast, where very few high mountains remain, erosion has been more pronounced because the basin in which the sediments were deposited sloped gradually eastward, with the result that the finest-grained particles accumulated in the east, forming softer, more erodible rocks.

Gondwanaland began to break up into separate southern continents about 140 million years ago. The Falkland Plateau drifted past the Cape, separating Africa from South America and opening up the Atlantic Ocean, while Africa, already resembling its modern outline, was moving rapidly northwards on a collision course with Eurasia. In the fynbos region the fragmentation of Gondwanaland resulted in faulting and the formation of a number of large basins, from Worcester in the west to Algoa Bay in the east.

1 The Cape Supergroup, the predominant rocks of the fynbos region, comprise a sandwich of sediments: layers of hard quartzite and sandstone alternate with bands of softer shale. Even within rocks of the predominantly quartzitic Table Mountain Group, such as may be seen on the Cape Peninsula, narrow bands of shale are evident.

2 The building of the Cape mountains occurred in a violent and dramatic period in the history of the fynbos region, when massive piles of sediment were thrust upwards in almost vertical folds. The mountains at Cogmanskloof in the northern Langeberg bear mute witness to the powerful forces that created them.

3

4

Subsequent erosion of the Cape mountains led to the deposition in these basins of the pebble-rich conglomerates, mudstones and soft sandstones of the Cretaceous Sequence, rocks which have yielded many fossils that provide a glimpse of life in those ancient times. Despite a latitude of between 50 and 55°S, the climate then was probably humid and subtropical. The landscapes were clothed in tall forests dominated not by flowering plants but by gymnosperms – plants that are similar to the yellowwoods of today – and a variety of dinosaurs roamed the fern-covered forest floor. The fact that similar floras and faunas existed on all the fragments of Gondwanaland (including Antarctica) suggests that at this stage a uniquely African biota had not yet evolved.

The first flowering plants (or angiosperms) appeared in the fossil record of the fynbos region 113 million years

ago, when the breaking up of Gondwanaland was well advanced, and by 80 million years ago they were the dominant plant forms in the fynbos region. Fossils of the earliest Proteaceae have been dated to about 95 million years ago and some ten million years later the flora of southern Africa was beginning to develop its own identity. For example, in the fynbos region, unlike on the other fragments of Gondwanaland, there is no evidence of pollen of southern beech trees (*Nothofagus*). However, some elements of angiosperm flora were common to already separated fragments of Gondwanaland, and the existence of Proteaceae and Restionaceae, for example, in Africa, Australia and South America suggests that dispersal must have occurred across the relatively narrow seas between these diverging landmasses.

By the end of the long beginning the climate in the

3 In the western part of the fynbos region the mountains strike in a northerly direction, from the Hottentots-Holland to the Cederberg. On the Kliphuisvlakte north of Tulbagh the quartzites are very hard, resulting in a fiercely broken and rugged landscape.

4 The east-west trending mountains of southern landscapes have softer contours than the western mountains, largely because the sandstones have a higher clay content and are consequently less resistant to erosion. This is evident in the rounded slopes that can be seen from the Swartberg Pass, north of Oudtshoorn.

fynbos region was uniformly moist and subtropical. The landscapes resembled those of the present, except that the mountains were probably somewhat higher and, for the most part, covered in lush forests comprising a mixture of southern Gondwanan and central African species. Only the catastrophic extinction of the dinosaurs, possibly the result of a collision between earth and a meteorite, interrupted the comparative mildness of this period. At this stage many different mammal species had evolved, and plants and animals were beginning to resemble their current forms.

THE MILD MIDDLE

The period we call the mild middle spans some 60 million years, which in terms of geological time-scales is not a particularly long time. However, this was an epoch of spectacular evolution, when distinctive faunas and floras appeared on the different landmasses of the earth. Although climates were generally mild by today's standards, there was a trend during this period of increasing aridity which undoubtedly increased the tempo of evolution.

Sixty five million years ago the fynbos region was located 5° further south than at present and the climate was warmer, wetter and much less windy. Conditions were benign throughout the world, and the globe was ice-free. The uniformly warm ocean and lack of ice meant that sea levels were much higher than at present and the shoreline in the fynbos region was located near the base of the mountains, with much of the current coastal plain being inundated. Large bays extended up to 30 kilometres inland from the present shoreline at what is now Vanrhynsdorp, in the Hopefield area, on the Cape Flats, at

1 The Cretaceous Sequence comprises masses of sediments deposited in large basins formed as a result of the fragmentation of Gondwanaland about 140 million years ago. The most common sediment is a pebble-rich conglomerate derived from the erosion of a younger Cape mountain chain and deposited in fast-flowing rivers which girdled these basins. Exposures of these rocks are readily visible today in the Heidelberg/Riversdale area, the Gamtoos and Sundays river valleys, and here near Oudtshoorn in the Little Karoo, where the pebbles are embedded in a matrix of reddish silt.

2 Southern beech trees (*Nothofagus*) have a long history in the southern hemisphere and are still important members of temperate rainforests in Australia, New Zealand and South America. Curiously, there is no evidence that this Gondwanan genus ever grew on the African continent. In a temperate *Nothofagus* forest in Chile grows a sapling of a species of *Podocarpus*, a genus widespread in the temperate rainforests of Africa.

4

3

Bredasdorp and Albertinia, and in the Algoa region of the Eastern Cape. The warm, wet conditions promoted chemical weathering, resulting in the development of deep soils, often with impermeable layers or hardpans that were rich in iron and silica compounds. Deeply weathered kaolin-rich soils, such as those in the Noordhoek Basin on the Cape Peninsula, also originated in the warm and wet conditions of the mild middle period.

At the beginning of this benign phase most of the world was uniformly forested. The fynbos region was clothed in subtropical forest, with Gondwanan trees of the Podocarpaceae, Proteaceae, Araucariaceae, Casuarinaceae and Cupressaceae families (although it is interesting to note that there are currently no araucarias or casuarinas indigenous to the African continent) as well as tropical trees, of the Anacardiaceae, Caesalpiniaceae,

Euphorbiaceae and Sapindaceae families. Palms and tree ferns also occurred. Fynbos elements represented in this ancient flora included members of the Proteaceae, Ericaceae and Restionaceae, and *Cliffortia* species of the Rosaceae. Also present were members of the Epacridaceae, close relatives of the Ericaceae which are now widespread in the fynbos-like kwongan of Australia but are extinct in Africa. In general the fossil record for this period gives the impression of a Gondwanan flora being enriched by tropical elements entering from the north.

About 35 million years ago the climate became drier and cooler. Temperatures began to drop in the southern seas and cold, deep-water currents developed. It is likely that over much of the fynbos region the forested areas gave way to a drier type of woodland which may have

3 During much of the mild middle period in the history of the fynbos region, landscapes were clothed in forests which were home to species of Gondwanan affinity (like this giant yellowwood tree) and those derived from tropical Africa.

4 The warm, wet climates of the mild middle promoted chemical weathering and the deposition of hardpans rich in iron and silica. We can see the remnants of these hardpans today as the silcretes and ferricretes (also known as ironstone, laterite or 'ouklip') which cap the hills of the southern Cape lowlands and Little Karoo. In the past these hardpans were buried beneath deep soils, but by a process known as landscape inversion they have now become prominent features.

included many fynbos elements. The dry interlude lasted only about ten million years and was brought to an end by the return of warm and moist conditions more typical of the mild middle period. These supported the growth of a mixed forest of gymnosperms and tropical angiosperms, including many palms. Its most striking feature was the high number of plant forms that no longer occur in Africa but still exist on other fragments of Gondwanaland, especially Madagascar, an island separated from Africa for at least 100 million years. Other plants growing in those early Cape forests are now extinct in the fynbos region but can be seen today in the more tropical parts of southern Africa. Yet among those ancient trees there were many that resembled forms which still occur in the forest and thicket vegetation of the fynbos region, such as the Cape chestnut (*Calodendron* species), the white stinkwood

(*Celtis* species), the waxberry (*Myrica* species), the olive (*Olea* species), the yellowwood (*Podocarpus* species), the Cape beech (*Rapanea* species), the white milkwood (*Sideroxylon* species) and the cedar (*Widdringtonia* species). Although Proteaceae and Restionaceae were widespread at this time, many other forms now prominent in fynbos were rare or absent.

Between 25 and 15 million years ago an event happened that was to have a profound effect on the fynbos region: Antarctica was finally separated from South America, allowing the development of the cold circum-Antarctic Current. The giant southern continent became isolated and, surrounded by icy seas, began freezing over. The mild middle period in the evolution of the fynbos region began drawing to a close about 16 million years ago, as permanently icy conditions were established in

the deep south. By 12 million years ago climatic conditions were deteriorating worldwide. The Benguela Current was in existence and cold ocean conditions along the west coast had an aridifying effect on the entire southwestern African region. Sea levels dropped, exposing large areas of sand which, as a result of the drier and windier conditions, were blown inland as large dunefields. Nutrients were leached from these deposits, which were to become the infertile, fynbos-clad sandplains that can be seen today on the lowlands of both the west and south coasts.

The generally cold conditions were interspersed with occasional warmer phases, when slowly rising seas deposited marine sediments such as the limestones of the Bredasdorp Formation. Now covering a large area of the south coastal lowland between Stanford and the Gouritz

Throughout the warm and wet mild middle there probably existed a form of proto-fynbos in localised patches on steep and dry rocky slopes and exposed peaks which were unsuitable for forest growth. It is likely that this early fynbos comprised members of ancient fynbos families such as the Penaeaceae, now represented by *Penaea dahlgrenii* from the Langeberg (**1**) and *Brachysiphon fucatus* from the Cape Peninsula (**2**).

3 Many of the trees which grew in the ancient forests of the mild middle no longer occur in the fynbos region or elsewhere in Africa, but still thrive in the rainforests of the biologically unique island of Madagascar. These rainforests represent a living museum of a long-past era and can provide many vital clues for unravelling paleoecological mysteries.

5

6

4

River, these limestones support a distinctive fynbos flora with numerous endemics adapted to the calcium-rich and alkaline sands derived from the marine limestone rocks.

About five million years ago the coastal lowlands were covered with open shrubland dominated by grasses, restios, geophytes and, for the first time, many members of the daisy family or Asteraceae. Forest vegetation occurred both near the coast, probably on dunes, and inland, as a gallery along the riverbanks. Its composition was not unlike the mixed afromontane-subtropical forests of today. Although casuarinas were still present, the tropical forms evident in the earlier deposits of the mild middle had disappeared. The inland plains were grassy woodlands which included many fynbos elements such as proteas, ericas and many other ericoid shrubs. The abundance of fynbos forms at this time suggests

the start of the rise to predominance of the fynbos flora.

The now-extinct herbivores of this ancient landscape are what one would expect in an environment which was a mosaic of shrubby grassland and woodland. The most common rodent was a molerat (*Bathyergus* species) whose presence indicates an abundance of geophytes on which it would have fed. There were a number of medium-sized grazers of the grassland, such as buffalo, hartebeest-like antelope and a three-toed horse (*Hipparion* species). Woodland-dwelling forms included bushpigs and nyala-like antelope. Large herbivores which lived in the woodlands included two elephant-like and three giraffe-like animals. A rhinoceros, an early ancestor of the white rhino, grazed on the salt marshes and floodplain grasslands, as did a hippopotamus. But most important of all in terms of the evolution of fynbos is that this period

4 Contemporary forms which grew in the old Cape forests include the Cape chestnut, the progenitor of the modern buchus.

Towards the end of the mild middle period, about ten million years ago, the earth began to cool and vast volumes of ocean were trapped in the icy wastes of Antarctica. Sea levels dropped appreciably, exposing sheets of sand which were blown into dunes, like these at Postberg, near Langebaan (**5**). Eventually, under the influence of drier and windier climates, the sand was blown inland to form the extensive sandplains which mantle parts of the west and

south coasts. On one of these sandplains, near Leipoldtville on the west coast, grow species such as *Lachenalia mutabilis* and *Grielum humifusum* (**6**).

provided the first evidence, in the form of burnt fossil bones, that frequent fires swept through the landscape.

A few million years later browsing animals typical of densely wooded conditions declined and were replaced by a great diversity of grazers, including zebras, wildebeest, hartebeest, springbok and gazelles. In their wake came, for the first time, the carnivores of the African savanna such as lion, hunting dog and spotted hyaena. It is also at this time that the black rhinoceros, a browsing species, entered the fynbos region, suggesting an increase in the abundance of low shrubs as opposed to grassy glades and dense woodland.

THE FIERY BIRTH OF FYNBOS

Between five and two million years ago the fynbos region had begun to resemble quite closely what we see today.

Climates had deteriorated worldwide; Antarctica was icy; and in the northern hemisphere large glaciers crept across the high-latitude lands. At this time a summer-dry, mediterranean-type climate like the present one developed in the fynbos region, as rain-bearing westerlies in winter alternated with dry southeasters in summer. This period also saw the increasing importance of fire, an ecological factor which played a crucial role in the evolution of fynbos species. Out of the ashes of the primeval rainforests, fynbos was born.

The past 1.5 million years of the world's history, during which fynbos species proliferated, have been characterised by fluctuating climates. There has, however, been a distinct pattern to these fluctuations: long glacial or icehouse conditions, lasting on average for 100 000 years, have alternated with brief, 10 000-year interglacial or

greenhouse periods. During the glacial times the polar icecaps expand, temperatures drop (by 5 °C on average), wind speeds are higher and conditions are generally drier. Sea levels also drop as a greater volume of the ocean's water is bound up in the icecaps. The reverse conditions apply during interglacials. The onset of glacial climates occurs over a very short period, perhaps a few hundred years, resulting in the rapid exposure of the sea floor and the consequent erosion of sediments and movements of sand dunes. There have already been about ten such glacial-interglacial cycles and, based on this periodicity, we are currently approaching the end of a warm interglacial phase.

The general aridification of the fynbos region and the associated increase in the incidence of fire was central to the spread of fynbos and the proliferation of fynbos

Without doubt, the onset of recurring fire, made possible by the development of a summer-dry or mediterranean-type climate about five million years ago, was the most important impetus for the replacement of forest by fynbos and contributed enormously to the diversification of the fynbos flora.

plants. Recurring fires would have destroyed vast tracts of drought-stressed forest and prevented the establishment of forest seedlings, which require long fire-free intervals to develop to maturity. Fire would also have fragmented populations of fynbos plants into small and isolated subpopulations, thereby promoting the evolution of new species. Rapidly changing climates would have augmented this process, also fragmenting plant populations. However, at no time in its history was fynbos subjected to catastrophic climate changes such as the extensive glaciations which caused the extinction of entire ecosystems over much of the northern parts of Europe, Asia and North America.

The fossil record from the fynbos region over the past 1.5 million years is concentrated on the lowlands, where suitable sediments accumulated. Furthermore, because

of technical limitations, accurately dated records are restricted to the past 70 000 years. Despite these shortcomings, it is possible to provide a general picture of glacial and interglacial environments.

The pattern which emerges is that conditions during an interglacial period were similar to those of the present, with the southern and southeastern parts of the fynbos region receiving much of their rainfall in summer while the western parts remained dry during the same season. Lightning strikes associated with thunderstorms, particularly in late summer, were largely responsible for fires. Fynbos had more or less the same distribution in the mountains and on the lowlands that it has today, with the warm, frost-free conditions and summer rain in the eastern parts resulting in the establishment of subtropical thicket and afromontane forest in favourable sites.

During glacial times, however, the northward movement of the high-pressure cells and the cooler temperature of the Agulhas Current resulted in a sharp decline in summer rainfall in the southern and southeastern regions. Only occasional deep fronts deposited rain, especially on lower-lying ground. Moreover, lower sea levels (the coastal plain was some 50 to 200 kilometres wider in the Agulhas area during the coldest part of the last glacial) meant that the mountains were further from the ocean, and orographic rainfall was thus reduced. With an overall lowering of the temperature by 5 °C, frosts were probably heavy in the lowlands, eliminating the more frost-sensitive subtropical and fynbos shrubs, and snow was widespread in the mountains, even at moderate elevations. In the western fynbos region, the greater frequency of westerly fronts and associated year-round rainfall may

By two million years ago landscapes in the fynbos region almost certainly resembled those of today. A time traveller to this site on the Cape Peninsula would have found it clothed in fynbos similar in appearance to the contemporary veld, but certainly harbouring different species.

1 2

have resulted in wetter conditions than those at present.

During the last interglacial, some 125 000 years ago, the fossil record indicates that browsers similar to those of today dominated the herbivore fauna in the valleys of the Little Karoo at the foot of the Swartberg range near Oudtshoorn. However, with the onset of glacial conditions the fauna changed dramatically across the fynbos region, and during the last glacial, between 75 000 and 12 000 years ago, grazers or open country species predominated. In coastal areas of the southern Cape, which are currently dominated by forest and thicket, common species included quagga, warthog, bontebok, black wildebeest and springbok, none of which occur there today. In the Little Karoo valleys further inland the glacial fauna comprised grazers such as quagga, mountain zebra, hartebeest and wildebeest. Then, with the establishment of the current

interglacial about 12 000 years ago, woodland species became more prevalent. Only about 6000 years ago did the contemporary fauna of grysbok, steenbok, klipspringer and mountain reedbuck appear, suggesting a reduction in grass and an increase in shrubs.

These inferred vegetation changes are corroborated by charcoal remains in the Boomplaas Cave in the Little Karoo. During the last glacial Middle Stone Age huntergatherers collected mainly asteraceous shrubs for firewood, suggesting that they were surrounded by some form of dry, grassy shrubland. In warmer times Later Stone Age people collected a wide variety of subtropical thicket shrubs, including species of *Euclea*, *Maytenus*, *Olea* and *Rhus*. Sweet thorn, currently the most common valley bottom tree, was the dominant source of charcoal only from 2000 years ago.

In the western fynbos region, fossil pollen from vleis in the Cederberg suggests that fynbos has been the predominant vegetation throughout the past 14 000 years. Unfortunately, the evidence barely extends into the last glacial. This is not the case for charcoal deposits from the Elands Bay Cave on the west coast, which date back in a long sequence to more than 30 000 years ago. The contemporary vegetation on the sandstone hill adjacent to the cave resembles that of the succulent karoo, with *Rhus undulata* shrubs and a mosaic of dry thicket (*Euclea racemosa* and *Pterocelastrus tricuspidatus*) and karoo Mesembryanthemaceae growing on the coastal sands below the cave. The most recent charcoals indicate that these thicket shrubs and the mesembs were collected for fuel. However, charcoal remains from the glacial period more than 20 000 years ago were dominated by species

Periods of glacial or icehouse climates, which lasted on average for 100 000 years and occupied 90 per cent of the past 1.5 million years of the fynbos region's history, were about 5 °C colder than the alternating warmer and shorter interglacial phases. During the glacials lowland areas supported large herds of grazing animals such as the quagga (now extinct), mountain zebra, black wildebeest, hartebeest and springbok, suggesting a vegetation that was much grassier than

that of the present interglacial. Only about 12 000 years ago, when the climate became warmer, did the contemporary browsing fauna, including the klipspringer (**1**), become established. In the depths of the glacial periods snow would have been a common occurrence on the mountains (**2**), lying year-round on the upper peaks and falling regularly at low altitudes during the winter.

of, amongst others, *Podocarpus*, *Kiggelaria*, *Cassine* and *Olea*, suggesting the widespread existence of an afro-montane scrub-forest. Even under the cooler conditions of a glacial climate, considerably more rain than the 200 millimetres per annum currently recorded for the Elands Bay area would be required to support this vegetation.

The differences observed in the climates between the western and eastern fynbos regions (see the chapter 'What is fynbos?') were probably exacerbated during the glacials which occupied more than 90 per cent of the past 1.5 million years. The fact that the species richness of fynbos landscapes in the west is double that of fynbos landscapes in the south and southeast is consistent with this scenario. In the west fynbos would have persisted throughout the glacials over most of the landscape. Further east, however, it would have retreated to the higher mountains where there was enough moisture to support it, and a dry asteraceous and grassy shrubland would have grown on the lower mountain slopes and lowlands in place of the fynbos, thicket and forest which occur there today. Only with the onset of warmer, wetter climates about 12 000 years ago would fynbos have spread from the mountains to occupy the lower-lying ground. In these regions there has simply been less time for fynbos species to proliferate, so the landscapes support fewer species than in the west, where fynbos has had a long and relatively uninterrupted history.

THE ORIGINS AND AFFINITIES OF FYNBOS

We are now in a position to give some tentative answers to the questions posed at the beginning of this chapter: how old is the fynbos and where does it come from?

Some ancient fynbos species can still be found in remote mountain localities. Known as palaeoendemics, they belong to ancient plant groups that are distantly related to the contemporary flora and include: *Grubbia rosmarinifolia* (**3**) of the family Grubbiaceae; the cycad *Encephalartos longifolius* (**4**) from the grassy fynbos region; *Sonderothamnus petraeus* (**5**) of the family Peneaceae; woody members of the Iridaceae such as *Nivenia binata* (**6**), *Witsenia maura* (**7**) and *Klattia stokoei* (**8**); and another irid, *Pillansia templemannii* (**9**).

We have shown that fynbos elements appeared in the fossil record soon after the evolution of flowering plants about 100 million years ago. They became steadily more abundant throughout the 60 million years of the mild middle period in direct response to climatic deterioration during this phase. Yet it was only after the inception of summer-dry climates and the widespread occurrence of fire, about two to four million years ago, that fynbos became the dominant vegetation type in the southwestern Cape. The exposure by erosion of the deep soils which developed during the warm, wet climates of the mild middle, and the leaching of nutrients from the soils deposited during marine transgressions during the same period, promoted its expansion and diversification.

Patches of proto-fynbos have probably clung to harsh sites in the mountains for 70 million years or more, and many ancient fynbos species can still be found, often occupying a small area in remote mountain localities. Called palaeoendemics since they belong to ancient (palaeo) plant groups which are distantly related to the existing flora, many of these species belong to the seven families endemic to fynbos: the Bruniaceae (although this is not strictly endemic, since one species occurs on the sandstones of Pondoland and southern Kwazulu-Natal), Geissolomaceae, Grubbiaceae, Penaeaceae, Retziaceae, Roridulaceae and Stilbaceae.

However, the bulk of narrowly endemic fynbos species are recently evolved ones with many close relatives, and are termed neoendemics. Certain families have produced a disproportionate number of neoendemics, foremost among them being the Ericaceae, Proteaceae, Rutaceae (buchus), Rhamnaceae (phylicas), Fabaceae (especially the genus *Aspalathus*), Polygalaceae (muraltias) and Rosaceae (cliffortias). On the lowlands neoendemics are usually associated with a particular soil type, such as the Bredasdorp Formation limestones which support at least 100 endemics with very restricted distributions. In the mountains local endemics are disproportionately clustered in the wettest sites of the higher mountain peaks, often in ericaceous fynbos. This pattern is certainly evident in the Langeberg, where numerous locally endemic Ericaceae and Proteaceae occur on the highest peaks and each peak often has its very own endemic species.

An intriguing aspect of neoendemism in the fynbos flora is that these species are associated with a predictable set of biological characteristics. A neoendemic is invariably a low shrub that is killed by fire and has seeds that are dispersed very short distances, mostly by ants.

1 Most species with narrow distributions in fynbos are neoendemics, or species which have evolved since the fiery birth of fynbos a few million years ago. A large proportion of them are low shrubs which are killed by fire and belong to the Ericaceae, Proteaceae, Rutaceae and a few other families, and many have seeds that are dispersed by ants. A species fitting this profile is *Serruria cyanoides* (Proteaceae), which is confined to the Cape Peninsula.

This package of traits is responsible for the rampant speciation of these evolutionary lines. Being killed by fire, the neoendemics are vulnerable to fire-induced population crashes. After fires unsuitable for their regeneration their populations decline dramatically, with the result that they are forced through a population, and hence genetic, 'bottleneck'. In these small populations new gene complexes can appear very rapidly, resulting in new varieties or even species. This 'catastrophic' speciation is further promoted by the existence of discrete generations – since the plants are killed by fire, they cannot exchange genes with their offspring – and the short dispersal distances minimise the chance of an invasion of genes from distant populations.

If a small satellite population is growing in some habitat which is in any way unusual for the species as a whole (such as a different soil type), or if environmental conditions are abnormally harsh during its establishment phase (such as a very dry year), natural selection may result in rapid speciation. In this way, fire and changing climates probably promoted speciation of the fynbos flora to produce the spectacularly rich plant life that we see today.

A discussion of the affinities of fynbos raises the question whether the fynbos flora is of Gondwanan origin. Certainly, there are a number of families and genera in fynbos which occur today on other fragments of this former supercontinent. Foremost among these are the Proteaceae and the Restionaceae, which are particularly well represented in Australia but also occur in other parts of the southern hemisphere. However, no fynbos genera belonging to these families occur outside Africa. Of the geophytic families,

Other shrubby neoendemics include *Agathosma thymifolia* (Rutaceae) from the Langebaan area (**2**); *Erica insignis* (Ericaceae) from the Swartberg and Anysberg in the Little Karoo (**3**); and *E. occulta* (**4**), an unusual species confined to a tiny area at Hagelkraal on the Agulhas Plain. Only in the winter-rainfall zone of the fynbos region are geophytes, such as *Hessea undosa* (**5**) from the Gifberg, common among neoendemics. *Protea holosericea* (**6**), known from a single population in the high mountains near Worcester, is a good example of the many dwarf to low shrub protea species which are neoendemic. This species is related to the more widespread *P. magnifica*.

1

2

3

the Haemadoraceae, which is centred in Australia, has two fynbos genera, while certain liliaceous genera which occur in fynbos, such as *Bulbinella* and *Caesia*, also have Gondwanan distributions. Of particular interest is the irid *Dietes* which has six species, five of which occur in Africa (two in the fynbos region) and a single one on Lord Howe Island, a tiny Gondwanan fragment situated between Australia and New Zealand. Among the Cyperaceae, *Tetraria* occurs in both Australia and the Cape, and there are strong links across the Indian Ocean between certain grass groups.

The key issue in explaining these links rests with the timing of the break-up of Gondwanaland in relation to the evolution of flowering plants. The general consensus is that flowering plants evolved long after connections between Africa and Australia had been severed, and that

the Australasian-Cape connections are the products of dispersal across a considerably narrower Indian Ocean. As pointed out in the previous chapter, the similarities between Australian kwongan and Cape fynbos are the result of convergent evolution. Direct links between the Gondwanan flora and that of the fynbos region are limited to the ancient gymnosperm genera *Podocarpus* and *Widdringtonia*, the latter being closely related to many Australian cedars.

As was also shown in the previous chapter, the fynbos flora is African, with fynbos-like vegetation occurring throughout sub-Saharan Africa, Madagascar and the Mascarene Islands. As the modern flora of Africa expanded about five million years ago, fynbos-like elements in tropical Africa would have retreated into the mountains. Then, as evidence indicates, they expanded their range

during the colder and drier glacial periods, when the savannas and forests retreated. The unusual combination of nutrient-poor soils, winter-wet climates and moderately long fire cycles (of about ten to 15 years) prevented other African vegetation types such as grassland, savanna and forest from displacing fynbos from its southwestern stronghold. They penetrated the region only during warmer climatic phases on relatively fertile, fire-free and summer-wet sites, which are mainly clustered in the southern and southeastern lowlands. Thus, although the Cape flora itself is restricted to the southwestern and southern corners of the continent, it can still be considered a persistent and richly diversified example of an African flora which existed, for millions of years, alongside the ancient African rainforests. It is little wonder, then, that most fynbos genera are of African origin.

Because flowering plants evolved after the break-up of Gondwana-land, fynbos groups which are present on other southern continents must have achieved their distributions from long-distance dispersal across ocean barriers that were considerably narrower than at present. Gondwanan elements in the Cape flora include the wild almond (**1**), the only African member of the subfamily Grevillioideae in the Proteaceae, a group which is common in Australia and South America; *Bulbinella* in the Asphodelaceae, which also occurs in New Zealand and is illustrated here by *B. divaginata* (**2**); and *Dietes* in the Iridaceae, of which five species are found in eastern tropical and southern Africa (two of these extend into the fynbos region where they grow on the forest floor) and one on Lord Howe Island between Australia and New Zealand. *D. iridioides* (**3**) is shown here.

4

6

7

5

This African stock was enriched to a limited extent by temperate Eurasian species which migrated down the elevated 'plant highway' created after faulting and vulcanism had formed the uplands of eastern Africa, about 15 million years ago. Thus fynbos includes some genera, such as *Alchemilla*, *Anemone*, *Festuca*, *Ranunculus*, *Scabiosa* and *Viola*, which have their highest concentration of species in Europe and southwestern Asia. It is tempting to include *Erica* in this group, but Ericaceae pollen was recorded in the fynbos region more than 65 million years ago, suggesting a long history for this genus in Africa as well as in Europe. The fynbos flora also includes a few genera with worldwide distributions. These cosmopolitans include *Eragrostis*, *Euphorbia*, *Polygala*, *Salvia*, *Senecio* and *Myrica*.

Despite the invasion of the fynbos region by certain wide-ranging genera, it is significant that some 193 other genera are endemic to the region, this being about 20 per cent of the total. This level of endemism is unusually high and characteristic of an area which has been isolated for a long time. It reinforces the view that 'island fynbos' has provided an opportunity for the spectacular and recent diversification of an old African flora whose species and genera are now densely packed in a modern vegetation covering an ancient, worn-down landscape.

The fynbos flora includes a few members of genera which have migrated down the East African uplands from Europe and southwest Asia. These include *Viola decumbens* (**4**) and *Anemone tenuifolia* (**5**). Other genera have worldwide or cosmopolitan distributions, and they include *Polygala*, represented here by *P. recognita* (**6**), and *Euphorbia*, illustrated by the dainty fynbos geophyte *E. tuberosa* (**7**).

4. FAMINE IN PARADISE

At first glance it appears incongruous – a botanical wonderland in an area where essential nutrients are very scarce; where summer drought dries out the topsoil for months; where recurring fires raze all in their path, transforming dense shrublands into blackened, smouldering moonscapes; where howling winds pummel ceaselessly for days or weeks on end; and where the amount of plant material produced is only marginally greater than in some deserts. These are definitely not the features that most people associate with paradise.

So what makes this vegetation exceptional in such unpromising conditions and what are its important characteristics? The first thing that anyone wandering in an average patch of fynbos notices is that it is quite easy to walk around, as there is a lot of open ground. Twigs and dead leaves lie undecomposed, forming a dry layer

underfoot. The leaves of the low shrubs are small and tightly rolled-under at the margins, and those of the larger, proteoid shrubs are bigger and strap-like, and thick, hard and leathery in texture. The stalks of the restioids are tough, and their leaves are wiry. Apart from the delicate flowers, plant parts are tough, hard to the touch and they often have spiky edges. Despite the awe-inspiring beauty of its landscapes and the enchantment of its exquisite flowers, the overall impression of the fynbos environment is one of harshness – a land of adversity.

Yet it is no contradiction that fynbos plants flourish in these harsh conditions. The stress-inducing factors are, in fact, responsible not only for the hard, spiky appearance of fynbos, but also for the amazing diversity of plant species, the spectacular array of colourful flowers of so many shapes and sizes, and the weird and wonderful

Fynbos plants have to cope with the harsh realities of poor, sandy soils, relentless summer sun, periodic drought and strong, desiccating winds. The effects of these forces are evident in the openness of the vegetation and the leathery, evergreen leaves of individual plants. This harshness is most pronounced on the arid fringe of the fynbos region, where both soil nutrients and moisture are scarce. The locally endemic *Leucospermum pluridens* grows in such an environment, on the northern slopes of the Outeniqua Mountains.

interactions between plants and animals. Every fynbos plant has a unique blend of features and attributes, many of which the astute observer will recognise as variations on the theme 'adaptations against adversity'. In this chapter we explain how the infertile soils, the aridity and heat of summer, and the strong winds have moulded the rich diversity of plant life in the fynbos.

THE LIMITED LARDER

Although different plants require varying amounts and combinations of mineral elements to grow and reproduce, all plants need a basic 'cocktail' of certain nutrients. Nitrogen, potassium, calcium, phosphorus, magnesium and sulphur (the macronutrients) occur in relatively high concentrations in plants and are essential for a large number of life-sustaining processes. Several other mineral elements

(the micronutrients) occur in much smaller concentrations, but are also essential. These include iron, chlorine, copper, manganese, zinc, molybdenum and boron. Other important nutrients, among them cobalt and sodium, occur in minute concentrations and are known as trace elements.

Of the macronutrients, phosphorus is particularly scarce in fynbos, and nitrogen, sulphur, calcium, potassium, boron, copper, molybdenum and zinc are generally also in short supply. Whereas fynbos plants are adapted to cope with these deficiencies, most crop plants are not, and for this reason their cultivation is not a viable enterprise in many parts of the fynbos region.

Why should there be a dearth of nutrients particularly in fynbos? The availability of minerals for plant nutrition is influenced by many factors, of which the composition of the soils is probably the most important. Their mineral

content depends in part on the rocks from which they are derived, the quartzites and sandstones of the Table Mountain and Witteberg groups, which themselves are deficient in minerals. They give rise to sandy soils with low levels of rock-derived nutrients such as phosphorus. The large particles of these sands allow water and minerals to drain rapidly through them. The pH of the soil – its relative acidity or alkalinity – is another factor in its capacity to hold minerals. In the acidic fynbos soils, in which hydrogen ions replace the positively charged ions of essential minerals that cling to soil particles, the minerals are easily washed out and lost to plants. Soil pH also influences the solubility of certain nutrient elements, and therefore to what extent they are available to plants. For example, elements such as iron and aluminium are most available to plants under acidic conditions, whereas others such as

Most fynbos grows in almost pure, sterile sand where no agricultural crop or garden plant would survive. Yet out of this impoverished substratum emerges the exquisite beauty of *Leucospermum prostratum*, a procumbent pincushion from the southwestern Cape coast.

calcium and potassium are most available in alkaline soils.

In the chapter 'What is fynbos?' we have already seen that different levels of soil fertility influence the distribution of the different vegetation types within the fynbos biome. But soil nutrients also influence the distribution of particular species. For example, locally endemic species such as *Leucadendron meridianum*, *Leucospermum patersonii* and *Protea obtusifolia* are confined to limestone outcrops in the southern coastal areas and cannot survive on adjacent soil types which have lower concentrations of nutrients, especially calcium and phosphorus. The juxtaposition of soil types of different origins, with different nutrient levels and different sets of plant species is an important factor determining the very high regional species richness in coastal areas such as the Agulhas Plain.

Besides varying from one place to another within the

biome, the availability of nutrients at a particular site also changes markedly over time. As plants decay they constantly add to the humus, thereby changing the content of the soil, its texture and thus its capacity to hold minerals and water. In most other ecosystems the agents of decomposition, notably fungi and insects, are most active in the warmer summer months, but in fynbos at this time of the year the topsoil is at its driest. Therefore, most decomposition takes place over a short period, mainly in spring and autumn, and this results in the very slow breakdown of plant remains (or build-up of organic matter).

Fire is probably the most important factor responsible for the recycling of nutrients in fynbos. When a fynbos community reaches a post-fire age of about 35 years nutrient levels in the soil are inadequate to support the growth of most fynbos elements. Consequently the

dominant plants start to lose vigour and the fynbos becomes 'senescent'. At this stage fynbos is especially susceptible to fire which, by returning mineral elements held in above-ground plant material and litter to the soil, is an effective revitalising agent. The recycled minerals are then rapidly incorporated into the post-fire regrowth.

The increase in nutrient availability after a fire is quite marked, but its magnitude and how long it lasts depend on the pre-fire vegetation, properties of the soil and the intensity of the fire. After a very intense burn phosphorus levels are higher but the availability of nitrogen is reduced, a situation which favours the growth of nitrogen-fixing legumes. These plants, which include many *Aspalathus* species, often germinate *en masse* and form dense mats after hot fires. After two or three years, as nitrogen levels in the soil increase, they are gradually

---

1 Unlike most woody plants, many fynbos shrubs – such as this as yet undescribed species of *Lobostemon* from the Riversdale coast – have relatively short lifespans. Should fynbos remain unburnt for 25 years or longer, most of the soil nutrients essential for plant growth become bound up in plant parts and litter; growth rates decline and the plants begin to senesce and die. At this stage a fire is needed to release these nutrients back to the soil, creating a brief spurt of fertility.

Because of the low soil fertility, many fynbos plants have interesting adaptations to enhance their efficiency in foraging for nutrients. Most legumes form partnerships with bacteria which fix atmospheric nitrogen in exchange for carbohydrates from the host plant. There are 27 genera and more than 600 species of fynbos legumes, including *Otholobium fruticans* (**2**), *Indigofera filifolia* (**3**), *Psoralea oligophylla* (**4**), *Aspalathus uniflora* (**5**) and *Podalyria calyptrata* (**6**).

replaced by other fynbos species. Nutrients, therefore, influence not only where different plants occur in the landscape, but also at what stage they dominate in the post-fire succession.

Adversity – the mother of invention

Since nutrients are very scarce in fynbos, plants need to be very efficient firstly in locating and absorbing those that are available, and secondly in using them to best advantage. For the first requirement, specialised nutrient-uptake mechanisms have evolved in many fynbos plants, some of the most fascinating of which are hidden below ground – where the plants have formed symbiotic partnerships with bacteria and fungi.

The activity of free-living bacteria in the soil stimulates the production of dense clusters of rootlets in hundreds of species of Proteaceae. These rootlets, termed proteoid

roots, improve the uptake of poorly soluble ions, notably those of phosphorus, iron and manganese, from the nutrient-deficient soils. Bacteria also stimulate the production of nodules, or small gall-like outgrowths, on the roots of legumes of the family Fabaceae, enabling the host plant to absorb atmospheric nitrogen which is otherwise unavailable to it. The bacteria, which live in the nodules, possess the enzyme nitrogenase which enables them to convert atmospheric dinitrogen gas into organic nitrogen. This in turn is passed on to the plant via the nodules. In exchange for this service, the plant provides the bacteria with carbohydrates. Many species of the Fabaceae are totally dependent on these root nodules, the most striking examples being members of the very large genus *Aspalathus*.

Fungi also have symbiotic associations with plant roots

---

7 A somewhat bizarre way of coping with nutrient poverty, at least for a plant, is carnivory. The sundews, such as this *Drosera cistiflora*, trap and digest insects on sticky glandular hairs on their leaves and use the nutrients thus derived to sustain their growth and reproduction.

8 Root parasitism, or nutrient theft, is another ingenious way of coping with scarcity. Fynbos has about 100 species of root parasites, mainly in the Santalaceae, but also including the beautiful *Mystropetalon thomii* (Balanophoraceae), or *aardroos*, which derives its nutrients from roots of Proteaceae.

which are termed mycorrhizas, from the Greek for fungus-root. The fungi in this partnership absorb phosphorus and other nutrients such as calcium, potassium, sulphur and zinc from the soil, and surrender some of these to their host plant in exchange for shelter and a supply of carbohydrates. What appear to be the roots of a mycorrhizal plant are in fact a tangle of delicate fibres clutching masses of soil particles; some of the fibres are indeed plant rootlets, but others are the mould-like hyphae of the fungi. More than 75 per cent of the plant species in the Cape flora form some kind of mycorrhizal association. In many of them the fungal hyphae have completely replaced the rootlets in the course of evolution, and the plants cannot survive without them. Besides their influence on nutrient uptake, the fungi also benefit the plants by detoxifying certain substances, deterring root

pathogens and protecting the root tips from the adverse effects of highly acidic conditions.

Having absorbed what nutrients they can from the poor soil, fynbos plants are like frugal housekeepers, using the nutrients sparingly and ensuring that none are wasted. They cannot afford to produce new leaves annually, and the leaves of some proteas remain on the plant for six or more years. Thus evergreen plants are often associated with – though not entirely limited to – nutrient-poor soils, whereas plants with drought-deciduous leaves (those that are shed from the plant when drought-induced stress becomes too severe) are uncommon in fynbos. In areas with richer soils, such as the dry coastal thicket near Saldanha, plants can afford to drop their leaves in summer because they have access to good nutrient supplies for manufacturing new ones in the autumn, in

1 Like legumes, ericas form partnerships with micro-organisms in order to improve access to essential nutrients. In the case of ericas, including this *Erica pinea* growing in Du Toit's Kloof, the relationship involves a fungus which forms an association with the plant's roots, termed a mycorrhiza.

On the more fertile soils such as coastal sands, nutrient poverty is less limiting to growth than in most fynbos soils. Many of the plants which grow in these richer soils are able to shed their leaves during the long, dry summer since they can afford to grow new ones at the beginning of winter. In thicket on the west coast near Langebaan (2), *Lycium ferocissimum* is in the early stages of shedding its leaves with the onset of summer. Similar habitats on the south coast (3) support

evergreen thicket which is dominated by species that are capable of exploiting both summer and winter showers in this non-seasonal rainfall zone.

6

4

5

7

8

time for the reliable winter rains. This is not a viable option in the rest of the fynbos region, where the soils are too poor. Moreover, in the south and southeast, where summer rains do fall, it is better for the plants to remain fully equipped with leaves so that they can take advantage of the rain whenever it comes. Thus, dry coastal thickets along the south coast consist almost entirely of evergreen species.

Once they have reached maturity, many fynbos species slow their growth rate in order to reduce their nutrient requirements. The restioid *Thamnochortus punctatus* goes a stage further, withdrawing 70 per cent of the nitrogen from dying mature culms into the rest of the plant.

When it comes to reproduction many fynbos plants are more generous in their allocation of nutrients, since it is important that their offspring have the best chances to survive and thereby ensure the continuation of the species. The seeds of proteas, for example, are large and packed with nutrients so that the seedlings can establish rapidly in the post-fire environment without first having to invest resources in leaf growth. For this expenditure to be worthwhile the odds must be strongly in favour of a given seed developing into a mature plant, and a number of strategies have evolved to ensure that this occurs. One such strategy is serotiny – the storage on the plant of nutrient-rich seeds in persistent woody cones. While on the plant, seeds are not vulnerable to many predators (although specialist seed-eating insects do attack the cones). Moreover, seeds are released *en masse* after fire when the heat of the flames stimulates the opening of cones. Thus, by confining seed release to the immediate post-fire environment, scarce seed predators such as

Although fynbos plants are generally conservative in their use of nutrients, they do lavish resources on their seeds, thereby ensuring adequate seedling establishment in the dry, impoverished topsoil. The Proteaceae, in particular, produce a few large, nutritious seeds which, in the case of *Leucadendron* and *Protea*, are stored in robust and woody cones. In *Leucadendron*, a dioecious genus with separate male and female plants, since the latter (4) bear the burden of repro-

duction by supporting the large cones, they need thicker stems and, as a result of allometric scaling, have larger leaves than male plants (5). This dimorphism is evident in the wind-pollinated *L. rubrum*.

The cones of Proteaceae species are fire-proof woody structures, formed from surplus carbohydrates, that protect the seeds on the plant for several years or until the plant dies. The seeds represent a major investment of nutrients and the allocation of carbohydrates to

their protection is a cost-effective adaptation for nutrient conservation. A few months after flowering the heads of *Protea repens* (6) dry out and the bracts contract, eventually forming a brown 'cone' (7). Some cones open before the plant dies as a result of insects boring into their bases and cutting off the moisture supply from the plant. Many, however, remain closed until a fire kills the plant. The cone opens a few days later, releasing the entire crop of seeds simultaneously (8).

fire-traumatised mice are overwhelmed by a surplus of food, and the chances of survival for an individual seed are greatly improved. Furthermore, seeds germinate in an environment where there is no layer of dense vegetation which might inhibit the growth of seedlings. Another strategy to promote successful germination is myrmecochory, whereby ants carry plump and protein-rich seeds beneath the soil, out of harm's way. This intriguing story is discussed further in 'Where are the animals?'

The timing of events in the life cycles of fynbos plants has also evolved to cope with nutrient shortages. For example, the time of flowering is critical for determining when flowers are ready to be pollinated and when seeds are available for dispersal and germination. In species that rely on animals for seed dispersal, seeds are released at the time which suits their dispersal agents. Thus

species such as leucospermums, whose seeds are dispersed by ants, flower in spring so that ripened seeds are released in summer when the ants are most active.

An excess of carbohydrates

The shortage of essential nutrients in fynbos does not affect photosynthesis, since there is sufficient water and sunshine to drive the process. It does, however, affect the use of carbohydrates (a large group of organic compounds including sugars and starches), which are the product of photosynthesis. The lack of nitrogen and phosphorus in particular limits the channelling of these foodstuffs into the usual activities of plant growth and maintenance, and they are used instead in the manufacture of mechanical structures and secondary compounds, producing some of the characteristic features of fynbos.

In many cases, the excess carbohydrates are routed

to structures that enable species to survive fires. For example, carbohydrates accumulate in underground organs such as rootstocks, bulbs and rhizomes, enabling plants to resprout after fire. They are also allocated to fire-resistant structures such as the cones of many serotinous proteas.

The sclerophyllous, evergreen leaves of fynbos shrubs probably evolved because they represent a cost-effective investment of nutrients in the form of carbohydrates. Rich in fibre, wax and cutin, they are not favoured by herbivores as they are poorly digested. Large amounts of silica in the leaves of restios have the same effect. Another use of surplus carbohydrates to reduce the impact of herbivory is in the production of secondary compounds. Many fynbos plants have high concentrations of polyphenols which have deterrent or toxic properties that protect the plant from herbivores, thereby preventing the loss

---

In fynbos, species' flowering times may be determined by the activity of their seed dispersers or by other biological requirements related to their seeds. For example, *Leucospermum oleifolium* (**1**), like many other plant species that rely on ants for seed dispersal, flowers in spring so that by summer, when the ants are most active, the seeds are mature. However, most *Protea* species, such as *P. laurifolia* (**2**), flower in late autumn or winter. Instead of being dispersed by ants,

their seeds are held on the plant for much longer, even for several years in the case of serotinous species. Seeds of the proteas generally take longer to mature than those of *Leucospermum* species, and it is possible that the advantage of having mature seeds by summer, when most fires occur, has led to winter-flowering in proteas.
3 Unlike other mediterranean-climate vegetation where flowering is largely restricted to late winter and spring, many fynbos plants flower

in midsummer. There are many possible reasons for this, including a higher proportion of summer precipitation (especially in the east). Most summer-flowering plants grow at higher (and cooler) altitudes or in damp sites. Shown here growing in a seepage zone high in the Koue Bokkeveld is *Erica inflata*, with its vivid midsummer display of delicate blooms.

of precious nutrients. Tiny glands on the surface of leaves, fruits and petals contain the oily polyphenols and are often visible as small bumps on the underside of leaves. Plants with these secondary compounds, including many species of the Rutaceae, emit the pleasantly aromatic or sometimes rather pungent smells that are so distinctive of fynbos. Other fynbos plants have high levels of tannin in their leaves, another unpalatable secondary compound that effectively deters herbivores. The tannins are water-soluble and give many fynbos streams their characteristic brown colouring. Interestingly, when the catchments of fynbos streams have mainly red- and yellow-coloured soils, the tannins are strained out and the stream water is clear.

By reducing herbivory, secondary compounds indirectly contribute to the slow rate of decomposition of plant litter in the fynbos. This in turn means that elements such as nitrogen and phosphorus are largely held in plant material and not released into the soil where they would be leached out. Only when the plant material burns in the next fire are these elements released to play their role in the next stage of the nutrient cycle.

A bizarre outcome of all the products of the excess of carbohydrates – and thus, indirectly, of the low nutrient level – is that fynbos is prone to fire, the major driving force in the dynamics of the vegetation. Slow decomposition results in enough fine dead material on the ground to carry a fire, thus increasing the flammability of fynbos. In addition, some plants produce high levels of volatile secondary compounds that make them more flammable, and many restioid species have layers of cuticular wax which also seems to increase their flammability. These

---

The shortage of nitrogen and phosphorus in fynbos soils limits the overall productivity of fynbos plants. However, owing to an abundance of sunshine and, in most habitats, adequate amounts of moisture, there are no constraints on the production of carbohydrates. Some of the surplus carbohydrates are channelled into the production of various mechanical structures that help fynbos plants to cope with adversity. The woody cones of *Leucadendron comosum* (**4**) protect seeds from predators and fire; the tough, thick leaves of *Protea convexa* (**5**) facilitate the efficient use of nutrients and reduce herbivory; and the thick bark of *Mimetes fimbriifolius* (**6**) helps the plant to survive fire.

Many fynbos plants, notably those of the family Rutaceae such as *Adenandra uniflora* (**7**), *Coleonema album* (**8**) and *Agathosma serpyllacea* (**9**), have distinctive smells that in some cases are pleasantly aromatic and in others are somewhat pungent. This characteristic fynbos fragrance, produced by tiny oil glands on the surface of leaves, fruits and petals, probably evolved to discourage herbivores.

10 The blister bush, a member of the carrot family or Apiaceae, is well known to, and carefully avoided by, hikers in the mountains of the fynbos region. Its leaves contain a substance that may have evolved originally to deter herbivores but also causes blisters on the skin of people who brush against it and then expose the skin to sunlight.

1

2

adaptations, apparently for self-destruction, in fact make fynbos self-perpetuating, since if fires did not occur at regular intervals of at least 40 years, fynbos could be replaced by forest species.

HOT DRY SUMMERS

In terms of quantity, the annual rainfall in the fynbos region is variable, ranging from less than 200 millimetres in the inland valleys to about 400 millimetres on the broad coastal lowlands, and from about 800 to more than 3000 millimetres in the mountains. In addition, the proportion of rain that falls in summer increases from the western part of the region to the east. Most fynbos areas, notably those in the extreme west with their true winter-rainfall climate, experience rainless periods during summer that last long enough to cause depletion of soil moisture, and

this in turn limits plant growth to some extent. Although summer drought in fynbos is not as intense as it is in some other mediterranean-climate regions of the world, fynbos plants show a wide range of adaptations for dealing with the stresses imposed by the heat and drought of the summer months.

Surviving through summer

In the mountains of the southwestern Cape the season of low rainfall and high temperatures extends from November to March. At these altitudes deep-rooted shrubs and even seedlings of shrub species such as proteas and cliffortias show little sign of stress during most summers. Plants with shallower roots, such as the restioids, experience drought stress more often, especially in deep sandy soils where the upper layer dries out quickly. The shortage of soil moisture seldom lasts long, however, as the

lightest of rains can rapidly replenish the moisture supply. Even in drier, northwestern mountains such as the Cederberg, where the rainfall is lower, proteoids show relatively mild water stress during summer.

Fynbos plants balance their water budgets when soil moisture is low by conserving energy, effectively assuming a lifestyle reminiscent of the Mediterranean region; they metabolise energetically in the early morning, rest through the hot midday, then resume activity in the late afternoon. At the height of summer the siesta period may be extended until sundown.

The stress of summer drought is further avoided by means of variations in the rooting systems of the different plants. Laborious investigations have shown that fynbos species display a range of rooting strategies, with some having long taproots that reach water at great depths,

---

1 Why does the water of many streams in the fynbos region resemble black tea and why are other streams not coloured in this way? When the soils in the catchment of a stream are sterile and strongly acidic, decomposition rates are very slow and organic matter, such as tannins from sclerophyllous leaves, combines with iron and aluminium to form organic complexes which stain the water. Should the catchment support less acidic soils that are reddish yellow, the

stream colour is white rather than black. This may result from the more rapid decomposition of complex organic compounds as well as from the soils' ability to strain out the tannins.
2 Only the low-lying areas of the western fynbos region experience the regular and severe summer drought that is typical of most mediterranean-climate regions. Shown here is a late summer aspect of fynbos in the Cederberg. There is an air of sullen endurance as

the plants conserve scarce moisture by ceasing all activity in the midday sun, a lifestyle which many human inhabitants of mediterranean-climate regions have enthusiastically emulated. Note that the shallow-rooted restioids are showing the most visible signs of stress.

3

4

5

whereas others have shallow, fibrous roots that capture water near the soil surface. Between these extremes are several other root types at intermediate levels. By sharing the soil moisture in this way the different growth forms in fynbos can coexist in a small area because they do not compete directly with each other for water.

Examples of deep-rooted shrubs are the tall proteas that dominate many fynbos communities. The roots of the adult shrubs, tapping soil moisture far below the ground surface, enable them to cope with dry periods, but seedlings are vulnerable, especially if their roots have not extended deep enough before the start of the summer drought. This is particularly evident in warmer, drier areas such as the coastal lowlands, where many seedlings often succumb. In most areas, however, if fires burn in late summer or early autumn (as is usual), seeds germinate during

the first winter and extend adequate roots before the onset of drought the following summer. Rapid root growth in seedlings is clearly advantageous, and is made possible by drawing on reserves in the nutrient-rich seeds.

Shrubs with shallower roots include most of the ericoid element of fynbos communities, such as ericas, buchus and species of *Cliffortia*, *Muraltia* and *Phylica*. The network of fine roots that many of these species have developed as part of their associations with bacteria and fungi to improve their ability to take up nutrients also serves to enhance their water uptake over an extended surface area in the soil.

The fibrous roots of restioids are also short, and the plants' growth is restricted when water is depleted in shallow soil during the driest time of the year. Indeed, of all the growth forms, restioids are most vulnerable to

prolonged periods of drought. To supplement the meagre moisture available in surface soils, many shallow-rooted restioids make use of their architecture to trap the dew and mist common in the mountains. The condensed droplets of moisture then run down the plant's smooth stalks to its base where they are absorbed by the roots. The dense tussocks of wiry culms that are a feature of *Thamnochortus punctatus*, for example, effectively intercept droplets of mist in this way.

Leaves are adapted in many different ways to coping with austerity. The permutations described below are all attempts to solve the dilemma faced by every plant: how to expose the greatest area of photosynthesising surface to the sun and exchange gases for photosynthesis and transpiration, while simultaneously conserving water and avoiding overheating.

The leaves of fynbos plants have many characteristics that enable them to cope with excessive solar radiation and associated heat stress. The silvery and finely hairy leaves of *Mimetes argenteus* (3) reflect radiation while the spines on the tips of the leaves of *Muraltia heisteria* (4) may conduct heat from the leaf to the atmosphere. The geophyte *Haemanthus nortieri* (5), which grows at the northern, arid edge of fynbos near Vanrhynsdorp, produces during winter large,

erect leaves that have minimal exposure to the sun during the warmest part of the day. Members of the genus which grow in cooler, southern areas, where heat stress is not a problem, produce prostrate leaves in order to maximise radiation loads in winter.

Close inspection of a sample of fynbos leaves will reveal considerable variety besides the obvious differences in shape, size and texture. The colour, sheen and hairiness vary, and the surfaces of some are covered with a layer of wax or scales. Some Proteaceae and Rhamnaceae species, for example, have hairs, or trichomes, on one or both sides of the leaf, whereas others, notably in the Restionaceae, have stomata buried in 'crypts' in the leaf. These are all adaptations to reduce the flow of air over the stomata, thereby reducing water loss. Epidermal hairs also increase the sheen on leaves, making them more reflective and helping to maintain lower leaf temperatures.

Leaf spines are a conspicuous feature in some fynbos species, especially those of the genera *Aspalathus*, *Cliffortia*, *Metalasia* and *Muraltia*. Their primary function is probably to prevent the loss of leaves to herbivores, but they also act like mini-conductors, dissipating heat from drought-stressed seedlings and thereby reducing mortality. Leaf spines are most common in dry areas.

Another adaptation for water economy that is evident in parts of the fynbos – although it is not nearly as prevalent there as it is in the adjoining karoo – is succulence, whereby moisture is stored in fleshy leaves or stems. Most succulent plants in fynbos are found in small fissures in rock cracks which contain small amounts of soil that dry out very quickly.

A small total leaf area helps to reduce heat build-up and water loss, and to this end thousands of ericoid plants have small leaves. Another leaf adaptation – seen in many *Erica* and *Phylica* species and thousands of other ericoids that experience some water shortage – is that both edges of the leaves are rolled under, almost meeting

1 Fynbos has a rich succulent flora which is mainly associated with dry and fire-free sites such as exposed cliffs and rock crevices. *Delosperma esterhuyseniae*, growing in a crevice in the Baviaanskloof, is one of the several hundred fynbos members of the Mesembryanthemaceae, South Africa's largest plant family.

Many fynbos shrubs have small leaves that are tightly rolled-under at the margins, leaving only a narrow longitudinal slit; these are known as 'ericoid' leaves because the design is clearly demonstrated in the Ericaceae, for example in *Erica bruniades* (**2**). Ericoid leaves lack stomata on the upper surface, and transpiration takes place only in the narrow chamber formed by the rolled leaf. A dense layer of fine hairs inside the chamber further reduces the flow of air over the stomata, and thus water loss. However, not all ericas have tightly rolled-under leaves. Species which grow in moist, shady habitats, such as *E. marifolia* (**3**), have less need to conserve water and thus have more open leaves.

in the middle. Moreover, the hard, waxy upper surface has no stomata or pores, these being concentrated inside the narrow chamber formed by the rolled-under leaf edges and protected at the slit-like opening by numerous interlocking hairs. This structure is very effective in reducing water loss. However, leaves of *Erica* species that grow in damp areas, such as *E. marifolia* and *E. riparia*, are flatter or 'open-backed'.

The branch arrangement of most fynbos shrubs is open rather than dense, a canopy design that allows for effective heat dissipation from the leaves. A good example of this architecture is found in the waboom whose leaves, in addition, are positioned almost vertically, exposing a maximum area of photosynthesising surface to the sun in the early morning and late afternoon, but a minimum during the hottest midday period.

WIND – HEAVEN'S BREATH?

Most parts of the fynbos region are bombarded by high-speed winds for a few months of the year, and summer gales are an integral part of the fynbos environment. The basic direction of the winds tends to be parallel to the coast, and they are fiercest at promontories such as Cape Point, Cape Agulhas and Cape St Francis which have very high mean annual wind speeds. Wind patterns in the mountains are more complex, partly because the prevailing winds are deflected by the Cape Fold Mountains, but also because differences in the heating of air over mountain slopes and valley bottoms produce local variations in the wind patterns. In autumn warm, dry, northeasterly berg winds blow outwards from the interior of southern Africa, sometimes causing temperatures to rise above 36 °C and significantly increasing the probability of fires.

Wind has played a major role in shaping the plant life of the fynbos region. For example, by affecting soil moisture and humidity, it influences local drought conditions and the probability of fire. Its drying action, especially when the weather is hot, removes humid air around the leaves and increases water loss through transpiration, often exacerbating the effects of drought. Howling gales cause mechanical damage to plants, and evolution has favoured the development of small compact shrubs. On the other hand, wind also disperses pollen and seeds, and many fynbos plants have adaptations for taking advantage of it.

Adaptations for riding the wind

Because of the low levels of nutrients available to them, fynbos plants have fewer options for seed dispersal. Not for them the large, juicy fruits typical of the more fertile

4 Strong winds are a characteristic feature of the fynbos environment and have played an important but largely unstudied role in shaping the ecology of the region. Here a gale-force summer southeaster at Cape Point ruffles a stand of *Elegia filacea*.

1

2

3

forests or thickets, that are dispersed by birds and mammals. Theirs is a low-cost option – their seeds are, more often than not, dispersed by wind. This dispersal mode requires that seeds must either be very small or have special structures that improve their aerodynamic properties. Seeds of some species possess both these qualities. For example, the orchids, of which there are over 200 species in the Cape flora, all have minute seeds in which the coat is thin, loose and drawn out into a delicate wing-like structure. Some erica seeds are small enough to be carried a reasonable distance by gusts of wind without having any special aerodynamic features. Larger seeds have a range of other structures that allow them to 'ride the wind'. Those of daisies of the Asteraceae are produced in a fluffy mass, with individual seeds suspended in a plume of white floss that slows their descent in still air and allows them to

remain airborne in windy conditions. Seeds of many protea species are covered with long straight hairs and are released into open, burnt patches. When dry and clean, the hairs catch the wind and form a 'sail' that propels the seed over the surface for 100 metres or more. However, the hairs soon pick up dust and ash which make the seed less mobile, and it is easily trapped by barriers such as rocks or the skeletons of burnt plants. Thus the dispersal distance is limited.

Some genera of fynbos plants show several adaptations for seed dispersal, each one the result of an evolutionary experiment in balancing the budget – a trade-off between thriftiness and effectiveness. An interesting example is the genus *Leucadendron* in the Proteaceae, which includes species with different adaptations for dispersal by wind. *L. stellare* has a hairy, nut-like seed,

similar to that of the proteas described above; *L. platy-spermum* has large, winged seeds which are carried almost 50 metres by the wind, but cannot tumble along the ground; and the small, wedge-shaped seeds of *L. rubrum* have plumed perianths and are borne considerable distances by the wind. All modes of seed dispersal have certain benefits, but the major advantage of dispersal by wind is probably the lack of dependence on any animal. This means that the plant does not have to produce costly substances to attract dispersers. Structures such as wings and plumes are cheaper to produce than fleshy fruits, and in fynbos this represents a viable option.

Wind also plays a role in pollination, with about 12 per cent of species in the Cape flora, representing some 156 genera and 26 families, being pollinated in this way. It is not clear why this apparently wasteful and random

1 Many fynbos plants rely on wind for dispersing their seeds, thus saving the cost of having to advertise to attract dispersers. The seeds (or, more accurately, fruits) of the tall silver tree are small 'nuts', about 1 centimetre long, each one equipped with a well-developed 'para-chute' which consists of the plumed perianth under which the seed is suspended by a 'life line' – actually the persisting style. This design

enables the seed to 'ride the wind' when it has been dislodged from its elevated launching site.

2 Clouds of pollen drift about a dense stand of the wind-pollinated *Erica hispidula*, a widespread and sociable species. About 5 per cent of ericas rely on the wind to carry pollen from anthers to receptive stigmas. Since the chances of a particular pollen grain being carried to a receptive stigma are immeasurably small, wind-pollinated species have rounded, egg-shaped flowers or open-mouthed corollas, and large, flat stigmas that often protrude from the tube. This greatly

4

method of pollination has evolved repeatedly from animal-pollinated ancestors. Whatever the reasons, pollination by wind requires specialised floral adaptations, and the evolution of these adaptations in 17 per cent of the plant families in the Cape flora has been an important factor in the development of the amazing floral diversity. For example, the 5 per cent of ericas that are wind-pollinated have rounded, egg-shaped flowers or open-mouthed corollas, large flat stigmas that often protrude from the tube, and no nectaries at the base of the ovary.

For wind-pollination to be effective, the species must be abundant so that there are enough receptive stigmas to receive the airborne pollen. Therefore, wind-pollinated species in fynbos tend to form dense stands. A good example of this is the very common *Erica hispidula* which is widespread throughout the mountains of the fynbos

region. Walking through a stand of these ericas often raises a cloud of pollen.

DIVERSITY IN THE LAND OF ADVERSITY

We often marvel at the amazing diversity of fynbos plant communities. But Nature's aim in designing these communities was certainly not to impress humans; the fact that fynbos does offer such a bewildering array of plant life for us to observe and enjoy is a fortuitous by-product. Many features of fynbos vegetation evolved to enable the plants to cope with the harsh features of their environment while drawing the greatest advantage from the opportunities provided by sporadic periods of abundance, especially those linked with the occurrence of fire. The ancestors of today's fynbos plants experimented in many ways to eke out an existence in this land of adversity. This

experimentation has taken them along many roads – some of which led to success, while others were dead-ends. The roads to success have taken some surprising turns, as the keen observer can discover by delving beyond the obvious in any fynbos patch.

---

improves the chances of a wind-borne pollen grain landing on a receptive stigma, but even this innovation in floral design is not enough to make wind an efficient option for pollen transfer – there must also be many more flowers in the area to intercept the wind-borne pollen. Wind-pollinated species in fynbos tend to form much denser stands than their animal-pollinated relatives.

3 Other wind-pollinated plant groups in fynbos include species of *Leucadendron*, *Cliffortia* and Restionaceae. The last-mentioned group is entirely dioecious (having separate male and female plants) and many of its species, such as *Staberoha distachyos*, have conspicuous floral bracts which facilitate the flow of pollen onto the hidden female flowers.

4 The theme of this chapter, adversity promotes diversity, is well illustrated by the profusion of fynbos plant life growing on the sterile and stony sand of a dry and remote peak in the Gamkaberg, Little Karoo.

5. THRIVING ON FIRE

To most people fire is devastating, a disastrous event which destroys vegetation, buildings and crops, threatens humans, decimates wildlife and leaves behind it a forlorn and blackened landscape. This description is, of course, apt for urban and agricultural landscapes where nature has been subdued and is managed to benefit humans. It is also true for many ecosystems, such as tropical rainforests and the temperate woodlands of northern Europe, where fire is an occasional and catastrophic event. But it certainly is not true of fynbos.

Fire is a natural and normal process in fynbos. As was shown in the chapter 'Origins', the very existence of fynbos plants can be attributed to the increasing importance of fire over the past few million years. They have lifestyles which have been shaped by fire – without it they perish,

leaving no offspring and confounding the biological imperative to reproduce. If it were possible to exclude fire from fynbos for a century or two, many of the landscapes would become densely infested with just a few dozen species of forest and thicket shrubs and trees.

It took botanists a long time to appreciate the role of fire in fynbos. Other than the pioneering research carried out by Margaret Levyns and R.S. Adamson between the two world wars, very little work was done until the mid-1970s. Since then a great deal of fire-related research on fynbos has brought to light a wealth of information that has been rapidly assimilated into policies and actions for the wise management of fynbos.

DIFFERENT TYPES OF FIRE

To talk about fire *per se* is to oversimplify this extremely

1 The sight of fierce flames and smoke-darkened skies engenders in most of us a primeval fear of the destructive power of fire. Yet in fynbos fire is a keystone process, an essential event which provides new opportunities for organisms to regenerate, produce offspring and then die back in anticipation of the next fire.

3

2

complex phenomenon. Ecologists refer rather to a fire regime which has four components: frequency (how often do the fires burn?); season (at what time of year do they burn?); intensity (how hot are they?); and size (what area do they cover?). Different vegetation types experience different fire regimes, depending on the source of ignition (e.g. lightning), the fuel load (the amount and arrangement of flammable vegetation) and climatic conditions (the length and intensity of the dry season).

The frequency of fynbos fires varies between four and 45 years, but on average most fynbos plant communities burn every 12 to 15 years. This frequency is determined by the rate at which vegetation grows (or the fuel load accumulates) after the previous fire. In most sites the regrowth of fynbos is slow as a result of low soil fertility and the scarcity of moisture, and there will be an interval of at least four years between fires. However, in relatively fertile sites where rainfall is higher – such as in the shale-derived soils on the seaward slopes of coastal mountains – fynbos may burn only three years after the last fire, especially in extreme hot and dry conditions.

In grassy fynbos in the eastern regions, where fuel accumulates more rapidly owing to the fast growth of summer-active grasses, fire frequency is, on average, higher than in the west, ranging between four and six years. In dry fynbos, on the other hand, where rates of regrowth are very slow, fire intervals can be long, averaging about 25 years. For most fynbos areas there is a 50 per cent chance that a fire will occur in 20-year-old vegetation and a 100 per cent chance that it will occur in 30-year-old vegetation.

The time of the year when fires burn is determined by

2 The life-giving nature of fire in fynbos is shown vividly by the beautiful blooms of *Haemanthus canaliculatus* erupting from the scorched earth shortly after a fire at Betty's Bay.

3 It is often said that as a management tool, fire is a bad master but a good servant. Here, on Devil's Peak, uncontrolled fires have burnt too frequently, eliminating many slow-maturing seedling shrubs and creating a grassy landscape with many weedy species.

the climate, the seasonal variation in the moisture content of the vegetation, and the availability of ignition sources. In the western part of the fynbos region the dry and windy weather conditions suitable for fires may occur at any time of the year but are generally most common in summer, when rainfall and humidity are low, and temperatures and wind speeds high. In the eastern regions, however, the higher summer rainfall and the generally drier winter weather, coupled with regular hot and dry berg winds between May and August, result in many fires during the cooler months. Throughout the fynbos region lightning, the principal natural source of ignition, is most likely in late summer and early autumn, when thunderstorm weather moves down from the northeast.

The intensity of a fire depends on the fuel load of the burning vegetation and the rate of combustion. On a hot and windy day very old veld, with lots of dead vegetation and a dense layer of fine litter, will support an intense burn. On the other hand, a fire in young veld on a cool, calm day will be much less intense. Fires in fynbos are more intense than those in grassland or savanna.

Although very large fires may still occur in the mountains, in lowland areas patch burning and barriers such as firebreaks, roads and croplands have considerably reduced the extent of modern fires compared with those of the past. In precolonial times it is likely that fires burned for many days and swept through millions of hectares of vegetation, but nothing on that scale is experienced today. The last of the truly great fires occurred in February 1867, after a very dry summer and during a period of unremitting berg winds. Having started near Swellendam, it finally died out more than a week later in the subtropical thickets near Uitenhage, some 500 kilometres to the east.

The 'average' fire regime in fynbos could be described as moderately intense fires occurring during the summer months at intervals of 12 to 15 years, and covering several hundred to several thousand hectares. However, this is a very broad generalisation, for each fire is unique, both in its properties and in its effect on fynbos. An appreciation of the variation in fire-related regeneration of fynbos plants is the key to unlocking many of the secrets of fynbos.

WAITING TO BURN

By the time a fynbos community has reached the age of about 15 years since the last fire and all its species have flowered and set seed for several successive years, it is ready to burn again. Let us examine a typical patch of mature proteoid fynbos growing on the lower slopes of the

In the dry and open fynbos of the inland mountains fuel loads are low and accumulate very slowly, resulting in much longer intervals between fires than in wetter fynbos communities. In these drier parts proteoid shrubs, including this undescribed species of *Leucadendron* on the lower slopes of the Klein Swartberg, are capable of living for many decades in the absence of fire.

southwestern Cape mountains, classifying its different categories of plants on the basis of their lifestyles and modes of reproduction. Our hypothetical community has a moderately dense overstorey of proteoid shrubs that are 2 to 3 metres tall; a dense understorey of ericoid shrubs and restioids 0.5 to 1 metre tall; and a sparse ground layer of grasses, dwarf shrubs and herbs in openings in the vegetation. All in all this sample patch includes about 100 species. There are almost no seedlings, apart from an occasional forest or thicket species seedling growing in the shade of a protea shrub.

The first distinction to be drawn is between the seeders (plants which are killed by fire and depend entirely on seed for regeneration) and the sprouters (plants which resprout from protected buds). In most fynbos communities the majority of species are sprouters. However, most

of the living material, or biomass, comprises seeders, which are usually the dominant shrub species. Further distinctions are based on the lifespan of a plant and its mode of seed storage.

Of the four proteoid shrubs in the community, three are seeders. One is a protea which stores its seeds in woody cones borne in the canopy of the plant. It flowers in winter and produces seeds which, lodged in the base of the cones, develop over several months so that they are ripe before the start of the peak fire season in late summer. Cones older than about three to four years open spontaneously, releasing their precious crop of plump, protein-rich seeds onto the ground where they are hungrily devoured by small rodents. The seed store in the canopy of this serotinous protea is not particularly large because very few florets (between 2 and 20 per cent) in a protea

flowerhead develop seeds, and many of these (up to 30 per cent) are eaten by insects which live in the cones. At 15 years old the protea is considered to be mature, and may be allocating 40 to 60 per cent of its annual growth to flowers and fruits. It would have started flowering at about five years old and about 30 years later flowering will begin to decline. After 45 years without fire plants begin to die, spilling their seed banks into an inhospitable environment. This programmed death by natural senescence (or old age) is an unusual feature of seeder shrubs in fynbos.

The leucadendron in our hypothetical community is also a seeding, serotinous shrub, with the same lifestyle characteristics as the protea. Leucadendrons, however, are dioecious, having separate male and female plants. Seed loads are usually much higher than those of proteas

A hypothetical community which is 'waiting to burn' would look very much like this patch of proteoid fynbos on the lower slopes of the Riviersonderend Mountains. Prominent shrubs are *Leucadendron laureolum* and *Protea repens*.

(partly to compensate for the lack of seeds on male plants) and levels of seed predation in the cones are much lower. Flowers appear later in the year than most protea flowers, and seeds take less time to ripen.

The third seeding proteoid is a fire-sensitive mimetes which, unlike the serotinous protea and leucadendron, drops its seeds onto the ground as soon as they are ripe. There they are collected by ants and buried, out of harm's way, down to 5 centimetres beneath the soil surface. Ants, being tiny and cold-blooded, prefer to locate their nests in open, sunny sites away from the shaded canopies of the tall, proteoid shrubs. The mimetes flowers in spring and its ripe seeds are shed in midsummer, when ants are active and before the peak fire season. Seed set in myrmecochorous (ant-dispersed) proteoids is very low, each flowerhead producing one to four large, protein-rich

seeds. The seed banks in the soil are not very large and adequate numbers for regeneration depend on annual inputs of seeds. Since the mimetes also has a lifespan limited to about 40 years, a fire-free interval longer than this will seriously diminish its potential for post-fire regeneration.

The next major group of seeding plants in our fynbos patch are the ericoid shrubs, with possibly as many as 15 species growing between the taller proteoids. These ericoids include one or more species of *Agathosma*, *Cliffortia*, *Erica*, *Metalasia*, *Muraltia*, *Passerina*, *Phylica* and many other genera, all of which have more seeding than sprouting species. Flowering occurs throughout the year, although there are peaks in spring and early summer. We know very little about how many seeds are produced each year in this group but the species with larger seeds,

1 A serotinous cone of *Leucadendron laureolum* in which plump and protein-rich seeds are stored until, as shown, fire stimulates their release.

2 Our hypothetical proteoid community includes a number of seeding ericoid shrubs such as *Erica borboniifolia*.

3

4

5

which are invariably myrmecochores (e.g. *Agathosma*, *Cliffortia*, *Muraltia* and *Phylica*), produce far fewer seeds than the smaller-seeded species (e.g. *Erica*, *Metalasia* and *Passerina*). Seed production also shows large year-to-year fluctuations. Seeds are shed mainly in the late summer and autumn, and most decay after having been buried for a year. Since most of these species, like the proteoids, become senescent in old fynbos, there is little chance of good seedling recruitment after a fire in 40-year-old veld.

The final group of seeding species comprises the 'fire ephemerals'. These plants appear during a brief period after fire, usually between one and several years, then perish and persist as dormant seeds in the soil. There may be as many as ten species of fire ephemerals in the fynbos patch, but as it is already 15 years old they would

have died by this stage. They are mainly annual, biennial and short-lived perennial herbs or soft shrubs belonging to many genera, including *Aspalathus*, *Erepsia*, *Helichrysum*, *Lobelia*, *Roella*, *Selago*, *Senecio*, *Thesium* and *Ursinia*. Perhaps the best example of a fire ephemeral is the Cape everlasting or *sewejaartjie*, so-named in Afrikaans because it usually disappears from the veld about seven years after a fire. Fire ephemerals grow rapidly, flowering profusely in the first few years and producing large numbers of tiny seeds which are capable of persisting in the soil until the next fire. There is no well-defined flowering period for this group, although many of its members flower in late summer and autumn during the height of the fire season. However, since these species are active in the early post-fire years, it is highly unlikely that fire will interfere with their reproduction.

Of the sprouters, comprising the majority of species in our hypothetical fynbos community, the first example is the waboom. This proteoid shrub is able to sprout from fire-resistant buds buried beneath thick bark on its branches as well as from an underground rootstock, or lignotuber. Unlike all the seeding species, individual waboom plants of different ages coexist in the fynbos patch since most survive fires. Flowering extends over the winter months and ripe seeds are shed in autumn: the waboom does not store the small number of seeds it produces in its canopy. As a generalisation, sprouting species produce fewer seeds than their closely related seeding counterparts, the widely accepted explanation being that since sprouters have to allocate scarce resources to the growth of lignotubers and thick bark, little is left for seed production. Moreover, since most individuals

Fynbos includes some 1000 species of fire ephemerals, plants which complete their life cycles during a relatively brief period after fire and survive until the next burn as dormant seeds. Included in this group are many of the everlastings, some of which are valuable cut flowers, such as *Edmondia sesamoides* (**3**), strawberry everlasting (**4**) and *E. pinifolia* (**5**).

1

of sprouting species survive fire, seedling establishment plays a relatively minor role in the survival of the species. Another important characteristic of the waboom is that it shows no signs of senescence in old veld. Indeed, individuals may live for centuries, and some magnificent specimens up to 10 metres tall can be found in secluded mountain valleys.

Our fynbos patch also includes a dozen or more low sprouting shrubs belonging to the ericoid genera already listed as including seeders (*Agathosma*, *Cliffortia*, *Erica*, *Metalasia*, *Muraltia*, *Passerina* and *Phylica*), as well as other genera such as *Clutia*, *Osteospermum*, *Otholobium* and *Pelargonium*. All of these species sprout from ligno-tubers and, unlike their seeding counterparts, many flower in the first year following a fire, drawing on their stored resources to attract pollinators to the fire-blackened

landscape. A particularly showy example of this lifestyle is the ubiquitous *Erica cerinthoides*. As would be expected, sprouting ericoids produce fewer seeds (and seedlings) than seeders. Some of these sprouters, like *Pelargonium cucullatum*, disappear when veld remains unburnt for very long periods.

Restios, sedges and true grasses make up a large proportion of the sprouters in our fynbos patch, and about 25 per cent of its species. Common genera which include sprouters in the Restionaceae are *Elegia*, *Hypodiscus*, *Ischyrolepis*, *Restio* and *Thamnochortus*, and in the Cyperaceae (sedges) *Ficinia* and *Tetraria*. Grasses are represented mainly by *Ehrharta*, *Merxmuellera* and *Pentaschistis*. Although there are a number of seeders in the Restionaceae (e.g. Riversdale thatching reed), there are very few among the sedges and grasses. Most

restios, sedges and grasses live for decades, although their foliage dies back in very old veld.

Geophytes, or bulbs, make up about 20 per cent of the species in our patch, and can be divided into two main categories on the basis of their growth and flowering patterns. For most species reproduction and growth are synchronous (i.e. leaves and flowers are present at the same time), and they are termed synanthous. For other species growth and flowering are uncoupled (i.e. leaves are lacking during the flowering period), and they are called hysteranthous. Hysteranthy is an evolutionary advancement over synanthy, and is advantageous in that it enables geophytes to flower outside the normal growing season, during late summer and autumn. Thus, flowers are produced at a time when few other species are in bloom and there is less competition for pollinators. In the case of the

1 As legumes, the many *Aspalathus* fire ephemerals form a symbiotic relationship with root-borne bacteria which are capable of extracting atmospheric (as opposed to soil) nitrogen. This additional source of nitrogen enables the plants to grow exceptionally fast. Some fire regimes favour these species, with the result that one or more of them germinate profusely. Large areas may become smothered in *Aspalathus*, resulting in the elimination, by competition, of the seedlings of many other members of the community, especially the seeding ericoids. In the Kogelberg *A. excelsa* forms a dense thicket three years after a fire. In a few years' time, however, this species will have disappeared from the scene.

red-flowered species of *Gladiolus* and *Tritoniopsis*, autumn flowering coincides with the period of peak abundance of their exclusive pollinator, the mountain pride butterfly. Among Amaryllidaceae species of the fynbos, hysteranthy and autumn flowering are associated with fleshy, non-dormant seeds which germinate immediately after dispersal, just in time for the winter rains. Exceptions in this family are the true fire-lilies, species of *Cyrtanthus*, which produce dry, dormant seed and are therefore not restricted to autumn flowering. Indeed, in keeping with their name, they flower immediately after fire, irrespective of the season.

Most fynbos geophytes are synanthous and flower during the cool, wet months when they are shunting starch from their photosynthetically active leaves to underground bulbs, corms and rhizomes. If rainfall is low

in a particular winter, as can happen in the non-seasonal rainfall zone from the Overberg eastwards, they may not accumulate sufficient resources in that season for flowering. Probably for this reason geophytes are most abundant, in terms of species numbers and individual plants, in the western fynbos region where winter rains are most predictable.

Our hypothetical patch of fynbos includes two hysteranthous species, a *Cyrtanthus* and a *Tritoniopsis*. The remaining species are synanthous and, with the exception of a species of *Aristea* and one of *Corymbium*, they have leaves which die back in the early summer months. A midsummer's walk through the tangled shrubbery of our patch would reveal no hint of its rich geophytic flora.

The final group of sprouters in our fynbos community comprises six or so species of forest and thicket shrubs

and trees. This complement of species depends on the distance from, and composition of, the nearest patch of forest or thicket, and could include, for example, at least one species of *Rhus*, wild olive, wild peach, mountain maytenus, blueberry bush and rockwood. Forest and thicket species differ from fynbos shrubs in having glossy green foliage and producing fleshy fruits which are dispersed by birds. Moreover, they are the only plants in fynbos which establish seedlings between, and not after, fires. In the fynbos patch most of these seedlings are found beneath the tallest shrubs, since these offer a perch for fruit-eating birds and provide a dense mulch of litter and the shaded conditions in which the seedlings thrive. Seedling growth, however, is very slow and few have reached a height of half a metre in the 15-year-old fynbos. A few mature wild olive and rockwood trees cling

Many sprouting shrubs flower most profusely almost immediately after fire when they do not have to compete with seeders for pollination. *Erica cerinthoides* (2) and *Pelargonium cucullatum* (3) are two conspicuous sprouters.

Some geophytes, especially in the Amaryllidaceae, are hysteranthous, their flowers appearing after the leaves have died back, as can be seen in *Boophane disticha* (4). Others, such as this *Lachenalia* species (5), are synanthous, their leaves and flowers evident at the same time.

1

2

Our hypothetical community includes a patch of thicket perched on a rocky outcrop which affords it some degree of protection from fire (**1**). Thicket plants have fruits which are dispersed by birds. In the candle-wood (**2**) the capsule opens to display brightly coloured seeds with fleshy arils which attract fruit-eating birds.

to a large sandstone outcrop which affords protection from all but the fiercest fires.

The patch of fynbos described, with its array of species and lifestyles, is reasonably representative of most fynbos communities. Serotinous proteoids are absent from some areas, such as those with swampy soils, high mountain peaks, arid fringes and coastal dunes. Forest and thicket species are not always present in fynbos and generally do not occur in the high mountains. Drier sites than the one described may support a higher proportion of seeding shrubs.

The next step is to let the patch of fynbos burn in order to observe the flush of reproduction which the flames unleash. Within the scope of this book it is impossible to do full justice to the exquisite subtleties of fire effects in fynbos, but we hope that this account will encourage you

to wander through recently burnt fynbos and blacken your clothes and hands in the quest to discover more.

PHOENIX ARISING

The fire has come and gone. Our patch of fynbos burnt in a midsummer wildfire driven by a gale-force southeasterly wind. The fire burnt all day, consuming about 1500 hectares of dry shrubland until it was brought under control by experienced firefighters backburning from a firebreak. Although it was a hot burn, differences in the fuel loads and variations in the weather conditions – particularly the wind speed – ensured that the intensity was uneven. In the hottest spots all but the thickest branches have been consumed and even the patches of thicket in their rocky refuges have been torched. However, there are also areas where scorched leaves and fine twigs remaining on

skeletons of the larger fynbos shrubs indicate that in patches the heat was less intense.

Destructive though it may appear, the fire has set in motion a chain of biological events which ensures the birth of a new fynbos community, rising like Phoenix from the ashes. A few days after the fire many hundreds of seeds of serotinous proteoids lie scattered on the ground. The proteoids' woody cones, opened by the heat of the flames, have spilled their precious seeds onto the blackened sand. There they will remain, blown by the relentless summer winds into small piles which collect against rocks, dead shrubs and any other obstacle. In such exposed situations the protein-packed seeds are vulnerable to the depredations of small rodents which have survived the fire and, in this barren environment, will value the nutrition they afford.

About two weeks after the fire there is already evidence of new life. The brilliant pink flowering stems of fire-lilies set against the blackened soil is a remarkable and beautiful sight, illustrating the contradiction of fire as the giver of life in fynbos. Fire-lilies, all members of the genus *Cyrtanthus*, are hysteranthous geophytes which flower immediately after fire, irrespective of season or the intensity of the burn. Most amazingly, it appears that smoke provides the stimulus for their flowering. The advantages of post-fire flowering are that the flowers are borne when there is little competition with other plants for pollinators, and seeds are produced when there is little pressure from seed-eating animals. However, as is customary in nature, there are also costs: pollinators, like pests, may be in short supply. Fire-stimulated flowering is widespread among sprouting fynbos species, but only the fire-lilies

3 As a fire burns its intensity may vary markedly, depending on the weather conditions and the fuel load. In some cases, especially during a mild spring or winter burn, individual plants may escape the flames, as this *Leucadendron laureolum* has done.

4 A landscape after fire seems devoid of life. A thorough search, however, will reveal survivors which escaped the flames by hiding under rocks or remaining in water, as did this Cape chirping frog.

have the flexibility to flower at any time of the year – and the inflexibility to have flowering restricted to the few weeks after fire.

Another two weeks pass, and young green shoots are thrusting up from the rootstocks and rhizomes of shrubs and restioids. Rates of regrowth are rapid since the fire occurred in summer, when most species were dormant, but their stored starch reserves were at a maximum. Not all sprouters have survived. Mortality is highest among the smaller individuals of waboom and other shrubs, and all the thicket seedlings have perished, indicating that longer fire intervals are required for the expansion of thicket in this area. The waboom shrubs and the mature thicket species are all resprouting from subterranean buds since the fierce flames have killed the more sensitive branch-borne ones. With time more and more sprouts appear as

plants begin to reclaim their place in our fynbos patch. At this stage, some three months after the fire, there is still no sign of seedlings.

Towards the end of April, four months after the fire, the first good rains of winter fall. Two days of soaking rain are followed by a sharp drop in the temperature as cold Antarctic air is drawn in from the south. The cool conditions are exactly what the fynbos seeds have been waiting for. Most do not germinate at temperatures above 20 °C, thus ensuring that seedlings will emerge not after summer showers, but only at the start of the winter rains when there is a good chance that the soil will remain moist long enough for the seedlings to establish.

For some fynbos seeds, such as those of the serotinous proteoids, low temperatures and moisture are sufficient to break their dormancy: for others, fire is essential.

Incredibly, the smoke from the fire has broken the dormancy of the many small-seeded species in our patch, including most Ericaceae, many Asteraceae and Restionaceae, and the fire ephemerals. Horticulturalists have discovered that germination is vastly improved when seeds are moistened with water through which smoke has been bubbled. What better proof of the dependency of fynbos on fire than smoke-stimulated germination! But smoke is not the only catalyst. As the flames moved through our patch they generated a pulse of heat which broke the larger seeds' dormancy, thus stimulating germination in species such as the mimetes and others with ant-dispersed seeds. Since these seeds were buried by ants, only very hot fires can provide the necessary heat to penetrate the soil layer and crack their hard coats, thus allowing germination to proceed. Similarly, the hard-coated

About a month after the fire the first shoots of sprouting shrubs, geophytes and restioids are thrust up from hidden rootstocks, rhizomes and bulbs, such as these of a watsonia (1). Much later, and after the first rains of the winter season, the first seedlings make an appearance. Tiny *Leucadendron laureolum* seedlings, with their protein-rich cotyledons and early leaves, emerge in front of *Spiloxene capensis*, a geophyte in the Hypoxidaceae (2).

3 One of the most spectacular sights in fynbos is the mass flowering of geophytes after a fire. Foremost among these are watsonias, which can brighten vast tracts of landscape after a summer burn. *Watsonia zeyheri* makes a beautiful display one year after a fire at Betty's Bay.

seeds of legumes, including *Aspalathus* species, also require a very hot burn. However, where the fire was intense many small seeds – which were concentrated in the top 2 centimetres of the soil – were killed by the heat. Thus, depending on the nature of the fire, some species win and others lose: hot spots favour big seeds, cool spots favour small ones. Since our fire was hot, it favoured the larger seeds, although occasional cool spots ensured the good germination of some small ones.

When fire consumed our patch of fynbos it left the soil surface exposed so that it is no longer buffered from temperature extremes by a protective mantle of green. These extremes are most pronounced in autumn when the days are warm and the nights cool – on some days the soil surface temperature rises to 50 °C and drops to 5 °C the same night. This considerable variation is responsible for breaking the dormancy of some species' seeds. The first seedlings to emerge are those of the fast-growing fire ephemerals whose small seeds are located close to the surface. Seedlings of the larger-seeded and more deeply buried myrmecochores take longer to appear, and also slow to get going are the Ericaceae seedlings whose tiny rootlets must first form partnerships with fungi to create nutrient-grasping mycorrhizas. In some places there are many hundreds of *Aspalathus* seedlings which, with their added source of atmospheric nitrogen, grow more quickly than any other species in the community.

The seedlings of serotinous proteoids begin to emerge about one month after the first rains. Lying on the soil surface, the seeds are particularly vulnerable to short dry spells during this establishment phase. When the soil surface dries out the naked seeds of leucadendrons, for example, are especially prone to losing whatever moisture they have taken up. Proteas, with their hard seed coats, are less vulnerable since they are better equipped to retain absorbed moisture. Germinants will often die if this desiccation happens shortly after the radicle or rootlet has emerged. During May the regenerating fynbos patch suffers two long dry spells with frequent dry berg winds which cause the death of many leucadendron and some protea germinants. At all stages of this establishment phase the seedlings of seeders are far more abundant than those of sprouters. For some sprouters, especially members of the Restionaceae, almost no seedlings are produced at all.

By the end of May some semblance of green brightens our sombre patch of blackened stems, and flowers of sprouting species are beginning to appear in profusion.

2

3

4

1

For a number of weeks now the brilliant crimson flowers of *Erica cerinthoides* have been visible on short, stout shoots emerging from buried lignotubers. The first synanthous geophytes to flower are delicate species of *Oxalis* which, unlike the spring-flowering members of this genus, produce non-dormant seeds. These germinate immediately after dispersal so that the new generation of plants can build up food reserves in their bulbs before the onset of drought during the summer months.

As the cold of winter gives way to the first warmth of spring, from mid-August onwards, more and more blooms appear. The most spectacular event in spring is the mass flowering of *Watsonia*, a geophyte in the iris family with a succession of beautiful flowers borne on stems up to 1.5 metres tall. In the years between fires only about 10 per cent of the plants bear flowers, but after a fire – especially one in summer or autumn when the bulbs contain maximum stored reserves – up to 80 per cent of plants flower, colouring entire hillsides in a breathtaking display. The stimulus for mass flowering in watsonias is apparently associated not with the direct effects of fire, but with the wide extremes in soil temperature experienced after the removal of vegetation. Researchers have discovered that mass flowering can be induced by clearing fynbos without the use of fire.

What are the advantages of these synchronised displays? Firstly, the mass of colour provides a strong signal to attract pollinators (seed set of this pollinator-dependent species is higher in mass-flowering than in normal populations); secondly, the enormous number of seeds produced are far in excess of the requirements of the snout

1 The fire-lilies encapsulate the contradiction of fire as a giver of life in fynbos. All are members of the genus *Cyrtanthus*, and all, like *C. ventricosus*, are hysteranthous geophytes which flower only within a few weeks after a fire, irrespective of the season of the burn.

Many fynbos geophytes flower profusely after fire, including *Bulbinella nutans* (2), *Oxalis luteola* (3), *Brunsvigia marginata* (4) and *Geissorhiza hispidula* (5).

5

6

7

8

9

beetles which burrow into the ripe fruits to consume seeds (seed predation is five times lower in mass-flowering than in normal populations). This tactic of producing occasional bumper seed crops which swamp potential seed-eaters with excess food, and thus ensure replenishment of the seed bank, is called predator satiation.

By the end of October all the species in our fynbos patch have appeared either as sprouts or seedlings. This is the time when the maximum number of species is visible in the community, for from now on some will disappear in a process of slow attrition, to persist underground as seeds, bulbs, corms and rhizomes. A large number of the species have flowered, including some of the shorter-lived fire ephemerals. For many geophytes and the single annual in our patch this will be the last reproductive event until the next fire.

Fire ephemerals contribute much to the beauty of fynbos in the first few spring seasons after a burn. Included amongst this group are species belonging to many different families and genera, such as *Othonna quinquedentata* (**6**) of the Asteraceae, *Roella ciliata* (**7**) of the Campanulaceae, *Hypocalyptus sophoroides* (**8**) of the Fabaceae, and the mauve *Selago spuria* (**9**) of the family Selaginaceae.

1

At this stage all seedlings are growing rapidly, using this benign period of adequate sunshine and moisture to extend their roots deep and wide so that they can forage for water in the dry months ahead. In general, the seedlings of sprouters grow more slowly than those of seeders because, even at this early stage, they are allocating valuable resources to rudimentary lignotubers rather than to increasing the spread of roots and shoots.

By midsummer, exactly one year after the fire, an air of silent endurance pervades our patch. The glorious floral extravaganzas have wilted to brown, papery stalks; the geophytes are dormant, leafless and hidden beneath the soil; the sprouting shrubs are established and firmly in place; and the seedlings are jockeying for position, for theirs is a summertime story. As was discussed in the chapter 'Famine in paradise', summer drought is not

particularly severe for adult fynbos plants. However, their shallow-rooted seedlings, like those in our post-fire patch, are affected far more severely and by autumn, having endured a long, dry summer, many of the seedlings have died. The extent of mortality is determined by the species, the microsite in which the seedlings grow and the genetic make-up of individual seedlings, for in this period of intense selection the weaker genotypes are weeded out and the less than suitable microsites are identified. An example of the latter can be seen where the seeds of serotinous proteoids are clumped around the blackened base of a restio tuft. The harsh radiation from the darkened surface adds an additional burden of heat to these large-leaved seedlings which, already losing large amounts of moisture through 'sweating', are struggling to balance their heat budgets. In these unfavourable sites

nearly all seedlings perish, whereas on surfaces of white sand many survive. Biological interactions also take their toll on seedlings, with faster-growing species overtopping and outmanoeuvring the slower ones.

The battle is on and the outcome is fraught with uncertainty: will the winter rains come late? Will they cease early or continue through to spring? We can only guess the outcome. The only bright beacon in the long, dry and anxious autumn is the brilliant display of the crimson-flowered *Tritoniopsis*, bravely parading its wares for the delicate mountain pride butterfly.

The first phase in the post-fire development, or succession, of fynbos comes to an end. Unlike succession in many other vegetation types, where there is a steady and reasonably predictable appearance of different species over time and where the establishment of the later

1 The 'youth phase' of succession in fynbos encompasses the five years after the establishment phase of the first post-fire year. This is the period when sprouters dominate, fire ephemerals begin to decline and many seeders produce their first flowers. Almost all the species in the community are visible and floral diversity is most pronounced.

species is facilitated by the earlier ones, succession in fynbos is self-replicating. Seed dispersal brings no new species into the community. Instead, fire stimulates the regeneration and appearance of species that were always present, albeit for some in a cryptic, below-ground form. There is, of course, a process of attrition during the course of succession as the shorter-lived species disappear. In the absence of fire and under certain fire regimes, some species may become locally extinct.

The next phase, the so-called 'youth phase', encompasses the four years after the first post-fire year. This is the period when sprouting restioids and shrubs dominate; fire ephemerals disappear; many seedlings of longer-lived shrubs die but the survivors produce their first flowers and seeds; and the vegetation cover (but not height) approaches its pre-fire levels. By the end of this phase most

sprouting shrubs have flowered several times, depleting their store of starch reserves in the process. From now on the emphasis is on regaining the pre-fire levels of reserves in anticipation of the next fire.

The fire ephemerals have provided some colour each spring and early summer, although without achieving the splendour of the watsonias' show. Dainty roellas, elegant erepsias and the prolonged displays of bright everlastings have been a welcoming sight each season, but they have now succumbed, their presence transformed to invisible seeds. The mass of *Aspalathus* seedlings has erupted into a prickly and impenetrable thicket of shrubs, about 1 metre tall. These fast-growing thickets have starved the slower-growing plants of light, killing many of them, especially the seedlings. Like the other fire ephemerals, *Aspalathus* has almost reached the end of

its lifespan but, through its effects on other species, it has made its mark on our fynbos patch. It has produced at least four crops of decay-resistant seeds which will lie in the soil, waiting for another hot fire. There is no guarantee that this will happen.

Towards the end of the youth phase many of the seeding ericoids begin flowering and start to replenish their seed banks, a crucial task since no viable seed from pre-fire times remains in the soil. The splashes of pink from flowering ericas in spring are complemented by the occasional brilliant red of a mimetes bloom and, in the last winter of the youth phase, a few protea and leucadendron plants produce their first flowers. The fynbos regrowth, dominated by sprouting restioids, has now covered most of the bare ground and there is again sufficient fuel to support a fire. At this stage, however, a fire would be

Slow-maturing proteoids such as *Leucadendron burchellii* (**2**) produce their first flowers towards the end of the youth phase. Another fire at this time can be disastrous for these species since they have not been able to build up large enough seed reserves for adequate regeneration. *Paranomus adiantifolius* (**3**), a faster-maturing species, is more tolerant of fires in the youth phase.

disastrous for seeding shrubs, since they have not had enough time to build up adequate seed reserves. Many of them would suffer severe population crashes or even become locally extinct.

The next stage in the post-fire succession of fynbos is the transitional stage, so named because it occupies the five years of transition from youth to maturity. This is the phase when all the late developers reach reproductive maturity and the seeding proteoids emerge to form the tall shrub layer. As the proteoid canopy develops it begins to shade out the lower storey of shrubs and herbs, with severe consequences for both seeders and sprouters. In the case of seeders, which depend on seed production for long-term survival, shading has a negative impact on flowering and therefore on the replenishment of their seed bank. Shading also reduces the capacity of plants to

1 During the transitional phase of fynbos succession all of the slow-maturing species reach reproductive maturity and the seeding proteoids emerge to form the tall shrub layer. However, some fire ephemerals, such as *Edmondia fasciculata*, remain conspicuous in open, rocky sites.

photosynthesise, thereby interfering with the ability of sprouters to build up starch reserves in their underground storage organs. Moreover, the shaded canopy disrupts mutually beneficial relationships between plants and animals. For example ants, which disperse the seeds of many seeding shrubs to safe sites, shun these densely shaded areas with the result that many valuable seeds are consumed by rodents. All of these interactions reduce the post-fire regenerative potential of the lower layer in our fynbos patch.

However, the emerging canopy does provide perch sites for birds which disperse the fruits of forest and thicket species. The seeds are deposited beneath the proteoids where the shaded, litter-rich and more fertile conditions provide conditions ideal for the germination and establishment of these shrubs and trees.

BACK TO NORMAL?

The mature phase of fynbos development spans approximately 20 years between the transitional phase and the onset of the senescent phase, when many of the longer-lived shrubs begin to die. During this phase flowering of the seeding proteoids reaches a maximum, but it is also the period when the risk of fire increases rapidly. Indeed, this is the time when fynbos is waiting to burn. We have returned, in our fynbos patch, to the beginning of the cycle.

The patch is now 15 years old, the age at which it last burnt. That fire set in motion a series of dramatic events which have run their course to produce a new patch of fynbos. Is this new patch different from the previous one or is it back to normal? The simple answer is that there is no 'normal' state. Each fire is unique in its effects on a particular fynbos community; each has its own peculiar

characteristics and is preceded and followed by weather conditions which are unique. With these environmental idiosyncrasies as the background to a flora rich in species and reproduction methods, there is little surprise that fire should have a profound effect on the relative abundances of fynbos plants.

For a number of reasons, the fynbos community now occupying our patch of hillside is substantially different from its predecessor. In the first place, the fire, occurring in the middle of a long, dry summer, was more intense than the previous one, which burnt in the middle of November after a cool, wet spring. Small-seeded species were negatively affected not only by the heat of the fire, but also by competition with dense *Aspalathus* thickets which were barely evident after the earlier cool, spring burn. Thus seeding species with large, soil-stored seeds

---

2 Autumn burns promote the good establishment of proteoid shrub seedlings, mainly because the short time between seed release from serotinous cones and germination after the winter rains reduces the loss of seeds to granivorous rodents. Here a dense mat of *Protea laurifolia* seedlings is evident beneath the skeleton of the parent plant after an autumn fire.

3 In fynbos, each fire is unique in its effect on the regeneration of different species, and there is no guarantee that our hypothetical patch will be identical in appearance and composition to its predecessor. This mosaic of different fires, as shown by the different veld ages, has profoundly influenced the species complement of the landscape at Chapman's Nek on the Cape Peninsula.

are generally more abundant in the later community than in the previous one.

Secondly, the different months in which the fires occurred had an important influence on regeneration patterns. The November fire occurred before the seeds in the cones of the serotinous protea had matured, but shortly after seed ripening in the serotinous leucadendron. Therefore, seedling establishment in the protea was relatively poor, since it had to rely on seeds in older cones, many of which had been consumed by insect predators. This was not the case for the leucadendron. Moreover, since the fire occurred in spring, seeds had to remain on the soil surface for a much longer time than after the summer burn and there was a considerably greater loss to rodent predators. The result was that the earlier community had a lower abundance of serotinous

proteoids than the contemporary one. The spring burn also resulted in a rather poor display (and lower seed production) of watsonias since it occurred at a time when insufficient starch reserves had been accumulated.

Thirdly, the climatic conditions during the regeneration phase after the two fires were different. After the spring fire there were excellent autumn and early winter rains, but the late winter and spring rains failed almost completely. After the summer fire good autumn rains were followed by a long, dry spell and then a return to wet conditions until late spring. These differences explain, among other things, a shift in the relative dominance from the serotinous leucadendron in the previous community to the serotinous protea in the contemporary one. Even though an average leucadendron produces twice as many seeds as a protea, and there were proportionally more leucadendrons

than proteas in the earlier community, the frequent dry spells during May after the summer fire had a disastrous impact on the leucadendron population.

These are merely some of the differences, and their causes, between the two communities – there are many more. The important point is that different fires favour different species and a variable fire regime ensures that all species persist and coexist in the long term. Extreme fires such as those which occur in the youth phase (before many plants have flowered) and the senescent phase (after many shrubs have died) can result in the local extinction of species. But these are relatively rare. Most fires occur in mature fynbos in the summer months, but even when a strict and regular fire cycle is imposed, the outcome is not readily predictable. The managers of fynbos ecosystems have to deal with this uncertainty.

1 Declining populations of the exquisite marsh rose prompted the first prescribed burn in fynbos. In 1968 a patch of senescent fynbos in the Kogelberg was deliberately set ablaze by the Forestry Department. The result was excellent regeneration of this critically rare species.

2 Many millions of hectares of fynbos are intensively managed, making it unique among the world's mediterranean-type ecosystems. Controlled burns, including the burning of firebreaks such as this one in the mountains near Grabouw, form part of the overall management scheme.

3

FIRE AND FYNBOS MANAGEMENT

This chapter has highlighted the crucial role of fire in determining the species complement and associated abundances in fynbos communities. If we wish to manipulate the abundance of particular fynbos species for some purpose – be it wildflower production, water production, grazing or nature conservation – the most practical and appropriate way of doing this is to manipulate the fire regime. Thus, management of fynbos equates to the management of fire.

Today, fynbos ecosystems are unique among the mediterranean-type ecosystems of the world for the intensity of management that is applied over vast areas of natural vegetation. These include the 1.4 million hectares of protected mountain catchments, wilderness areas and nature reserves in the mountains, as well as the nature

reserves and some flower farms on the lowlands. The chances are very much in favour of any given fynbos area having a fire-based management plan. This was not the case until relatively recently.

There is a very long precolonial history of the use of fire to manipulate fynbos communities. For tens of thousands of years San hunter-gatherers practised 'fire-stick' farming, whereby fynbos was burnt to increase – and make more visible – populations of edible geophytes such as watsonias. Fire was also used for hunting, both to flush animals towards sites where they would be captured and killed and to attract them to newly burnt veld. The arrival of Khoi-khoi pastoralists and their livestock in the fynbos region about 2000 years ago heralded a new era in fynbos fire management. Burning to improve grazing for their cattle and fat-tailed sheep became widespread on the

lowlands and lower mountain slopes. It appears that the Khoi-khoi were astute veld managers, with an intimate knowledge of good grazing areas and their management requirements. Sadly, we have no specific details of their protocols, but it is likely that, on the coastal plain at least, they burnt mainly in autumn as they moved from the mountain foothills to overwinter on the coast.

European colonisation of the fynbos region saw the first penalties for the indiscriminate use of fire. Thus started a process of attempting to control fire by preventing it – a hopeless task in a fire-prone environment. Early *trekboere* probably copied the veld management practices of the Khoi-khoi, from whom they would have learnt their veld-lore. However, as farmers became settled into legally delineated units they could no longer trek across the countryside in search of good grazing. Instead they

---

3 In parts of the Cederberg management is aimed at the preservation of the rare Clanwilliam cedar. Populations of this impressive tree, which is endemic to the Cederberg, have declined markedly over the past 100 years due to overexploitation and to high-intensity summer fires which destroy all juveniles and most adults. Although seedling recruitment is good after these hot fires, managers feel that adult mortality is unacceptably high. Accordingly, they have subjected some areas to short-frequency (four-year), low-intensity winter burns to minimise the death of adults. The drawbacks of this approach are that seedling establishment after winter fires is poor and that the surrounding fynbos is burnt at a frequency and season that is totally inappropriate. To help counteract the first disadvantage, seedling establishment of the cedar is supplemented by artificial plantings. The Clanwilliam cedar is unusual among fynbos plants in that its biology is out of phase with normal fynbos fire regimes, and it may well be an ancient endemic that adapted to climatic conditions of the past.

resorted to patch burning, whereby veld was burnt as often as possible in order to maintain a large area of young veld, the stage which has the highest grazing value for livestock. Fuel loads were low and fires spread unevenly across the landscape, resulting in a mosaic of patches of different ages. This 'matchstick farming', so-called because 'management' amounted to the throwing of burning matches into the veld from horseback, persisted on a wide scale until the 1950s. Thereafter there was an increasing trend for planted pastures to replace veld-based grazing and it was not long before fynbos management lapsed into neglect.

In the early part of this century the view of the fledgling scientific community was that fire in fynbos was destructive and inimical to its preservation. In 1924 a meeting of the Royal Society of South Africa, which included various prominent Cape botanists, condemned veld burning in fynbos, and this was to lead to an attempt to ban fires. In 1945 the Royal Society published a report on the preservation of fynbos which included the first serious suggestion of controlled fires. Four years later P.G. Jordaan of the University of Stellenbosch published the first of a series of papers which described and explained the effects of fire frequency and season on the recruitment of seedlings of *Protea repens*.

By the early 1960s botanists had come to realise that fire was essential for the preservation of fynbos. The first prescribed burn in a mountain catchment was carried out in 1968 in the Kogelberg in order to promote seedling regeneration in a senescent population of the critically rare marsh rose – and it worked! In the same year the Forestry Department accepted prescribed burning as a management practice in fynbos mountain catchments under state control. The Mountain Catchment Act of 1970, which resulted in the proclamation of privately owned mountain catchments, greatly extended the area of fynbos subject to mandatory fire management.

At present the management objectives for catchment areas (as well as other conservation zones) emphasise the conservation of ecosystems and species to preserve biodiversity; to control alien plants; to ensure the sustained yield of high quality water and minimise erosion; to provide opportunities for the wise utilisation of resources (e.g. wildflowers, recreation); and to promote environmental education and cultural conservation (e.g. archaeological sites). These are laudable goals, but how can they be achieved?

Firstly, any potential conflicts between these goals

Sustainable wildflower harvesting requires careful management which need not be in conflict with biodiversity conservation. Over-harvesting, especially immediately before a fire, can reduce seed stores and bring about the local extinction of economically important species. Here workers are harvesting *Erica irregularis* near Gansbaai on the Agulhas Plain.

must be identified. One possibility is a conflict between water production and conservation. Farmers in the lowlands who depend on mountain water have long held the view that frequent burning of fynbos increases the water yields from catchments. However, research has shown that fire cycles of 12 to 15 years are most appropriate for meeting water needs without degrading catchments as a result of excessive erosion. Fires at these frequencies are also optimal for conservation – so there is no conflict between these two goals.

Another potential conflict could arise between conservation and utilisation, specifically the harvesting of wildflowers. The removal of blooms and cones for the cut-flower and dried-flower industries has a negative impact on post-fire regeneration. Seeds are precious resources in fynbos and their continual removal invariably creates

problems. However, the careful management required for the sustained production of wildflowers is not incompatible with conservation goals. Fynbos farmers are encouraged to remove only 50 per cent of the flowers and cones of serotinous Proteaceae every alternate year and to avoid picking at all in the year before a prescribed burn. While this can be enforced on public land, the same does not hold on privately owned catchments. Problems arise when owners wish to burn more frequently than they should in order to encourage valuable fire ephemerals such as the Cape everlasting; when market forces encourage them to overharvest rare but desirable plants such as *Brunia albiflora*; and when they spray veld plants to eliminate insects on export flowers.

How, then, do fire regimes fit into fynbos management programmes? Research has shown that the fire regime

which ensures that the maximum number of species persists in fynbos is one of summer fires on a 12- to 25-year rotation. By this stage, when fynbos is in the mature phase, all species have reproduced for several seasons and there is no sign of senescence. There are, however, practical problems associated with this fire regime. Managers of catchments which abut on farmlands and towns need to minimise the fire hazard in order to avoid destruction of crops and infrastructure. The simplest way to do this is to reduce fire intensity by keeping fuel loads as low as possible and by burning under cool, windless conditions. This would translate into short (five- to ten-year) rotation burns in spring, autumn and winter – and these would have disastrous consequences for fynbos biodiversity.

To overcome this problem a compromise has been

The most intensive fire management is required where fynbos abuts on densely populated urban areas, such as on the Cape Peninsula. Ironically, much of the Peninsula mountain chain is haphazardly managed, resulting in the proliferation of dense stands of alien plants which, when burnt in one of the innumerable wildfires which sweep through the area, create an unacceptably high fire hazard.

1

reached. Firstly, fire intervals can be kept to a safe (for fynbos) minimum by applying a simple rule of thumb: a fire should take place only when half the population of the slowest-maturing species in an area (which is usually a serotinous proteoid) have flowered for three successive seasons. In most fynbos areas this translates into an eight- to 12-year rotation.

Secondly, fires have been scheduled for the autumn months (March and April), after the peak season for fire hazard but still within the safe zone for fynbos regeneration. However, the weather during these months can be very fickle – in the western fynbos region only 12 days on average during this period have suitable weather for prescribed burning. Furthermore, autumn burns strongly favour the recruitment of serotinous proteoids since the time between seed release and germination, or the time

that seeds are exposed to predation by rodents, is kept to a minimum. Thus, autumn burns may result in dense thickets of proteoid shrubs which would have an adverse impact on understorey species. Ideally, the fire regime should be variable so as not to consistently promote any single group of species. This could be achieved by introducing an occasional spring fire into the burning schedule. In practice, wildfires inevitably confound burning programmes and, in doing so, introduce the necessary variation.

Fynbos managers require a wide variety of up-to-date and accurate information and maps to manage their lands effectively. For example, they need to know the age of the veld, the identity of alien plants and the degree of infestation, and the location of rare and endangered species in each management block in their catchments.

Information such as this enables them to make decisions about which blocks should be burned; which require alien control before and after fires; and when and where to control the spread of wildfires. Effective decision-making can only occur if the information base is accurate and regularly updated.

Recently a computer-based management system has been developed which is tailor-made for fynbos mountain catchments, but can be applied just as well elsewhere in the fynbos region. All the relevant information is stored in a personal computer which the manager uses to generate overlay maps showing management block boundaries, post-fire vegetation age, and the distribution and density of alien weeds. It also has a routine to calculate the fire hazard in different vegetation types and a system for planning control operations for alien species. This highly

1 In the eastern fynbos regions such as the Baviaanskloof, where grasses are abundant and livestock ranching is practised, there is a strong incentive to burn veld on a 4- to 5-year rotation to promote grass growth. This causes the extinction of slow-maturing seeders, many of which are local endemics. Where this management system is applied the fynbos is dominated by sprouters such as *Leucadendron salignum*, *Leucospermum cuneiforme*, restioids and tropical

grasses, and in mountainous terrain it results in high rates of erosion. Fortunately it is prohibited in proclaimed mountain catchments.
2 In the Outeniqua Mountains the proteoid and ericaceous fynbos is surrounded on all sides by commercial forestry plantations and croplands, and alien plant infestations are widespread. Because of the need to reduce the fire hazard and to synchronise fires with alien control programmes, intensive management is required. This amounts to

sections being burnt under controlled conditions to create a relatively small-scale mosaic of similar-sized blocks of different veld age. Disadvantages of this system are that management is intensive (and, therefore, expensive); the high number of burning operations leads to a high risk of runaway fires; and, because of its complexity, the programme is easily confounded by wildfires.
3 The Koue Bokkeveld mountain catchment is remote, inaccessible

sophisticated technology provides the manager with easy access to the relevant data and generates a schedule for assigning priorities for planned fires. The system is constantly and inexpensively updated so that the wisdom gained by a particular manager is preserved for posterity. The implementation of this computer-based system will greatly increase the cost-effectiveness of managing fynbos catchment, an important consideration in an era of dwindling expenditure in the public sector.

The management of fynbos ecosystems has come a long way in the past 50 years: from ignorance and fire exclusion to knowledge and fire management. Although there is still much to be learnt about fire in fynbos, we now know enough to establish a set of simple rules on when and how to burn. Ironically, these advances in our knowledge and in its wise application for realising management

objectives have matured at a time of severe budget cutbacks, and for many catchments (and nature reserves on the lowlands) funds are inadequate to carry out fundamental management routines. This is alarming. Yet, as we detail in the final chapter, the scientific management of fynbos catchments is the most cost-effective way of ensuring that fynbos yields, on a sustainable basis, its economically valuable resources.

and free of alien invaders. Much of it is privately owned and artificial ignition of the veld is common but not problematic, since most of the fires occur at appropriate intervals and in the correct season. The approach here is to control the wildfires according to local circumstances of veld age, hazard to property and accessibility. This is termed adaptive interference fire management. Although the fire regime is dominated by wildfires, it may be supplemented with

intentional burns when and where they are required.

4 Remote mountain catchments which are state-owned and abut on non-flammable vegetation represent an ideal opportunity to allow the natural fire regime (where fires are started only by lightning and rockfalls) to occur without interference. The central assumption here is that such fire regimes are optimal for the maintenance of fynbos biodiversity. This 'natural fire zone management' is applied in some inland

mountain catchments such as those in the Swartberg (shown here) which are free of alien plants and are surrounded by succulent karoo.

5 As the smoke settles from another fynbos fire we feel uneasy about the consequences. Yet, in fact, a new cycle has been initiated and some species, dormant for many years, will soon have their chance to display their wares. Fire in fynbos is natural, but in today's world of human domination it needs to be managed.

1

6.WHERE ARE THE ANIMALS?

Why are there so many plants in fynbos and yet, apparently, so few animals? Large and medium-sized animals are conspicuous by their absence, and it is quite possible to spend a full day in the fynbos without seeing a single one. Not here will you find the lions, leopards and cheetahs, rhinos, elephants and giraffes that attract thousands of visitors to other parts of southern Africa. The fynbos vegetation, on its nutrient-poor foundation, simply cannot support the substantial food requirements of the larger animals. Nevertheless, it does provide suitable niches for many smaller, less obvious ones, and these, in their own way, are just as fascinating. One of the attractions of fynbos lies in the subtlety of its animal life and in the intricate relationships between the plants and the many small creatures that, as they feed on the plants, often render some vital service in return.

THE FYNBOS FAUNA

Mammals

About a third of southern Africa's 280 mammal species have been recorded in the fynbos region. Some – including the black rhinoceros, buffalo, red hartebeest, eland, lion and elephant – roamed the area when the European settlers arrived at the Cape, but were rapidly eliminated. Most survive in other biomes, but for the endemic blue antelope elimination in 1800 meant extinction. Many other species that are still found in fynbos have greatly reduced ranges and occur in much smaller numbers because of the large-scale removal of the natural vegetation that supported them. The most widespread antelope species in the Cape mountains are the common duiker, grysbok and klipspringer, while on the lowlands the endemic bontebok grazes, and in a few reserves in the eastern

1 Unlike in the savannas of South Africa, the fynbos fauna is neither conspicuous nor charismatic. Nutrient poverty, seasonal drought and recurring, intense fires set a ceiling on the abundance and diversity of larger animals in fynbos landscapes. However, animals, and especially small ones, play essential roles in the maintenance of fynbos plant biodiversity. These plant-animal partnerships are often difficult to observe but provide a delightful reward to the patient naturalist.

The plant-straddling web of an orb-web spider in the early morning light provides an apt example of the subtlety of animal life in fynbos.
2 The sandy soils of the fynbos region provide a habitat for a number of small burrowing mammals such as moles and molerats. The Cape golden mole, an insectivore endemic to Namaqualand and the south-western Cape, feeds on earthworms as well as insects and forages in ridge-like tunnels it creates near the soil surface.

part of the region the Cape mountain zebra still occurs in small numbers. The leopard is the only large predator left, and the few that remain are now confined to the mountains where they are very rarely seen.

There are more medium-sized mammals in fynbos, including the chacma baboon, the porcupine, the honey badger, the antbear and two genet and four mongoose species. Cape clawless otters are still reasonably common in lakes and marshes and along rivers and streams, but because of their secretive behaviour they are seldom seen. A far more common sight is the rock dassie or rock hyrax, sunning itself on an exposed rock or boulder in the mountains. Other smaller mammals that are fairly well represented in fynbos are shrews, elephant shrews, moles, molerats, dormice, mice, rats and gerbils. Of the three molerat species that occur one, the Cape dune molerat, is

endemic. Generally, however, endemism is low among mammals, with only seven other species qualifying.

Birds

There is not an unusual diversity of birds in fynbos, and although about 250 species (excluding seabirds) have been recorded in the region, most of these are not associated specifically with fynbos vegetation. The fact that many of these species are found in other biomes throughout southern Africa indicates that they do not rely on any features peculiar to fynbos for their existence. The uniform structure of fynbos vegetation is one reason for the lack of diversity among the birds, since it provides fewer different kinds of opportunities (or niches) for foraging, breeding and other activities than, say, forest or savanna does. Another reason is the basic shortage of food available and the lack of variety in its composition. There is, for

3 Although large-spotted genets are fairly common in the fynbos biome, they are seldom seen as they are almost exclusively nocturnal. They usually occur in riverine forest where they feed on a variety of insects, small birds and mammals, and wild fruits.

4 The shy and nocturnal grysbok is endemic to the fynbos region where it lives in thicket and dense shrubland along the lower mountain slopes, in kloofs and along the coast. It is a selective feeder,

foraging for palatable grasses, herbs, leaves, fruits and pods.

5 The bontebok, which is closely related to the blesbok of South Africa's grassland biome, is endemic to the southwestern lowlands of the fynbos region. In the past these large antelope occurred in many herds that roamed the grassy renosterveld lowlands of the Overberg, but hunting and the loss of their habitat to agriculture reduced their numbers almost to the point of extinction. Active efforts to conserve

bontebok have resulted in a dramatic rise in their numbers over the past few decades, and today they occur in several reserves and on many private farms. Bontebok are almost exclusively grazers, preferring short, palatable grasses that grow on clay-rich soils. Where this fodder does not exist, such is in the Cape of Good Hope Nature Reserve on the Cape Peninsula, they spend much time feeding in the strandveld where the soils are more fertile than in fynbos.

example, little to attract fruit-eating species into a fynbos environment.

Most patches of fynbos are usually rather bleak places for birders, especially during midsummer. Only six bird species are endemic: the Cape rockjumper, Victorin's warbler, the Cape sugarbird, the orangebreasted sunbird, the Cape siskin and the protea canary. Of these, the sugarbird is probably the species most people associate with fynbos since it is the most conspicuous and the noisiest, especially in autumn and winter when the long-tailed males display across their territories in protea shrublands. Another typical fynbos species is the orange-breasted sunbird, a tiny bird which darts among flowering ericas as an iridescent splash of colour. Together with the insect-eating Cape robin, the spotted prinia and the ned-dicky, these form the core of the bird life in many fynbos

1 Lesser doublecollared sunbirds visit mountain areas in the western Cape only during summer and autumn to feed on the nectar and insects in the flowers of several forest trees, as well as those of the Proteaceae and Ericaceae. During the rest of the year they live in the lowlands, especially in coastal thicket, where they breed.
2 Victorin's warbler, one of six birds endemic to the fynbos region, is secretive but fairly common in densely vegetated habitats. Its lively,

bubbling song carries across many a fynbos-clad valley at dusk.
3 A common resident in a wide variety of habitats in the fynbos region, the Cape robin may be found in forests, dense protea shrubland and subtropical coastal thicket, as well as in stands of alien trees.
4 Parties of the endemic Cape siskin rove widely in search of food and are regularly seen at high altitudes where they feed on the seeds of grasses, sedges and restioids.

5 Confined to rocky habitats of the southwestern and southern Cape mountains, the endemic Cape rockjumper nests under rocks and in clumps of bergpalmiet, and is invariably seen bounding from rock to rock before disappearing quickly into the undergrowth.
6 The protea canary, another fynbos endemic, is a little-known species which, although reasonably common in tall protea shrublands, is unobtrusive and frequently overlooked. Its winter diet comprises

communities throughout the year. Another two specialist nectar-feeders often associated with fynbos are the malachite sunbird and the lesser doublecollared sunbird. However, they have marked seasonal movements and are not confined to fynbos.

Some smaller animals

About 30 snake, six tortoise (including one endemic), 30 frog and toad (including nine endemic) and about 30 freshwater fish species (half of which are endemic) also occur in fynbos. Lizards have been poorly surveyed outside the southwestern corner of the biome, but at least 50 species are known to occur and agamas, skinks, geckos and chameleons are fairly well represented. Most numerous, and diverse, of all are the invertebrates – the insects, spiders, scorpions and molluscs of all shapes, sizes and forms. Every patch of fynbos is home to many

hundreds of these tiny creatures. Ants in particular are well represented, with 45 species alone having been recorded from the Jonkershoek Valley near Stellenbosch.

Levels of endemism are much higher for invertebrates than for vertebrates. This can be readily understood if one likens the less mobile invertebrates to immobile plants; only the vertebrates, being larger and more mobile, are able to move in and out of the fynbos environment. Invertebrates, and to a greater extent plants, have to stay on their fynbos 'island' and evolve new species to survive.

Animals and fire

The intense fires that burn large tracts of fynbos every five to 40 years pose major problems to all animals. Some perish, and this has given rise to the belief that fire brings only death and destruction to animals. However, many escape the heat and flames by fleeing to safe sites such

mainly dry protea seeds, while in summer it also feeds on smaller seeds, fleshy fruits, flowers and buds. The nectar of species such as *Protea repens* forms part of its diet too.

7 There are about 30 snake species in the fynbos biome, none of which are endemic. The puff adder occurs in a wide variety of habitats and, because its large size, lazy demeanour and apparent preference for lying on footpaths make it more conspicuous, it is probably the

most frequently encountered venomous snake in the region.

8 The endemic arum lily frog is, as its name suggests, closely associated with arum lilies which grow in vleis and other damp areas. Suckers on the frog's toes enable it to cling to the inside of the chalice-shaped flower, where it preys on insects attracted to the lily's spike.

9 This graceful crag lizard, an endemic species associated with the Cape Fold Mountains, occurs from Nieuwoudtville in the northwest of

the fynbos region to the Kammanassie Mountains in the east.

10 The rather secretive Cape skink feeds on large insects that it captures on the ground, usually in open, sandy areas.

11 Although a fire-charred landscape may appear to be devoid of life, many small creatures, such as this southern rock agama, survive by hiding under rocks or in holes. They emerge soon after the fire to forage on insects made conspicuous by the absence of vegetation.

1

as rocky outcrops, underground burrows, or relatively fire-proof riverine forests.

A few weeks after a fynbos fire many signs of animal life are visible. Birds such as longbilled pipits and Cape siskins often feed in recently burnt fynbos, the former on insects and small animals and the latter on seeds released from cones by the heat of the fire. Burnt fynbos also attracts mammals, and the grey rhebok and klipspringer, for example, may be seen feeding on the soft new growth.

Although most mice, rats and shrews survive fires by sheltering under rocks or dashing away from the worst of the flames, they migrate to unburnt patches of vegetation – notably forest along streams and in rocky terrain – from which they make brief forays into the burnt-out areas to feed on seeds and other titbits. Thus populations of small mammals in a burnt area of fynbos decline immediately

after a fire, remaining low for about nine months before they increase again, and to levels higher than the pre-fire ones, as more food and cover become available.

Birds are less vulnerable to fire than many other animals simply because they can usually fly away, both to avoid the flames and, after the burn, to find new sources of food and nesting sites. Some, instead of fleeing, feed opportunistically at the fire's edge, hawking insects that are flushed by the approaching flames.

The life cycles of many fynbos animals are finely tuned to the cycle of fire. Some breed predominantly in the late autumn and winter months, after the fire season, and thus avoid exposing their young to fire. Eggs of the endemic geometric tortoise, for example, hatch mainly in April and May when the greatest danger of fire is past. Birds that build nests in fynbos are susceptible to losing their

broods if a fire occurs before or after the young hatch, but in the southwestern Cape they breed mainly between July and October, well outside the summer fire season. The Cape honeybee, a very important pollinator of many fynbos plants, is another animal whose biology is in harmony with the rhythms of fynbos. By forming mobile reproductive swarms in the spring months, when most plants are flowering and fire incidence is low, they improve their chances of rearing a brood successfully and thus of colony reproduction.

FYNBOS AS FOOD

The environmental conditions that are peculiar to fynbos, notably fire and the nutrient-poor soils, mean that the quality of its vegetation as a food source is generally poor. Even 350 years ago, before the Europeans arrived with

1 The geometric tortoise, or *suurpootjie*, is the only endemic tortoise species in fynbos, and one of the rarest in the world; according to a recent survey, only between 6000 and 8000 individuals remain. Its breeding cycle is timed so that its hatchlings emerge in late autumn, when they are less likely to be caught in a fire.

2

3

their guns, the herds of large grazing mammals in the fynbos and renosterveld were smaller than those that roamed the grassland and savanna landscapes further north. The more nutritious renosterveld supported larger numbers of herbivores (which in turn provided food for the larger predators), but the loss of these natural grazing lands to pasture and wheatfields has meant that only those herbivores that can live on what the fynbos provides have survived in the region.

Grasses are scarce, especially in the western part of the biome, and those that are available are of poor quality, with abysmally low levels of crude proteins and phosphorus. Important trace elements such as copper, cobalt and manganese are also deficient in many areas, especially in summer. Foliage thus forms the normal diet of the majority of fynbos antelope, but the leaves of most shrubs are

tough and leathery and some, such as those of the common and widespread *Cliffortia* and *Muraltia* species, are spiny too. Other plants protect themselves by producing chemical compounds which make them unpalatable to a large number of animals. Consequently bulk feeding is not an option for fynbos herbivores; they must focus their attention on the more palatable parts of the plant and those where nutrients are concentrated – the fruits, seed pods and flowers – as well as on the first flushes of relatively nutritious growth after fire. Food sources such as these are widely scattered in space and time, and to take advantage of them many fynbos browsers have physiological or behavioural adaptations that enable them to locate, consume and digest what is available, and to exist in small numbers.

The most common antelope in the Cape mountains –

2 Steenbok are fairly common in relatively open habitats throughout the fynbos region. Like the other small antelope that live in fynbos, they are selective feeders, choosing nutrient-rich plant parts even if it means making occasional forays into vineyards which adjoin their habitat.

3 The Cape mountain zebra, which was rescued from extinction in the 1930s, used to roam widely in the drier mountain regions of the southwestern to southeastern Cape. Today there are several populations in the grassy mountains of the eastern fynbos region and in the Bontebok National Park and the De Hoop Nature Reserve. Like other zebra, it is a bulk-feeder, requiring large amounts of grass for adequate sustenance.

1

the common duiker, grysbok and klipspringer – are well adapted to the spartan fare of the fynbos. They have slender muzzles which enable them to select those parts of the plant which give them the highest food value. Selective feeding is a time-consuming process, but the animals' small size and, therefore, relatively low daily food requirements allow them to be fussy – they are the gourmets among antelopes.

The endemic bontebok and the Cape mountain zebra, on the other hand, are predominantly grazers and, requiring greater sustenance because of their greater bulk, they cannot afford the luxury of selecting only the choicest morsels. They also live in larger groups than the common duiker, grysbok and klipspringer, and must rely on extensive tracts of vegetation to survive. The fragmentation of natural areas by agriculture has meant that these large

herbivores can no longer migrate across the region as they did in the past and they are now confined to reserves which provide year-round forage. Most of these reserves are on the more fertile soils of the lowlands (e.g. the Bontebok National Park near Swellendam) and in the eastern mountains where summer rainfall promotes the growth of grasses (e.g. the Suurberg range north of Port Elizabeth). The mountains of the western part of the region, where there are still large tracts of fynbos, cannot support high numbers of bulk-feeders.

Some fynbos animals solve the problem of getting enough nutrients by feeding on almost anything that is available. The chacma baboon is probably the most familiar of these generalist feeders, as it is common and its search for food often brings it into contact with humans. Baboons feed on the flowers of a number of *Protea*

species by breaking off the flowerhead and sucking the nectar, as well as on the underground parts of a number of fynbos geophytes. They also devour insects and scorpions. Despite this catholic diet they experience a shortage of food in some areas at certain times of year, and it is then that the conflict between humans and baboons arises. On the Cape Peninsula they have learnt to beg from tourists, leading to potentially dangerous situations, and elsewhere they also raid farmers' crops. The predicament of baboons, probably more than that of any other fynbos animal, is symptomatic of human disruption of animal communities in the region.

Because of the scarce plant resources and therefore low herbivore numbers, large predators require very extensive home ranges in fynbos. The only large predator is, in fact, the leopard, and in the Stellenbosch area, for

1 Chacma baboons are still common in parts of the fynbos region, where they feed on a wide range of plants as well as on insects and scorpions. Despite their catholic diet they seem to experience a shortage of food in some areas at certain times of the year. In the Cape of Good Hope Nature Reserve they have shown an innovative way of overcoming the food shortage by harvesting mussels, limpets and other marine animals on the reserve's rocky shore.

This is the only record of primates other than humans foraging in the intertidal zone.

2

3

example, a leopard may have a range of between 380 and 480 square kilometres, which is more than ten times the average home range of a leopard in the savanna biome. Their natural food is scarce and their habitat has been encroached upon for extensive livestock farming. Leopards are shot every year, and their numbers continue to decline steadily.

At the other end of the scale, small herbivores – rodents such as the striped mouse, the vlei rat and the Namaqua rock mouse – are numerous in fynbos. They prosper by exploiting one of the biome's few nutritious food sources, the seeds, and in doing so they play an important role in the regeneration of many fynbos species. Seeds of fynbos plants are very rich in essential elements such as nitrogen, phosphorus and potassium, and in some groups nearly half the plant's annual uptake

of phosphorus is shunted into the seeds. As was discussed in the chapter 'Famine in paradise', fynbos plants pack their seeds with nutrients in order to give their seedlings as good a chance as possible to establish and thrive in a nutrient-poor environment and thus maintain their places in the community. In animals a number of innovative means have evolved to enable them to exploit every phase in the development of the seeds, from pollination to germination.

In order to germinate the seeds must reach the soil safely, but there are many opportunities for hungry animals to intervene. And intervene they certainly do. For example, the larvae of many insects regularly consume more than 80 per cent of seeds stored in the cones of species such as *Protea repens*. The adults lay their eggs in the protea blooms when the flowerheads are open. After the cones

2 The striped mouse is common over a wide range of habitats throughout the fynbos biome. This seed-eating rodent, along with several others, plays a major role in controlling the regeneration of many shrub species by consuming a large proportion of the seeds that are released after fire. The number of seedlings that establish is determined to a large extent by the length of time between the fire and the onset of cool, wet weather that triggers germination – the

longer this period, the more seeds are consumed by hungry rodents, and the fewer survive to germinate.
3 The leopard is one of the many large mammal species whose population size and distribution range in the fynbos region have shrunk drastically as human numbers have increased. Scratch marks on trees and spoor along paths are all that hikers are likely to see of these magnificent animals. However, stock farmers whose

land adjoins mountains have closer contact with them. Consequently a number of leopards are trapped and shot by farmers every year.

1

have closed and the seeds have matured, the larvae hatch and burrow into the seeds to enjoy a protein-rich meal.

Seeds that do reach the ground fall prey to rodents, which play a major role in the regeneration of serotinous proteoids, regulating whether or not entire shrublands re-establish after fire. The magnitude of the role they play depends on the time of year at which the fire burns. When a fire sweeps through a patch of fynbos at the end of a long dry summer its heat bursts open the cones of serotinous plants. The seeds are released and fall to the ground, vulnerable to the depredations of the hungry rodents. The sooner the first autumn rains fall, the sooner the seeds can germinate and 'escape' from the seed-eaters by developing into seedlings. These grow and mature and the proteoids return. The period between the fire and the first rains is critical: if the fire occurs in spring,

the released seeds lie exposed on the ground for months, waiting for the rains and cool temperatures of winter to initiate germination. During that time the rodents can consume the entire crop, thereby preventing the stand of proteoids from regenerating.

Another relatively rich food source for fynbos animals is represented by the fleshy underground bulbs, corms, rhizomes and tubers in which more than 16 per cent of the plants of the Cape flora – the geophytes – store their nutrients. These 'subterranean food packets' are the staple diet of many fynbos inhabitants, including baboons, francolins and molerats.

The composition of fynbos bird life and the behaviour of many species are determined largely by the distribution of food in time and space. Although fynbos is very rich in plant species, relatively few of these are used directly by

birds, and the scarcity of certain types of food is a major reason for the low diversity of birds. For example, parrots, louries, rollers, hornbills, barbets and woodpeckers are poorly represented in fynbos because large insects and fleshy fruits, a major part of their diet, are rare. There are no specialist fruit-eaters among fynbos birds, but generalist feeders such as the Cape bulbul, Cape white-eye, and redwinged starling are the most important fruit-eaters in most areas, and other species such as the southern boubou and protea canary also consume fruit at certain times of the year. Trees and shrubs of forest and thicket patches are the major source of fleshy fruits.

Although fynbos plants in general produce little in the way of fruits, some do provide birds with other important foods. Tall proteas such as *Protea nitida* and *P. repens* yield copious supplies of energy-rich nectar in winter and

1 Cape sugarbirds, endemic to the fynbos region, are specialists of the Proteaceae, visiting and pollinating species with a wide variety of floral designs. They probe into bowl-shaped flowerheads (such as *Protea cynaroides*), closed flowerheads (*P. speciosa*) and cup-shaped (*P. nitida*) and chalice-shaped ones (*P. neriifolia*), as well as the pincushion-like heads of *Leucospermum* species such as this *L. catherinae*, an endemic of the northwestern mountains. The

sugarbirds' stiletto-sharp claws enable them to grip onto branches and flowerheads and to continue feeding (and pollinating) even when strong winds force other birds to take cover in the undergrowth. Most proteas flower during winter, and at this time of year large numbers of sugarbirds gather on the lower mountain slopes to breed. In early summer the flowering period is over and they disperse, often into suburban gardens with summer-flowering shrubs.

this, together with the insects associated with it, attracts a wide array of birds to the showy bushes. Most conspicuous are the Cape sugarbird and orangebreasted sunbird, specialist nectar-feeders in the proteoid shrublands.

To ensure a year-round supply of food, many birds are itinerant, roving the countryside in search of sustenance. Orangebreasted sunbirds, for example, congregate at lower altitudes from autumn to spring when they feed on the nectar of proteas and other species, but in summer they move to the higher slopes where they are attracted to the many erica species that flower in the cooler, moist mountain conditions. Birds that are resident in most fynbos areas occur in relatively sparse populations and either feed mainly on insects, or are generalist feeders with an extensive diet that includes insects, fruit, nectar and seeds. Of the six species endemic to the fynbos

region, the protea canary and Cape siskin feed predominantly on seeds, the Cape sugarbird and orangebreasted sunbird on nectar, and the Cape rockjumper and Victorin's warbler on insects.

The degree to which food limits bird distribution is clearly seen if one considers how many birds have moved into the fynbos biome since habitats have changed through human influence and have provided new opportunities for foraging and breeding. Approximately a third of the present complement of birds in the fynbos arrived only in the last 100 years, and many of these have been here no more than 50 years. A large proportion of the 'new' species roost or nest in trees which are scarce in natural fynbos but occur in parks and gardens, and most of them feed on insects that have become more abundant in certain transformed environments, such as irrigated

pastures. None of them rely on natural fynbos resources for their survival – a severe indictment of the quality of 'fynbos cuisine'!

PLANT-ANIMAL INTERACTIONS
Pollination

Many types of mammals, birds and insects play a major role in fynbos that is frequently overlooked by the casual observer – they pollinate the flowers. Recent studies have shown that there is intense rivalry between plant species for the attention of pollinators, whose numbers are often so low that many flowers go unpollinated. This is particularly apparent for geophytes which bloom just after a fire, when pollinators are especially scarce. Competition for the attention of animal pollinators has been one of the major driving forces in the evolution of the great diversity of floral

---

2 Geophytes are an important source of food for many mammals in the fynbos, including molerats, porcupines and humans. It is somewhat unusual for birds to feed on geophytes, but for the francolins of the fynbos region – including the Cape francolin which is endemic to fynbos and parts of the adjacent succulent karoo – bulbs, tubers and corms form a large part of their diet.

3 Energy-rich nectar is produced by thousands of fynbos plant species to attract animals to visit and thus pollinate their flowers. Several animals have learnt how to exploit this valuable resource without 'paying' for the privilege by making contact with the stamens and pollen presenters – these are the 'nectar thieves'. Carpenter bees are adept at stealing nectar from species such as *Watsonia tabularis*.

4 Butterflies are uncommon in fynbos, probably because the leathery and nutrient-poor leaves of this vegetation provide little food for their foliage-feeding larvae. They are also not important pollinators of fynbos flowers. An important exception is the mountain pride butterfly which is strongly attracted to red flowers and is the exclusive pollinator of many autumn-flowering geophytes. It is shown here visiting the succulent *Crassula coccinea*.

designs in fynbos. The currency of this rivalry is nectar.

Energy-rich nectar is produced by thousands of fynbos plant species to attract animals to visit their flowers and pollinate them. But how do plants ensure effective pollination without providing a 'free lunch' to every visitor? Clearly, the reward of nectar has to be appropriately advertised to ensure that the correct pollinators are attracted, and the different species' advertising campaigns also contribute to the plethora of floral designs.

Some plants have gone the 'generalist route' and, like many proteas, are pollinated by both birds and insects. Other species have much stricter relationships with their pollinators. Several geophytes which grow at high altitudes and produce red flowers in autumn are pollinated predominantly (or exclusively in the cases of at least 15 species) by a single butterfly species, the mountain

pride. This butterfly is attracted to anything red, be it a backpack, a shirt or a flower. Red is not a colour that usually attracts insects, but this fixation enables the mountain pride to locate the red-flowered, nectar-bearing plants which are widely scattered in the dry autumn landscape. The dependence of so many different plants on one butterfly species for pollination is probably unique in the world. The mountain pride even visits aloes and red-hot pokers which, having flower shapes designed for pollination by birds rather than butterflies, thus provide it with a 'free lunch'.

About 430 plant species in fynbos are pollinated by birds, a figure that represents about 75 per cent of all southern African plants adapted for this form of pollination. Of these species about 100 belong to the genus *Erica* and 79 to the family Proteaceae. Many of the long-

1 Of the six sunbird species that occur in the region, the orange-breasted sunbird is the most dependent on fynbos vegetation. Just as the Cape sugarbird is a Proteaceae specialist, this tiny sunbird, weighing only 10 grams, is an expert on ericas, of which there are about 100 bird-pollinated species in the fynbos. In some ericas, such as this *Erica viridescens*, the corolla tubes are strongly curved to match the sunbird's bill.

3

tubed, red-flowered species of *Watsonia* are also pollinated by birds. The main agents are the Cape sugarbird and several of the sunbirds, with the former visiting about 300 protea flowerheads every day during autumn and winter to satisfy their energy requirements. Sunbirds are also attracted to the flowerheads of many protea species, but their shorter bills seldom allow them to effect pollination. They and other birds such as Cape bulbuls, Cape rock thrushes, redwinged starlings, Cape white-eyes, Cape weavers and yellowrumped widows are known as 'nectar thieves' since they feed on the proteas' nectar by inserting their bills through the side of the flowerhead, thus avoiding contact with the pollen presenters.

Sunbirds are more effective at pollinating ericas, and they have a close association with the *Erica* genus. The flowers of many of the species have straight or curved

tubes and are predominantly red, pink and white, orange, yellow or green. The tubular flowers of some of the species have strongly curved corollas that match the bill shape of the orangebreasted sunbird, the chief bird pollinator of ericas in fynbos. Because birds are much heavier than insects, most of the bird-pollinated ericas are relatively robust shrubs with sturdy stems that provide a perch for the bird.

About 80 per cent of the 526 *Erica* species that occur in the Cape flora are pollinated by insects, including bees, flies and thrips. Many of the ericas with flask-shaped flowers – such as *E. ampullacea*, *E. fastigiata*, *E. jasminiflora* and *E. shannonea* – are pollinated by flies with a long proboscis, and these have a higher concentration of nectar than ericas pollinated by other insects such as bees. They differ from their bird-pollinated cousins in

that the mouth of the flower tube is smaller, and its lobes are large, star-shaped and spreading, often providing flies with a landing platform and a foothold while they insert their long tongues into the tube to reach the nectar.

Ericas are by no means the only species pollinated by insects; indeed, the vast majority of fynbos plants rely on insects for this service. Beetles, flies, bees, moths and butterflies are the main agents, although other insects, such as earwigs and thrips, may also play important roles. Protea flowerheads often contain hundreds of insects of many species, some of which eat nectar and pollen or prey upon other insects in the flowerheads. Some are important pollinators in their own right, whereas others aid in pollination by attracting birds to the flowerheads to feed on them.

The showy flowers of many proteas are their billboards

About 80 per cent of the 526 ericas in the Cape flora are pollinated by insects. The shape and behaviour of different insect pollinators has influenced the evolution of flower form in ericas, resulting in a spectacular diversity of blooms. Whereas bees pollinate ericas with short, urn-shaped flowers such as *Erica obliqua* (**2**), long-proboscid flies – including horse flies, tangle-wing flies and bee flies – are important pollinators of many tubular-flowered species. A horse fly visiting *Erica irbyana* (**3**) finds the flower's narrow tube just wide and long enough for its tongue to reach the nectar.

for luring birds and insects to the irresistible nectar. But some species have dull, unassuming flowerheads that hang close to, or even lie on, the ground. No bird is going to be attracted to flowers such as these, but another group of animals is. About 35 *Protea* species have sweet, fleshy floral bracts which, unlike those of the bird- and insect-pollinated proteas, are low in tannins and, to a mouse at least, tasty to eat. These low-lying proteas also produce yeasty-smelling nectar which is highly attractive to certain small rodents. Moreover, the flowers provide nectar at times of the year when other foods that the mice eat, such as seeds, are scarce. The striped mouse, the Namaqua rock mouse and Verreaux's mouse are probably the most important visitors to species such as *P. acaulos* and *P. subulifolia*. The nectar of mammal-pollinated proteas is rich in sucrose, whereas the bird-pollinated species provide their flying visitors, which require more energy, with a 'quick fix' nectar containing fructose and glucose.

Flower mimicry is a device used by some plants to ensure that they are pollinated without having to provide nectar in exchange. It is a common phenomenon in other mediterranean-climate regions of the world, but less so in fynbos, probably because food is scarce. Pollinators visit flowers too often for 'charlatans' to become established. There are, however, a few striking examples, such as the rare orchid *Disa fasciata* which is very similar in form and colour to the more common China flower *Adenandra villosa*. By mimicking the latter, the orchid has greatly improved its chances of being pollinated. Another orchid, the nectarless *Disa ferruginea*, is also involved in mimicry, closely resembling *Tritoniopsis triticea* in one part of its

Insect pollination, which has been poorly studied in fynbos, is a topic in which amateur naturalists can make an important contribution to our knowledge of fynbos ecology. We know very little about the plant-pollinator relationships such as those illustrated by a painted lady butterfly on *Scabiosa africana* (**1**); a tachinid fly on *Hessea monticola* (**2**); a honey bee on *Polygala fruticosa* (**3**); and monkey beetles on *Moraea tulbaghensis* (**4**).

5 Pollination by non-flying mammals is a syndrome associated almost entirely with Proteaceae growing in fynbos and the ecologically similar kwongan of southwestern Australia. Proteas which are visited by rodents have dull, bowl-shaped flowers that usually lie on the ground or are hidden amongst the foliage; emit a yeasty odour; and produce copious amounts of sucrose-rich nectar. *Protea humiflora*, in this case visited by a Namaqua rock mouse, is a good example.

6

7

range and the red-hot poker *Kniphofia uvaria* in another. The mountain pride butterfly visits the orchid expecting to feed on an abundant supply of nectar, leaves unsatisfied, but does effect pollination.

Dispersing seeds

Seed dispersal by animals is usually a mutually beneficial arrangement – plants gain through the transport of their seeds to favourable establishment sites, while animals feed on some fleshy titbit attached to the seed. In fynbos the most important dispersers are ants, and they are attracted to seeds which have fleshy white appendages called elaiosomes. The fats, proteins, starches, sugars and vitamins contained in the elaiosomes are all gourmet products for these tiny invertebrates.

The dispersal of seeds by ants, or myrmecochory, is a most intriguing feature of fynbos ecology. A single spe-

cies, the pugnacious ant, is found virtually throughout the fynbos region and is dominant in most communities. Although at least another eight species disperse seeds, the pugnacious ant is by far the most important dispersal agent. It carries the seed into its nest, devours the fleshy elaiosome and discards the rest, leaving the seed underground and safe from predators until conditions are suitable for germination.

Two vegetation types, fynbos and Australian kwongan, have the highest incidence of plants with ant-dispersed seeds in the world. When trying to discover why this should be so, ecologists first looked at the two overriding environmental features of fynbos and its Australian equivalent: recurring fires and nutrient-poor soils. Were there associations between these features and myrmecochory? Some ecologists argued that seeds buried by ants avoid

Most of the goblet-shaped protea flowers are adapted for bird pollination. These flowers, which are actually agglomerations of many florets surrounded by bracts, are mini-ecosystems with a constant and congenial climate, a generous supply of pollen and energy-rich nectar, and a wide range of micro-niches. It is not surprising then, that protea flowers harbour a diverse community of insects. One member of this community is the nectar-feeding Cape scarab beetle – seen here on *Protea cynaroides* (**6**) – which is also an effective pollinator. Others include mites (**7**) which occur in their thousands. Although they hitch rides on pollinators such as sugarbirds and beetles, mites seldom transfer pollen themselves. They may, nonetheless, be important in pollination because the sugarbirds that feed on the nectar also eat the mites, and in probing for them come into contact with more stigmas, thus collecting more pollen.

1

2

being destroyed by fire. However, the fire-prone vegetation types on fertile soils that adjoin fynbos and Australian shrublands lack ant-dispersed species, so fire cannot be the primary reason for the evolution of myrmecochory. Nor could the answer lie in the quality of the soil for, far from carrying the seeds from nutrient-poor to nutrient-rich sites, the ants transport them from richer sites beneath the canopy of adult plants to less fertile ones in the open where they prefer to have their nests.

A common factor of ant-dispersed species is that they have relatively large and nutrient-rich seeds, and there is strong evidence that myrmecochory evolved to prevent the loss of these valuable assets to predators. An interesting natural experiment was established when the alien Argentine ant invaded small areas of fynbos. Unlike the indigenous species, it eats elaiosomes on the soil

surface, leaving the seeds exposed and vulnerable to predation by rodents. In fynbos invaded by the Argentine ant seedling regeneration of ant-dispersed plants after fire is much less successful than in uninvaded fynbos.

Although myrmecochory prevents seed loss due to predation, it cannot counter the effects of low seed production and the rapid depletion of seed stores. There are many ant-dispersed species in most fynbos areas, but the plants are generally scattered and not found in abundance. They also have common features in that most are dwarf, small-leaved shrubs that are killed by fire and produce seeds that are relatively large and few in number and are short-lived. Being entirely reliant on these small stores of seeds for reproduction after a fire, the plants are highly vulnerable to population crashes, since the climatic conditions following a burn are not always suitable for

regeneration. A plant that is vulnerable to population crashes is also susceptible to the development of new genetic structure, and this leads ultimately to speciation – the formation of new species.

Rates of speciation are faster in small populations than they are in large ones. Not only do ants disperse seeds over short distances (usually less than 10 metres) but, as most myrmecochores are insect-pollinated, pollen is also transferred over relatively short distances. The result is that plant populations easily become genetically isolated, which further enhances speciation. Thus one can say that the large number of ant-dispersed species in fynbos stems less from the ecological advantages of this method of dispersal than from the fact that it is associated with features which promote speciation.

Another plant-animal interaction which facilitates the

Floral mimicry, which involves the superficial resemblance in form or colour of one species to another so that the first gains some advantage, is strangely uncommon in fynbos. One example is the similarity between the red orchid *Disa ferruginea* (**1**), which produces no nectar, and *Tritoniopsis triticea* (**2**), which produces nectar in abundance. The mountain pride butterfly is 'fooled' into visiting the orchid and effecting pollination, without being paid for this service.

4

process of reproduction in fynbos involves geophytes and molerats. It was originally thought that when the Cape dune molerat was feeding on the corms of various geophytes it was simply exploiting a good source of nourishment. There is, however, another side to this story – the plants have capitalised on being the favoured food of molerats, making use of the animals to disperse their underground organs. Some iris species produce two separate clusters of corms: the larger cluster entices the molerat and, if it is completely consumed, the spine-tipped corms from the second one can still reproduce. Moreover, when a molerat finds the large tasty corm body it rips off the rough outer covering and begins to eat the corm segments immediately. Many of the segments are dislodged in the process and later take root.

Having eaten its fill, the molerat carries some corm segments back to its nest to store them. In doing so it drops some along the way, and leaves others in its hoard uneaten. These sprout too, with the result that the geophyte, aided by the molerat, has successfully dispersed its corms away from the parent plant.

Although not a hospitable environment for large animals, fynbos does provide sufficient sustenance for hundreds of smaller, inconspicuous creatures. The sustenance is not supplied free of charge, however, but in many cases on condition, as it were, that some service be rendered in return. The partnerships forged between plants and animals are fascinating, and although the significance of many has been discovered in recent years, there are no doubt many other interactions which have yet to be observed and explained.

3 The Cape dune molerat is a large rodent that feeds on the bulbs, corms and rhizomes of geophytes and is confined to the sandy lowland soils of the southwestern fynbos region. It lives in burrows up to 100 metres long, making its presence conspicuous by throwing up large mounds of excavated sand. More importantly, as it feeds on the corms of geophytes or carries corm segments to its underground hoard it inevitably drops some, and these will take root. Thus the molerat

plays a role in the dispersal of geophytes' underground organs.
4 More than 3000 fynbos plant species have seeds that are dispersed by ants. Only the kwongan flora of southwestern Australia has similar levels of ant dispersal, or myrmecochory. The influence of a tiny creature such as the pugnacious ant, shown here moving an elaiosome-bearing seed of *Leucospermum cordifolium*, is far out of proportion to its size. By burying the seed beneath the soil, out of reach of hungry

predators, the ants promote good post-fire regeneration of the largely reseeding and locally endemic myrmecochorous flora. Such subtle but vitally important plant-animal interactions are a hallmark of fynbos.

1

2

7. THE INVADERS

In many respects the fynbos region is like an island, cut off from the rest of sub-Saharan Africa as much by its unique combination of infertile soils, winter-wet climate and recurring fires at relatively long intervals as by its position in the southwestern corner of the continent. The effects of this insularity are seen most clearly in the fynbos plants since, being sedentary, they are unable to escape the harsh ecological forces. Indeed, as has been explained in previous chapters, they have thrived in the face of adversity, producing new species which have evolved to cope with the stresses imposed by their environment. About 6000 plant species, nearly 70 per cent of the total flora, occur nowhere else, representing the legacy of a long and isolated evolutionary history. Most species that are not endemic to the fynbos 'island' occur in vegetation types other than fynbos, such as forest, renosterveld or

subtropical thicket. These either do not burn or occur on more fertile soils and are therefore not as effectively isolated as fynbos. Just as fynbos species are 'locked inside' their island, plants from other African biomes, unaccustomed to the harshness of the fynbos biome, have been unable to penetrate it.

However, as was discussed in the chapter 'What is fynbos?', there are areas elsewhere in the world that experience climate, soils and fire regimes similar to those of fynbos. Organisms in these areas, having adapted to cope with similar stresses, would in theory be able to establish in the fynbos environment, but in the past were prevented from settling there by their inability to cross vast tracts of ocean. Then came voyages of discovery, the age of sea travel and, in modern times, the crumbling of communications barriers. The splendid isolation enjoyed

1 Humans first entered the fynbos region about half a million years ago. These early invaders were hunter-gatherers, sparsely distributed across the landscape in small groups. Their descendants, the San, decorated the hard, sandstone walls of caves with beautiful paintings that depicted images induced during trance-like religious experiences. However, there is no doubt that the elephants and other larger mammals illustrated in this rock art from the Cederberg roamed freely in the nearby Olifants River valley before they succumbed to the guns of the Europeans.

by fynbos came to an end when humans deliberately transported plants from these similar environments across the seas and introduced them into fynbos. Those who made the introductions could have had little idea of the disastrous long-term effects of what they were doing. And, because fynbos had not been regularly invaded by plants from adjoining biomes during its development, its defences against the incursion of invaders when the barriers were finally breached were very poor. This explains, in part, why alien vegetation has established so successfully in the southern and southwestern Cape.

But plants are not the only intruders: animals too have made an impact. Nor should we forget that humans have been the most influential invaders of all in the fynbos. Like other colonising organisms, they initially battled to survive in an alien environment. Unlike other invaders, however,

humans were able to use technological innovations to help them manipulate the natural environment and impose their will on it. In doing so they paved the way for the invasion of fynbos by other organisms.

HUMANS – THE MOST SUCCESSFUL INVADERS

Humans (or their ancestors) invaded the fynbos region from further north in Africa for the first time about 500 000 years ago. They faced many difficulties, and in fynbos in particular they had to cope with the shortage of food, the intense fires and the summer drought. They were also easy prey for large predators, which at this early stage included a sabre-toothed cat. Initially they stayed in the more fertile valleys and the coastal lowlands where food was easier to find, but by the Middle Stone Age (about 120 000 years ago) they discovered that fire encouraged

the proliferation of geophytes such as watsonias, the bulbs of which were an important food source. Armed with this knowledge, they were able to colonise areas that had previously been inhospitable and moved into the mountains where they occupied rock shelters.

When colder glacial conditions engulfed the fynbos region about 75 000 years ago populations of Middle Stone Age people dwindled significantly, and it was only much later, from about 21 000 years ago, that the human population in the fynbos region began to increase again. These people were hunter-gatherers of the Late Stone Age, and they were using relatively sophisticated stone tools and bows to hunt mainly wildebeest, zebra and eland. They were also starting fires to encourage more palatable growth for their grazing prey. By 14 000 years ago, at the end of the last glacial period or ice age,

2 With their more fertile soils and warmer climates, the lowlands of the fynbos region have borne the brunt of human settlement throughout time. Here, cultivated land on clay-rich soils nestles beneath the peaks and infertile slopes of sandstone mountains which, even to this day, have escaped the scars of agriculture.

hunter-gatherers had organised themselves into groups which scoured small areas of land for anything edible. Since they were operating at a level close to the carrying capacity of the environment, some major change in lifestyle was needed if their populations were to increase.

The change came with the introduction of domesticated livestock from north Africa. Domestic sheep arrived about 2000 years ago and cattle some time later, driven by people speaking Khoi-khoi dialects related to the central Kalahari languages spoken by the San. By the time Bartholomeu Dias sailed along the southern coast of the continent in 1488 there were substantial herds of cattle and sheep in the fynbos region. Almost 200 years later, when Jan van Riebeeck landed to found a settlement, an estimated 20 000 head of cattle as well as an undetermined number of sheep were reported to have been

driven to the shores of Table Bay. The sparse coastal grazing could not support this number of animals for long and they were soon moved to new pastures. Indeed, the generally poor grazing of the fynbos region meant that the Khoi-khoi were compelled to remain nomadic pastoralists, constantly moving to new grazing sites as the old ones became depleted. These movements imposed a system of rotational grazing on a large scale which probably maintained the quality of natural pasturage on the more fertile lowlands.

At this stage, Bantu-speaking people had not penetrated the fynbos region to any extent. The cultural traditions of the Xhosa were deeply rooted in sedentary agricultural practices – they grew crops such as millet, sorghum and later maize, all of which required summer rainfall, and they reared cattle. The fynbos environment

west of the Sundays River was unsuitable for the cultivation of these crops, and the grassy fynbos could not support permanent populations of cattle. Agriculture in the fynbos region had to await the arrival of the Europeans with their wheat and barley, cereals that are adapted to winter-rainfall conditions. Thus, the eastern border of the fynbos region in the southeastern Cape formed a natural barrier between the nomadic-pastoralist Khoi-khoi and the agro-pastoralist Xhosa. This boundary remained relatively static at about the Sundays River for more than 1000 years.

After the arrival of the Europeans in Table Bay, the activities of the Dutch East India Company began to interfere with the lifestyle of the Khoi-khoi and eventually resulted in their demise. The advent of the newcomers also marked the start of the rapid invasion of fynbos and the conquest

Merino sheep were introduced to the Cape in 1789 and their numbers expanded rapidly, especially after 1840 when the demand increased for wool to supply the mills of Britain's Industrial Revolution. The best grazing for these, and the fat-tailed sheep of the Khoi-Khoi that preceded them, was the renosterveld, originally quite grassy but very quickly degraded by the settled pastoralism of the European invaders. As early as 1773 Carl Peter Thunberg, the

'father of Cape botany', noted the proliferation of the unpalatable renosterbos in the Overberg which the colonists attributed to their sins against God.

by humans of an environment hostile to them. Initially the *trekboere* learned elements of plant and livestock lore from the Khoi-khoi, gleaning their expert knowledge of the timing and location of the best grazing and incorporating it into their European-style farming practices. They too became semi-nomadic pastoralists, spending the summers on the lower mountain slopes and migrating to the coast in winter. However, as more and more land was purchased and enclosed, settled agriculture took over and was to lead to the severe depletion of the natural pastures. Crop plants from Europe that could be grown in a winter-rainfall climate were introduced and arable farming expanded rapidly into the Boland valleys. By the mid-1800s the transformation of renosterveld to pasture and the cultivation of cereals was well advanced, and it accelerated swiftly when mechanised agriculture expanded in the Swartland

and Overberg after the Second World War. Today, more than 95 per cent of the renosterveld has been lost to the plough in these areas.

Technological innovations in agriculture have increased the yield of edible foods a thousandfold compared with the natural sustenance provided by fynbos, and just as the carrying capacity of the land has grown, so too has the human population. Towns and cities have expanded, transforming expanses of indigenous vegetation into paved roads, suburbs and industrial parks. This rapid urbanisation is posing a direct threat to at least 263 plant species.

As the human population in the fynbos region grew and means of transport improved, so more organisms were introduced to the region. The European settlers satisfied many of their needs for food, shelter and an

aesthetically pleasing environment by using alien plants and animals to replace indigenous species that had less direct value. Without these introductions, humans could not have colonised the fynbos, since supplies from the local larder did not meet their needs. Many introduced species fared poorly at the Cape, but some found conditions here much to their liking – so much so that they grew more rapidly and reproduced at much faster rates than they had done in their natural ranges. The unexpected environmental and economic impact made by some of these newcomers created problems that we are grappling with today.

ALIEN ANIMALS

Very few of the many animals that have been introduced to the fynbos region either accidentally or as livestock,

Today the renosterveld in the Overberg and elsewhere has almost entirely been replaced by winter-growing cereals introduced from Europe. We have very little knowledge of the plants and smaller animals that inhabited these rolling clay-rich plains, and it is likely that many are now extinct.

1

2

pets or game can be said to have become invaders. Those which have increased in number and expanded their ranges are confined mainly to areas modified by humans, especially where alien plants have established. Only the Himalayan thar, a goat-like animal that roams Table Mountain, has posed a significant threat to natural communities in recent times. In the early 1970s its heavy browsing caused accelerated soil erosion on a small part of the mountain, but since then a sustained extermination programme has held its numbers in check.

Whereas the relatively pristine tracts of mountain fynbos have remained free of introduced bird species, lowland areas, which have already been transformed by agriculture, alien plant invasions and urbanisation, have suffered greater ecological impact. For example, the European starling competes for nest holes with native bird

species such as the olive woodpecker. There is, however, no clear indication that competition such as this has led to the local extinction of any native species.

Among the invertebrates the two most widespread invaders are the Argentine ant and the white dune snail, whose occurrence is also clearly linked to patterns of human disturbance. The ant in particular has had a detrimental effect on the regeneration of certain fynbos plant species, as has been described in the previous chapter.

Introduced animals have, on the whole, failed to make any great impact on natural fynbos for two main reasons: the shortage of nutrients and the pressure from generalist predators. The nutrient shortage has impeded the spread of grey squirrels, feral pigs, starlings and various invertebrates into fynbos, and where they do occur it is on alien rather than natural vegetation that they feed. Feral pigs,

1 Seventeenth and early eighteenth century Dutch and Huguenot settlers created in the Cape a distinctive building and landscape architecture. Here the elegant homestead of the Boschendal estate near Stellenbosch is girdled by plants imported from Europe – vines, oaks and pines – some of which are now invaders of fynbos. This type of 'europeanised' landscape is now regarded as part of the Cape's cultural legacy.

2 European starlings were introduced to South Africa by Cecil John Rhodes in 1897. He released a small number of them in Cape Town as part of his programme for 'improving' the amenities at the Cape. The starlings soon became established and bred prolifically, rapidly extending their range as their numbers increased. By 1910 they had crossed the Cape Flats and less than 50 years later they had spread throughout the fynbos region.

3

4

5

for example, occur only in plantations of introduced trees or in extensive marshes, and European starlings feed on the seeds of the rooikrans, a native of Australia. Almost all the alien invertebrate herbivores which have successfully invaded the region feed only on introduced plants, and have therefore remained pests of agriculture, forestry and horticulture. In this respect the high levels of secondary compounds in fynbos plants have probably proved to be effective deterrents to introduced invertebrates. The only alien mammal which has successfully invaded fynbos, the Himalayan thar, is pre-adapted by its home environment to a low-quality diet.

Predators, too, have limited the success of alien animals in the region, with leopards, for example, possibly contributing to the failure of feral pigs as invaders. Another reason for the successful invasion of Table Mountain by

Himalayan thars is probably that all large carnivores on the Cape Peninsula had been eliminated before the thars set foot on the mountain.

INVASIVE PLANTS – THE GREEN SCOURGE

The threat posed by invasive alien plants to the survival of fynbos species, and the fynbos environment as a whole, cannot be overstated. Without adequate measures being taken to control this green scourge, many – if not most – fynbos species face certain extinction in the next 50 to 100 years. Since the establishment of the Cape Colony in 1652 the European settlers deliberately set about introducing alien plants, in the first instance to provide fresh produce but also for fuel, shelter and to 'europeanise' the landscape. Most of these foreign plants behaved themselves, dutifully performing important functions on farms

and in parks and gardens. Indeed, much of the prosperity of the fynbos region can be attributed to income generated from plants such as wheat, barley, grape vines, deciduous fruit trees and pines.

Of the many thousands of species that were introduced, only a handful spread and became troublesome weeds. With a few exceptions these were trees and shrubs from regions of the world with similar driving forces to those of fynbos: recurring fires, summer drought and nutrient-poor soils. Thus, fynbos has been invaded by pines from the Mediterranean Basin and California, and by wattles and hakeas from the sandy and summer-dry areas of Australia. Because they are adapted to cope with similar conditions, these species are biologically equipped to overcome the barriers which prevented other species from invading the fynbos 'island'. Moreover, they

---

3 Grey squirrels, originally from North America, arrived in South Africa via England, also as part of Rhodes's scheme to populate the Cape with 'familiar' animals. The squirrels spread rapidly from Cape Town and are now common throughout the Boland as well as on the Cape Peninsula. They depend on alien trees, notably oaks (as shown here) and pines, for food and habitat, and have not invaded natural vegetation.

4 A pair of Himalayan thars, native to Asia, escaped from the Groote Schuur estate on Table Mountain in the late 1930s. They liked conditions on the mountain, increased rapidly, and by the early 1970s occurred in large enough numbers to cause serious soil erosion. Because there are no corridors to other areas with suitable habitat, the thars have not spread from the Cape Peninsula to the mountains beyond the Cape Flats.

5 Most plant invaders in fynbos, like this cluster pine from the Mediterranean, are well suited to cope with the poor soils and recurring fires of the fynbos landscape. For reasons that still puzzle ecologists, there are few fire-adapted trees indigenous to fynbos. The greater height, rooting depth and sheer mass of alien thickets are responsible for their disastrous impacts on fynbos ecosystems: loss of biodiversity, reduction in water yield, increased fire intensity and greater soil erosion.

1

perform better than the indigenous species, for they arrived at the Cape without the predators and pests which control their population sizes in their home territories. Unhindered by seed-eating and leaf-devouring animals and the normal array of pathogenic microbes, populations of the aliens could grow exponentially. Consequently, the aliens have much larger seed stores and better seedling establishment than fynbos species and are thus better equipped to expand their populations after each fire. Other than on true islands (such as Hawaii), there is no place on earth where alien trees have invaded native vegetation to the same extent as they have in the fynbos region.

The detrimental impact of alien plants on fynbos species and ecosystems has been – and still is – enormous. No fewer than 750 fynbos plant species currently face extinction because of the aliens' spread, a scale of threat unparalleled in the world. And, unless drastic steps are taken soon, a cascade of extinctions is inevitable. Quite apart from annihilating individual species, the invaders have totally altered the dynamics of coastal sand dunes, accelerated riverbank erosion, changed fire regimes and reduced the flow of precious water in fynbos streams.

Effects such as these have direct economic costs which are only now being fully understood. For example, alien invasions not only reduce the ecotourism potential of fynbos landscapes, but also deplete the potentially exploitable genetic stock of wildflowers and medicinal plants. Fighting fires is more expensive – and much more dangerous – in alien thickets than in fynbos, which is more accessible and has lower fuel loads. Moreover, certain aliens promote water repellency in fynbos soils. This factor, together with a low to non-existent cover of sprouting (and soil-binding) fynbos plants beneath a canopy of aliens, results in severe soil erosion after fire: in uninvaded fynbos erosion seldom occurs. Perhaps the most important effect of all is that of alien plants on the water yield from mountain catchments, springs and vleis: dense stands of invaders reduce it by as much as 100 per cent in extreme cases. In the water-starved environment of the fynbos lowlands this is a serious matter.

Invaders of the coastal lowlands

When flying low over the coastline of the southwestern and southern Cape one sees, between sprawling coastal resorts, a mass of untidy greenery set against the lighter hues of strandveld and fynbos. This vegetation comprises mainly the invasive Australian wattles known as rooikrans

---

One of the greatest changes to the sandy coast of the fynbos region has been the stabilisation of pristine mobile dunefields – such as this one in the De Hoop Nature Reserve (**1**) – with alien plants, especially the Australian acacia, rooikrans. In this process sand which once fed beaches has become trapped, resulting in the erosion of the shoreline – and a financial headache for many coastal communities. Dune stabilisation using aliens was started on the Cape Flats in the mid-nineteenth century; these plants are now the predominant cover in almost every area that has escaped urbanisation, even in this small nature reserve along the False Bay coast (**2**).

and Port Jackson willow, or simply 'Port Jackson', shrubby trees that dominate the 7600 square kilometres of sandy coastal lowland between Saldanha Bay and Port Elizabeth. Whereas rooikrans thrives on the calcareous coastal dunes and in limestone habitats, Port Jackson is most abundant on acid sands and in wetter sites, and is also inexorably creeping up the lower sandstone slopes of the coastal hills and mountains.

Both species hail from the sandy coastal parts of southwestern Australia where the climate and soils are very similar to those along the fynbos coast. In its home territory rooikrans forms a much smaller shrub than in the Cape, and is confined to the fringes of mobile dunes and the first vegetated dunes above the high-tide mark. Port Jackson grows on acid, swampy sands in Western Australia in conditions strikingly similar to those occurring in parts of the Cape Flats. Like rooikrans, this species seldom achieves in its native habitat the height and healthy stature of Cape specimens.

Originally introduced in about 1850 to stabilise mobile sand dunes on the Cape Flats, Port Jackson and rooikrans were later planted, under the auspices of the Forestry Department, on active dune sands all the way from the west coast sandveld to Algoa Bay. Planting continued until the late 1960s, when both species were used in an attempt to fix the pristine dunes of the Agulhas Plain and beyond. Bags of rooikrans seeds were supplied at no cost to strandveld farmers who wished to propagate the trees for shade and as sand-binders. Ironically, the same farmers or their descendants have now identified these wattles as the principle threat to the growth of wildflowers and restioids used for thatching, as well as to grazing and other agricultural practices along the fynbos coastline.

Rooikrans and Port Jackson are only two out of approximately 900 Australian acacia or wattle species, and among the many that are well adapted to fire. Each year Port Jackson plants produce many thousands of seeds which accumulate in the soil and may persist for decades. Fire stimulates germination, and after a burn literally thousands of seedlings emerge. Since ants disperse the seeds over relatively short distances, invasion progresses as a steady outward movement from established individuals. At the same time clumps of trees grow thicker, in the process suppressing all indigenous species within them. From time to time new nuclei are established when seeds are dispersed by wind or birds. Like most aliens, Port Jackson thrives best in disturbed sites such as abandoned agricultural fields and gravel quarries, and

3 Although named after a cove near Sydney in New South Wales, Port Jackson willow hails from the sandy coastal plains of Western Australia, where the climate and soils are similar to those along the Cape coast. It was introduced to stabilise the sands of the Cape Flats and elsewhere in the fynbos region and is now the most troublesome weed of the lowlands. An orgy of spring blooms brightens the otherwise dull and impoverished thickets of this species.

4 Released from the pressure of indigenous predators and pathogens, a mature Port Jackson willow produces many thousands of seeds each year, several orders of magnitude more than it does in its home territory. The hard-coated seeds accumulate in the soil, germinating mainly after fire when many seedlings emerge, ultimately to form an even denser thicket.

much of its recent spread along roadsides and in building sites originated from seeds lying dormant in quarries. The plants survive even the most intense fires, and rapidly regain their pre-fire stature and reproductive potential.

Rooikrans has a similar biology to Port Jackson, but germination is not entirely dependent on fire. Seedlings can establish in the intervals between fires, mostly under tall, fruit-bearing thicket shrubs such as taaibos and white milkwood which are common in coastal landscapes. Most, however, establish after fire, as illustrated by the 4000 seedlings which were counted under a single mature rooikrans tree two years after a fire in the De Hoop Nature Reserve! Moreover, the seeds, encircled by a fleshy red aril, attract indigenous fruit-eating birds such as sombre bulbuls and redwinged starlings, and thus may be carried considerably longer distances than Port

Jackson seeds. This factor, together with inter-fire seedling establishment, enables rooikrans to invade more rapidly than Port Jackson. However, there are two features of rooikrans which make it easier to control than Port Jackson: it does not sprout after fire, and few seeds persist in the soil for longer than a year.

Both these wattles have had a severe impact on lowland fynbos ecosystems in many different ways. Their tall stature and dense shade eliminates almost all indigenous species, resulting in a sterile monoculture of untidy trees. Their large size also means that their fuel load is greater, so that when they burn the fire is extremely intense and difficult to control. Being both thirsty and deep-rooted, rooikrans and Port Jackson are responsible for drying up valuable wetlands, posing a serious threat to urban settlements which depend on these aquifers for their water

supplies. Also, being legumes, they supplement their nutrition by fixing nitrogen (which partly explains their rapid growth compared with most fynbos species), thereby enriching the soil in which they grow. This increased soil fertility prevents the re-establishment of many fynbos species, even long after the wattles have been cleared.

It can't be denied that Port Jackson and rooikrans do have their uses. They are the foundation of a thriving fuelwood enterprise which, in the Greater Cape Town area, was valued at R27 million in 1992 and provides the only source of income for many destitute people. Unfortunately, harvesting for fuelwood is likely to have little impact on controlling the spread of these aliens. Studies on the Cape Peninsula have shown that the amount of wood removed each year is much less than the annual growth, and it is already saturating the market. The industry is

---

1 Because of their greater fuel loads, alien thickets burn more intensely than fynbos does. Very hot fires such as this one which swept through a rooikrans thicket near Cape Hangklip destroy all soil-borne seeds, thus creating a lifeless surface that is vulnerable to wind and water erosion.

2 Rooikrans seeds are surrounded by a bright red aril, a fleshy substance highly attractive to fruit-eating birds such as this sombre bulbul. The unfortunate consequence of this trait is that seeds of this species are dispersed much further from the parent plant than other wattles, thereby hastening the rate of invasion.

3 An interesting consequence of the spread of alien thickets into the more open fynbos of the Cape coast has been an increase in the numbers of caracal, or *rooikat*. This solitary and secretive predator has benefited from the better cover afforded by the aliens. Coastal landowners attribute the declining numbers of indigenous antelope to increased predation from this animal.

4

5

largely a subsistence and informal one and would have to remain so, as any attempt to manage it in terms of systematic harvesting or fire control would price the product out of the market. The beneficial role of wattles in dune stabilisation is suspect, given that this practice usually creates more problems than it solves, and that indigenous species have proved to be more effective sand-binders. Some farmers extol the virtues of wattles as fodder plants, and rooikrans is regarded as a valuable shade tree in the drier areas of the west coast. However, the advantages of alien plants must be balanced against their costs, and the long-term benefits of alien control definitely outweigh any usefulness that the plants may have in the short term.

Invaders of streams and rivers

Legumes with hard seeds and other species with water-dispersed seeds have invaded the banks of streams and rivers throughout the fynbos region. The most pervasive and destructive of these aliens are the black wattle and blackwood, both indigenous to southeastern Australia; the Port Jackson willow; the stinkbean from southwestern Australia; and sesbania which hails from Argentina and southern Uruguay. Oleander, a native of seasonally dry riverbeds in the Mediterranean Basin, has invaded similar habitats in the drier parts of the fynbos region. The first two species, however, do have some commercial value: the black wattle is used to produce tannin, mainly in Kwazulu-Natal; and blackwood is used as a timber in the production of high-quality furniture in the southern Cape.

Periodic scouring by floods not only disperses seeds of the invaders, but breaks their resistant coats, stimulating germination *en masse*. In this way, many thousands of seedlings appear at the end of the rainy season and

4 Many alien plants are not without their uses. Rooikrans and Port Jackson form the basis of a thriving formal and informal fuelwood industry. In 1992 the firewood and charcoal markets in the Greater Cape Town area consumed 60 000 tonnes of fuelwood of these species, comprising a turnover of R27 million. They are also harvested for subsistence fuel in informal settlements.

5 Black wattle, a native of southeastern Australia, was widely planted in the southwestern Cape as early as the 1850s for its tannin, which is used in the production of leather, and as a source of shelter and wood. This species has now invaded watercourses throughout the fynbos region, where it obstructs the flow of water, especially during flooding. This leads to erosion and river diversion, transforming the watercourse into a diffuse system of shallow streamlets and destroying the indigenous riparian vegetation.

develop into dense stands that obstruct the flow of water, especially during flooding. Because of the obstructions, watercourses are eroded and well-defined rivers are transformed into diffuse systems of shallow streamlets and trickles. The consequent deposition of sterile river sand and the widening of the streambed create ideal surfaces for further expansion of the aliens and, in a continuing cycle, the zone of water-wasting trees is increased.

Mountain invaders

Alien infestation of the mountains affects about 9000 square kilometres of fynbos, mainly on the lower, wetter slopes which adjoin farmland, forestry plantations and other sources of alien plants. The major culprits are pines, hakeas and wattles. Of the pines, the most aggressively invasive species are the cluster pine, the aleppo pine and the Monterey pine. The first two are natives of the

Mediterranean Basin where they grow in fire-prone forests, and the Monterey pine is naturally restricted to a tiny area south of San Francisco in California, although it is now the most widespread forestry tree in the world.

Three hakeas, all Australian members of the protea family, are pest plants in mountain fynbos. Like the pines, as well as many indigenous Proteaceae, these species are serotinous, storing their seeds in woody structures borne on the plant canopy. The most widespread species in fynbos is the silky hakea, a shrub or small tree which, in its native southeastern Australia, grows in the understorey of fire-prone eucalyptus forest on nutrient-poor soils. The other two species, rock hakea and sweet hakea, originate from kwongan, the southwestern Australian vegetation type equivalent to fynbos. Wattles have also invaded mountain fynbos. The chief spoiler of this group is the

long-leaved wattle, native to the coastline of southeastern Australia, but Port Jackson, blackwood and the black wattle are becoming increasingly troublesome too in some mountain areas.

Of the alien species mentioned above, the three most widespread in the mountains are the silky hakea, the cluster pine and the long-leaved wattle, and to understand why they are so successful as invaders it is necessary to look closely at their biology. Dense thickets of silky hakea mar the landscape in most mountain ranges between Cape Town and Port Elizabeth. Unlike many of the other invaders which owe their widespread occurrence in mountain fynbos to large-scale propagation by humans, this prickly shrub has dispersed naturally and rapidly from a few planting sites. Introduced in about 1830 for use as a hedge plant and sand-binder and as a source of fuel, it is

1 It is thought that sesbania arrived in South Africa only about 45 years ago. This attractive legume from Argentina and southern Uruguay, which was widely planted as an ornamental, spread at a phenomenal rate along streams in the fynbos region. By the early 1980s a survey of the rivers on the lowlands of the western Cape showed this species to be present along 64 per cent of the sampled length of rivers.

2 Blackwood, another acacia introduced to South Africa from southeastern Australia almost 150 years ago, was widely planted in the southern Cape forests to supplement the very limited supply of good quality timber from indigenous tree species. Timber of this species now usually makes up more than half the total amount harvested from southern Cape forests every year. Unfortunately blackwood has spread along streambanks and wooded areas in many parts of the

fynbos region where it forms dense thickets that disrupt many features of the invaded ecosystems.

3

4

the major invader of mountain fynbos and now covers almost 4800 square kilometres, or 14 per cent, of this habitat. The secret of its success lies in the huge numbers of seeds that it produces.

The silky hakea seldom achieves its 50-year lifespan. Having thin bark, the plant is easily killed by fire and does not resprout. Fire, however, is essential to its reproduction, for only after the plant has died do its woody cones (also known as follicles) lose moisture and split open, releasing their store of seeds within a few days. The seedlings establish rapidly and the young plants flower for the first time at the age of two years, accumulating viable seeds about one year later. In the absence of specialised seed-eating insects, the silky hakea's seed production in fynbos is prodigious. A dense thicket can contain 9000 shrubs per hectare and, even if each shrub carries only 200 seeds,

after a fire up to 180 seeds are released per square metre. If only one seed out of 200 survives to maturity the population remains static; if any more survive (and they usually do) the population grows at an alarming rate.

Most of the seeds drop to the ground near the adult plant to form dense daughter stands, but some are carried long distances, perhaps even several kilometres, by gusts of wind. These establish isolated colonists which, after the next fire, are in turn surrounded by daughter stands. Thus the spread of silky hakea is achieved in two ways: existing stands become denser and increase in size as more seeds disperse outwards, and satellite populations form when seeds are carried further away. Eventually these populations coalesce to form the continuous stands that cover many Cape mountains.

The cluster pine, introduced to the Cape in about 1680,

3 Some of the impacts of alien plants in the fynbos region are clearly shown in this scene from the mountains above Villiersdorp. Water derived from mountain catchments nearby is stored in the Thee-waterskloof Dam where it supports agriculture on the distant lowlands and whence it is transported to Cape Town to supply a rapidly growing human and industrial demand. Cluster pines, which have probably spread from adjacent plantations, are in the process of

choking this catchment. If left unchecked, these invaders will reduce water yields and destroy ecotourist opportunities, at a great cost to the economy of the Western Cape.
4 Hakeas, Australian members of the Proteaceae, were introduced to the Cape between 1840 and 1860 and planted as ornamentals, hedge plants and for fuelwood. Three species, but especially the silky hakea, have invaded fynbos. Like many fynbos proteas, the

silky hakea is serotinous, storing its nutritious seeds in woody structures termed follicles. These follicles remain closed until the plant dies or (more usually) is killed by fire, when hundreds of winged seeds are released.

was widely planted throughout the fynbos region for timber, shade and shelter. Foresters and hikers also scattered large numbers of seeds in the mountains in a misguided attempt to 'europeanise' the treeless landscape. Because it has been here for so long and has been so widely planted, the cluster pine has invaded most fynbos communities, often forming mixed stands with silky hakea and other alien species. Like the hakea, it begins to produce seeds at an early age and by the time a fire occurs each tree may have a store of several thousand seeds. The entire store of winged seeds is released within a few days of the fire, and although most drop to the ground and germinate close to the parent plant, some are borne considerable distances by the wind to form new populations.

The third of the most widespread aliens in the mountains, the long-leaved wattle, shares features with two other Australian wattles, Port Jackson and rooikrans. However, it is more like the former in that fire is necessary to stimulate its seeds to germinate, and it accumulates a large, viable store of seeds in the soil. The long-leaved wattle's seeds are more attractive to birds than those of Port Jackson, but they are not as brightly advertised as those of the rooikrans, with their red arils. Nor does the wattle enjoy as long a fruiting season as rooikrans. These factors suggest that the species is not adapted primarily for seed dispersal by birds, although redwinged starlings have played an important role in its invasion into mountain fynbos.

MORE PLANT INVADERS?

With the benefit of hindsight, it is possible to identify the biological characteristics of an aggressive plant invader in fynbos and thus produce an 'identikit' for screening other species for their invasive potential. High-risk species are those adapted to recurring fires at intervals of between five and 40 years, and capable of growing in infertile soils in regions which experience summer drought. Species that produce large numbers of easily dispersed, protein-rich seeds which would be eaten by specialist seed predators in their native habitat are also good candidates for invading fynbos. The 'model' invader of fynbos would begin to produce seeds at an early age, preferably between three and five years, so that it could ensure an adequate seed store before the next fire. It would also be a tall shrub or a tree, capable of exploiting soil moisture which is unavailable to the smaller fynbos plants.

The other mediterranean-climate regions of the world, particularly those in Australia, have many hundreds of plants which fit this description. There are many more

1 Silky hakea has invaded about 14 per cent of mountain fynbos. Rates of invasion by this species are very rapid, with each fire in which it is burnt resulting in a massive increase in its population size. The indigenous proteas, such as *Aulax umbellata* and *Leucadendron xanthoconus* growing here in the Klein River Mountains near Stanford, are no match for these marauding invaders.

2

3

4

species of pine, hakea and wattle which could overrun fynbos as effectively, if not more so, than the present complement of invasive plants. Since we are already battling to contain the spread of the aliens that have already invaded fynbos, it is plain that every effort should be made to keep these potential invaders out of the region – we cannot afford to experiment with any introductions which appear even remotely dangerous.

Unfortunately some potential invaders have recently been introduced and are threatening to become pests in the southwestern and southern Cape. One group comprises *Banksia* species which hail from Australia, where they occur in fire-prone shrublands and woodlands with mediterranean-type climates. The genus belongs to the Proteaceae and, like other members of the family, produces wind-dispersed and protein-rich seeds which are stored in woody cones on the plant canopy. In the plants' home territories the seed numbers are kept in check by parrots and weevils, but in the Cape these specific predators do not occur. Many banksias have been introduced to the fynbos region where they are being cultivated, orchard-style, for their magnificent flowers. One species, *Banksia ericifolia*, has started to invade fynbos in the Elim area of the Agulhas Plain. In fynbos eight-year-old plants produce about 16 500 seeds, more than 12 times the number produced by 25-year-old plants in the species' natural range near Sydney!

RESTORING THE BALANCE

The control of invasive shrubs and trees is the largest single task facing the managers of natural areas in the fynbos region. It is a task that was first tackled seriously by officials of Cape Nature Conservation and the Department of Forestry only in the early 1970s, when it was realised that many nature reserves were becoming overrun by aliens, and when attempts were made to eradicate them in mountain catchments by means of prescribed burning. On private land, however, and despite an increasing awareness of the problem, very little is being done to control this scourge. The high cost of clearing the aliens by mechanical means compared to the potential income that could be generated from fynbos veld is a major disincentive for control on privately owned land. Based on labour costs (at 1994 values) of R120 per worker per day (including salaries and overheads), the cost of clearing a dense infestation is about R2500 per hectare. However, the cost of preventing an alien invasion by removing seedlings and occasional individuals amounts to

2 The cluster pine is easily distinguished from other pines in the fynbos by its long, stout, light green needles that are borne in pairs. This pine from the Mediterranean Basin was one of the first tree species to be introduced to the Cape, probably arriving in the 1680s.
3 The seeds of the long-leaved wattle are long-lived; this and its prodigious seed production in the absence of natural enemies results in the accumulation of very large seed banks in the soil under adult trees. The seeds have small elaiosomes that facilitate their dispersal by ants, but they are also dispersed in water and in soil, for example in river sand used for building. Although the seeds lack the fleshy aril which makes rooikrans so attractive to birds, redwinged starlings do eat and disperse some seeds – and this has allowed long-leaved wattles to spread into the mountains.
4 Most of the alien plants that have invaded large areas in fynbos were introduced more than 100 years ago. Many others that have been introduced more recently have the potential to cause as much damage as the current invaders. Alien plants may be present in low numbers for many years before starting to spread. Lest we allow fynbos to become transformed to this kind of alien-choked community – which includes Port Jackson, Spanish broom, cluster pine and feathertop grass – we need to guard against potential new invaders.

a mere R20 per hectare per year. Only ignorance and apathy on behalf of landowners and budget-allocating bureaucrats prevent the large-scale application of optimal maintenance management to control invasive plants in the fynbos region.

Over the years managers of state-owned land have developed excellent skills in the mechanical and chemical control of invasive plants. These depend on an understanding of the biology of the invasive in relation to fire, mechanical removal and chemical treatment. There are many 'tricks of the trade' which work for some species, and in some areas only. However, a general principle is that the control of aliens should begin with lightly infested areas and be integrated into the fire management programme. A combination of alien control and fire management ensures that after a burn systematic follow-up

action is taken to remove seedlings and apply herbicide to the resprouts. The major forms of control are: cut-and-leave, cut-and-burn, burn standing, and chemical control.

The most effective control of invasive pines and hakeas, none of which sprout after fire, is the cut-and-burn method. Mature plants are cut down, stimulating the release of seeds from cones and follicles. Once all the seeds have germinated, the stand is burnt in order to kill all the seedlings. For wattles which do not sprout, such as the long-leaved wattle and rooikrans, the best control methods are cut-and-burn or burn standing. Fire stimulates the germination of soil-stored seeds and subsequent seedlings must be removed, either mechanically or by spraying with chemicals. In very dense stands which have been burnt standing, it is often impossible to get to the seedlings, and in cases such as this cut-and-burn

is the best method. For sprouting wattles such as Port Jackson, black wattle and blackwood, resprouts from adult plants must be treated with chemicals.

Fire is not a realistic option for the integrated control of sesbania and stinkbean since they grow in riverine habitats which seldom burn. Purely mechanical control of these two species is largely ineffective, but research indicates that biological control may prove to be the answer. The cut-and-leave method is more successful where aliens occur amongst vegetation that seldom burns, such as in the mosaic of fynbos and thicket that occurs on coastal dunes. It is particularly effective against rooikrans, the seeds of which decay rapidly in the soil. However, follow-up action is essential in order to ensure that all newly established plants are removed before they begin to produce seeds.

Although mechanical clearing of dense stands of alien trees and shrubs in fynbos is very expensive it is, in many cases, the only practical way to remove these thickets. The first stage of clearing is carried out about a year before a scheduled burn. Most seedlings of serotinous invaders are killed by the fire, and seedlings of plants which store their seeds in the soil must be manually or chemically controlled. Regular follow-up operations are required to remove any seedlings missed in the first removal, and those that establish between fires.

Considerable progress has been made in restoring fynbos to invaded sites throughout the region. Silky hakea and cluster pine have been cleared from many thousands of hectares in the mountains. Pines and other invasives have been removed from Table Mountain, and spectacular progress has been made in clearing wattles and other species from the Cape of Good Hope Nature Reserve on the Cape Peninsula. Even in sites that had been densely infested with aliens, some form of fynbos, albeit poor in species, has re-established. Yet this progress has been achieved at great cost to the management authorities, and in recent years budgets have shrunk in real terms, with less money available for a problem that is increasing exponentially in terms of both spatial scale and funding requirements. Despite what has been achieved, it is not being alarmist to say that the battle against alien invasive

plants in the fynbos region is being lost, and hopelessly so. The financial implications of this ecological disaster are profound.

Firstly, the mechanical and chemical war against aliens must be sustained at all cost. Initial efforts need to concentrate on the relatively cheap option of preventative management: alien-free areas must be kept free of aliens. Secondly, the biological war against aliens must be stepped up. South Africa is a world leader in research on the biocontrol of invasive organisms, and scientists have established that the application of biocontrol is relatively straightforward. Introduce, from the home country, specialised pest organisms which keep the population of the invader under control in its native habitat; keep these pests in quarantine and conduct trials to ensure they do not attack closely related plants indigenous to the host

country (for example, South African acacias in the case of biocontrol agents for Australian wattles); then release them and monitor their impact on the invasives. There have been some spectacular biocontrol successes against invasive plants in the fynbos region.

Perhaps the most successful (and certainly the most conspicuous) biocontrol programme has been on the long-leaved wattle. The snout beetle *Melanterius ventralis* and the bud-galling wasp *Trichilogaster acaciaelongifoliae* were introduced from Australia and, after the mandatory period of quarantine, were released: the wasp in 1982 and 1983 at 120 sites throughout the wattle's range in southern Africa (most of them in the fynbos region), and.the beetle in 1985 at 12 sites in the southwestern Cape. The wasp induces bright yellow-red galls on the flowering stems, thus reducing seed production to very

It is feasible to restore invaded landscapes to a state reminiscent of their pristine glory. This is especially true of hakea-invaded sites where spectacular success has been achieved in some mountain catchments. In the Outeniqua Mountains fynbos has returned after the removal of impenetrable thickets of silky hakea.

low levels, while the snout beetle attacks any unripe seeds that do form. Working in tandem these two agents reduce seed production (and therefore seed stores in the soil) by 99 per cent. Eventually the plants are weighed down by a mass of galls which cause branches to be stripped ungraciously, and they die. The two agents have spread very rapidly through the fynbos region, and almost every long-leaved wattle has succumbed to their attack, or is about to.

Biocontrol also holds great promise for reducing the invasive potential of silky hakea and preventing re-infestation of cleared areas. Research into the natural insect enemies of the species in Australia revealed several potential biocontrol agents. Three were eventually released after careful host-specificity tests, the most successful of which has been the weevil *Erytenna consputa*. About

8000 adult weevils were released in small groups at more than 100 sites in the fynbos between 1971 and 1981, and colonies established at 80 of them. The weevils can destroy more than 80 per cent of the annual seed production, and in conjunction with a leaf weevil and a seed moth, are contributing to the control of silky hakea. A pathogenic fungus, *Colletotrichum gloeosporioides*, which is thought to be indigenous to South Africa, also plays a role by killing adult plants and seedlings. Silky hakea mortality due to this fungus was first noted in the late 1960s and is now evident throughout its range in fynbos. Large numbers of shrubs are killed by the fungus but large-scale dieback occurs only in scattered localities. Spore suspensions of the fungus were distributed by firing coated shotgun pellets into dense thickets and by spraying from helicopters. Symptoms are now evident in

virtually all silky hakea stands but dieback is sporadic, making it difficult to incorporate this pathogen into integrated control strategies. The fungus nevertheless forms a valuable supplementary control agent, and methods are still being sought to improve its contribution to the war against silky hakea.

Attempts are also being made to curb the spread of sesbania by means of biocontrol. In this case three snout beetles have been introduced, each of which attacks different parts of the plant and together reduce its vigour. One, *Trichapion lativentre*, was released in the 1970s; the adults feed on the leaves, flowers and young pods while the larvae develop in the young flower buds. The other two, *Rhyssomatus marginatus* and *Neodiplogrammus quadrivittatus*, were released in 1984; larvae of the former develop in immature pods whereas those of the latter

1 Biological control is undoubtedly the most cost-effective method of curbing the spread of aliens. An indigenous biocontrol agent – a fungus – kills silky hakea, infecting the leaves and stems of the invader and causing a brown discoloration. It seems likely that all alien plants will eventually become colonised by indigenous pests and pathogens and their numbers will be held in check. However, this may take several centuries: in the meantime we need to speed up the process with

introduced biocontrol agents, thereby reducing harmful impacts in the short to medium term.
2 In 1982 a pteromalid wasp was released in southern Africa for the biological control of the long-leaved wattle. The immature wasps develop within the flower buds and induce the plant to produce characteristic globular swellings (galls) instead of normal flowers and fruits.
3 The biological control of sesbania has been achieved by means of

three species of snout beetle. The adults of all three species feed on the growing stems and leaves, while the immature stages of each species destroys a different part of the plant. The larvae of *Neodiplogrammus quadrivittatus* (shown here) bore through mature branches and stems. In combination the three beetle species have reduced the density of many infestations of sesbania and have arrested the spread of the weed.

bore through mature branches and stems. It is this kind of multi-pronged attack that holds great promise for reducing the threats posed by invasive alien trees and shrubs in fynbos.

A recent and unusual biocontrol agent is the gall rust *Uromycladium tepperianum*, a fungus introduced from Western Australia to control Port Jackson. It causes galls on the invader, reducing seed production and vigour, until heavily galled plants eventually die. Between 1987 and 1994 Port Jackson plants were inoculated with fungal spores at several hundred sites in the fynbos region, and although the fungus spread slowly at first, it has increased dramatically in recent years.

Research is currently being carried out on the biocontrol of several other invaders. Suitable seed-feeding snout beetles of the genus *Melanterius* have been identified for the control of blackwood, black wattle and stinkbean, and these should be released shortly. Since the first two species have economic value and are planted on a commercial scale, it is necessary to restrict biocontrol to seed predation only. The same restriction applies to rooikrans which is valued as fuelwood, and a suitable seed-eating biocontrol agent for this species is being sought. Contrary to fears that this will threaten the fuelwood industry, a substantial reduction in seed numbers will prevent the post-fire development of impenetrable and thin-stemmed rooikrans thickets which have no commercial use.

Biological control is not a 'quick-fix' solution for the problem of aliens in fynbos. The introduction of each new agent is a time-consuming process, and even when introduced it needs time to become established and reach population levels that will have a noticeable impact on the weed. For effective and long-term control of invasive plants, biocontrol must be integrated with mechanical and other forms of control which, in turn, must form part of a fire management programme. This requires appropriate planning and cost-effective implementation of policies. Biocontrol will never eradicate an invasive species, but it can reduce population levels to such an extent that control measures are no longer a major drain on management budgets. What is clear, however, is that without a commitment to wage war against the aliens, we will lose the fynbos.

4 The peculiar brown swellings that now adorn many Port Jackson trees in fynbos are the fruiting bodies of a fungus which is one of the many natural enemies of Port Jackson in Western Australia. Symptoms of the fungus are becoming increasingly obvious in thickets of Port Jackson where infected plants deteriorate and eventually die.

5 The greatest threat to the fynbos is the relentless march of alien plant invaders across its landscapes and, in the process, the destruction of valuable biodiversity and other ecosystem services such as the supply of clean water. Here, below Constantiaberg on the Cape Peninsula, another fire has stimulated the further spread of aliens which will soon suppress the fynbos in their path. Right now, there is little doubt that the war against aliens is being lost, and hopelessly so. The human inhabitants of the fynbos region must be made aware that their future well-being is inexorably tied to the effective control of these alien invaders.

1

8. EARNING ITS KEEP

What is the value of fynbos? This is a question that is being asked more and more frequently by planners, conservationists and landowners who are having to make decisions on the future of areas of fynbos that are still unspoilt. The decisions they make cannot be based simply on people's aesthetic judgements about fynbos, since these differ enormously and are usually emotionally charged. Instead, they need to consider the monetary value of the goods and services that can be derived from fynbos ecosystems, as well as to weigh up the costs and benefits of different forms of land use. Only if this is done can conservation compete with development on equal terms. To some people placing a monetary value on fynbos may seem offensive, but it should not be considered so. As will be shown in this chapter, looking at fynbos in financial

terms holds the only promise for the long-term conservation of this unique natural asset.

In order to achieve sustainable development, a stock of capital assets no smaller than the present stock must be left for the next generation. In the past only capital that was man-made was considered to have any value; environmental assets were regarded as worthless. Thus South Africa's natural capital, with its great diversity of goods and services, was allowed to become degraded, without consideration being given to any economic value it may have had.

The relatively new and rapidly growing discipline of environmental economics, however, is explicit about placing monetary value on natural as well as man-made capital. Contrary to the fears of many purists that the monetisation of natural habitat can only lead to its exploitation and

1 The sheer beauty of fynbos arouses in most of us a desire to preserve it so that future generations might also enjoy its splendour. How much would we be prepared to pay to ensure the long-term conservation of this lowland landscape near Stanford? What is the value, in monetary terms, of the flora, fauna and ecosystem services (such as water production and tourism opportunities) which this landscape holds? Unless we begin to value fynbos in monetary rather than emotional terms, conservation will struggle to compete with forms of land use that degrade fynbos.

degradation, it is far more likely to provide a boost for conservation.

There are several reasons for this. Firstly, natural habitats provide a wider variety of uses (in terms of food, energy, building materials, cut flowers, water supplies, and recreation and tourism opportunities) than transformed areas do, and these can generate more income. For example, the sustainable harvesting of natural forest products in Malaysia provides 11 times more income per unit area than intensive agriculture does. Secondly, as the area occupied by natural habitat is irreversibly reduced, so the value of the goods and services which flow from these habitats increases. How often do we read now of 'Land for sale: includes valuable fynbos', when only a few decades ago fynbos was regarded as useless? Thirdly, there is still a great deal of uncertainty surrounding the

functions and benefits of natural habitats and biodiversity. The present stock of plant-based drugs, for instance, has been derived from only 90 species, while half a million plant species, including almost all the fynbos ones, remain to be tested. Given the potential economic benefits of fynbos plants, precautionary measures must be taken to protect this genetic stock of information.

Unfortunately, environmental economists have not been very active in the fynbos region and comparisons between the costs and benefits of conservation and those of other forms of land use are not readily available. Nonetheless, there can be no doubt that fynbos can earn its keep as a provider of food, shelter, flowers, recreation and water. Before exploring how it does so, we take a brief look at the state of the fynbos ark – what has been lost and what is left.

THE STATE OF THE ARK

When Europeans first settled at the Cape in the seventeenth century they found an environment which was far from pristine. Since arriving in the fynbos region some 125 000 years ago, humans have, in various ways, had a profound influence on fynbos ecosystems. However, it was only under European settlement that vast tracts of natural landscape were transformed irreversibly into crop monocultures and were invaded by an assortment of alien trees and shrubs. Today more than 95 per cent of the renosterveld of the Swartland and western Overberg has given way to cereals and pastures. About 60 per cent of lowland fynbos has been spared the plough and pavement, but 36 per cent of the remaining habitat is invaded to some extent by alien plants. Holiday resorts continue to encroach on the endemic-rich fynbos on coastal dunes.

2 Coastal resort development is a good example of how poor planning and short-term financial gains have degraded the fynbos-ocean interface, an ecological zone that has, if properly managed, great potential to generate income in an ecologically sustainable way. Unsightly suburban sprawl extends across the coastal fynbos at Pringle Bay below the Kogelberg, in the very heart of the Cape flora.

3 Many lowland habitats in the fynbos region have been degraded or transformed. More than 95 per cent of the renosterveld in the western Overberg, for example, has been destroyed. Only small fragments of indigenous veld remain.

Only in the inaccessible and infertile mountains do large areas of untransformed fynbos remain, and even here alien plants are spreading at an alarming rate, especially in the wetter coastal ranges.

As far as individual species are concerned, many fynbos plants and some animal groups are distinguished by their natural rarity and their small geographical distributions. The combination of these biological features and the extensive loss of natural habitat has resulted in the fynbos region having one of the highest concentrations of Red Data Book species in the world. These species are classified as critically rare, endangered, vulnerable or extinct, and their presence in large numbers serves as a warning to conservationists that remedial action is required. There are a massive 1406 Red Data Book plant species in the fynbos region, 29 of which are classified as

extinct. In the animal sphere, 37 mammals, or 29 per cent of the fynbos total, are Red Data Book species, as are 21 bird species (7 per cent); 17 reptiles (16 per cent); 7 amphibians (18 per cent); 12 freshwater fish (43 per cent); and 54 butterflies (23 per cent). The fynbos ark is shipping a lot of water!

Without doubt the greatest threat to fynbos vegetation is invasion by alien plants, followed by agriculture and urbanisation. The last-mentioned is especially important in the Cape Town area and along the coastal strip. Birds and mammals are threatened mostly by hunting and poisoning, whereas commercial collecting and water pollution are the most serious threats to reptiles and amphibians respectively. Butterflies are especially vulnerable to agriculture and urbanisation which destroy their breeding sites. Alien fish predators such as trout are the

main threat to the freshwater fish of the fynbos region.

How adequately is fynbos conserved? Approximately 19 per cent of the fynbos region (including areas of renosterveld, succulent karoo and afromontane forest adjacent to fynbos) is conserved in 244 nature reserves. Although this may seem quite healthy, the geographical distribution of conserved areas is highly biased: about 95 per cent of conserved land is in the mountains, protecting about 50 per cent of mountain fynbos. The conservation status of renosterveld is dismal, with only 0.6 per cent of its original extent conserved, and for lowland fynbos the situation is only marginally better, with only 4.5 per cent of its original area included in nature reserves. It is estimated that the present configuration of reserves protects about 80 per cent of all fynbos plant species. Research by conservation biologists has identified an optimum network of

Because of its enormous plant biodiversity, high endemism, numerous species that grow in small populations and severe threats to the indigenous flora, fynbos has an extremely high concentration of rare and endangered, or Red Data Book, species. The Greater Cape Town Metropolitan Area has the highest concentration of Red Data Book species in the world. Here 92 species occur on the rapidly urbanising Cape Flats and 171 species, including *Hessea cinnamomea*

(1) and *Staavia dodii* (2), grow on the Peninsula mountain chain. Fynbos also harbours many Red Data Book animal species, including 94 vertebrates and an unspecified number of invertebrates. The exquisite Table Mountain ghost frog (3) is one of the former, clinging to existence in a few isolated populations.

4 The Agulhas Plain, a lowland fynbos area south of Bredasdorp, has great floral wealth and endemism but no adequate reserve network. A relict population of *Leucadendron stelligerum*, one of the approximately 100 plant species endemic to this embattled region, is almost obscured by weedy renosterbos but manages to survive at the roadside.

5

reserves for conserving the remaining species in the smallest possible area. Priority areas for additional fynbos reserves are mainly on the lowlands and include the Cape Flats, the Malmesbury, Hopefield and Piketberg areas of the west coast, the Agulhas Plain southwest of Bredasdorp, the coastal plain south of Riversdale, the coastal strip south of Humansdorp, and the dry fynbos in the Bokkeveld, Gifberg and Witteberg mountains.

Another vital question is whether fynbos reserves are large enough to protect all the component species in the long term. Large areas can support more species than smaller ones firstly because they usually include a greater range of habitats, but also because certain species require a minimum area of habitat to support a critical population size. Below this population size a host of factors reduce the species' chance of long-term survival. We

know very little about the critical population sizes of fynbos plants and animals, but it is reasonable to speculate that the continued fragmentation of once-extensive fynbos habitat into isolated 'islands' will lead to the extinction of many fynbos organisms.

Conservation biologists have used natural experiments to assess the effects of habitat fragmentation on fynbos plant biodiversity. In the Knysna area, fynbos occurs as small 'islands' in a 'sea' of afromontane forest. The surrounding forest acts as a barrier to the dispersal of most fynbos plants and, in this respect, is similar to a plantation, cropland or urban area. It was found that the smallest islands had only one quarter the number of species that occurred in a patch of continuous fynbos, or 'mainland', of a similar size on the nearby Outeniqua Mountains. This island effect disappeared in fynbos

patches of 600 hectares or larger, suggesting that reserves should be at least this size to preserve the full complement of the wet proteoid fynbos of Outeniqualand. Interestingly, the species which were absent from the smaller islands were fire ephemerals and low shrubs – precisely the group which thrives on short fire rotations. The absence of fire in the small fynbos patches, owing to the relatively large perimeter of fire-proof forest, was responsible for the loss of these species. The message here is that small, isolated fynbos reserves should be burnt at regular intervals to maintain their species diversity.

The dependence on recurring fire was confirmed by a study on the Agulhas Plain, where fynbos on limestone outcrops (the 'islands') occurs in a 'sea' of fynbos on acid sand. Unlike the Knysna situation, the 'islands' and the 'sea' here are equally fire-prone. Although outwardly they

5 Today true wilderness experiences in the fynbos region are only possible in the mountains, which have about 50 per cent of their area conserved. Even in the relatively densely populated southern Cape coastal strip it is possible to slip away to ascend Cradock Peak and enjoy this magnificent view to the east along the Outeniquas and beyond to the seemingly endless ranges of the eastern Cape mountains.

1

2

seem similar and harbour the same pollinators and dispersers, these two fynbos communities have entirely different floras. Only on limestone outcrops of less than 15 hectares were significantly fewer species found than in areas of similar size on an adjacent limestone 'mainland'. We do not know whether these small fragments would support viable communities if surrounded by a sea of pesticide-drenched cropland. However, under these circumstances many of the animals responsible for pollinating fynbos flowers and dispersing fynbos seeds would disappear, and the plants dependent on them could well become extinct.

Nonetheless, there does appear to be a case for preserving patches of fynbos less than 15 hectares in extent, provided that an appropriate fire regime is maintained. Such small reserves would protect small populations of

fynbos plants. Many fynbos species are naturally rare, some having total populations of less than 50 individuals. This natural rarity suggests that these species may be immune to factors such as genetic impoverishment which cause extinction in small populations of other organisms, and they may persist indefinitely in small reserves.

At the other end of the scale, there is no doubt that larger mammals require very large reserves in fynbos. As was explained in the chapter 'Where are the animals?', this results from the poor grazing quality of fynbos and, therefore, a very low carrying capacity for herbivores. For example, 30 000 hectares of fynbos is required to support a viable population of about 500 Cape mountain zebra. A family unit could be supported in a reserve of about 300 hectares, provided that individual animals could move, via corridors of natural habitat, to adjacent

1 Ecologists have studied plant biodiversity on naturally isolated fragments of fynbos such as the *eilande* (islands) within the Knysna forest and, shown here, the limestone outcrops within a 'sea' of acid soils on the Agulhas Plain. These studies have demonstrated the likely effects of human-induced fragmentation of fynbos landscapes on loss of biodiversity.

2 The fact that many fynbos plants are naturally rare and restricted not only makes them vulnerable to extinction should their habitats be destroyed, but also suggests that their populations may persist in very small reserves. Fortunately, many of these naturally rare species grow on upper mountain slopes where they are relatively safe. This male *Leucadendron bonum* plant is one of the 50 to 60

individuals of this species that are confined to a few square kilometres on high mountain terrain at Gideonskop, near Ceres.

3

reserves where they could breed with other populations.

In the renosterveld, a more fertile habitat, reserves to support viable populations of larger mammals could be considerably smaller than in fynbos. However, the large-scale transformation of renosterveld and the high cost of land in the habitat mean that reserve expansion there is no longer feasible.

About 20 per cent of reserves in the fynbos region are larger than 10 000 hectares but, with the exception of De Hoop Nature Reserve on the Overberg coast, these are all in the mountains. Indeed, with less than 5 per cent of its area transformed, and the existence of extensive corridors between reserves, the mountains are the only remaining areas suitable for the long-term conservation of larger herbivores and top predators in the fynbos region. Some 40 per cent of fynbos reserves are less than 500 hectares

in extent and 17 per cent are smaller than 50 hectares. Most of these smaller reserves are on the lowlands, and every effort should be made to maintain them as core conservation zones, integrating them with private nature reserves, conservancies and flower farming areas.

A large proportion of the fynbos region, about 80 per cent, is privately owned and encompasses substantial tracts of lowland fynbos, including all the habitats identified as conservation priorities. Small statutory and private nature reserves are scattered haphazardly throughout the region but, because funds are limited, the purchase of land for additional statutory reserves is not a realistic option. Yet the conservation status of this lowland area is critical: the Agulhas Plain, for example, is home to a unique form of dry fynbos, known as Elim fynbos, and harbours 100 plant species which occur nowhere else. Much

of it has been ploughed up and most of the remaining fynbos has been overrun by alien plants. Without intervention, entire habitats and many species will disappear within the next two to three decades. What is to be done?

The solution lies with the landowners themselves. The breakthrough will come when they and the communities which live on the land are persuaded by market forces that fynbos can be an 'engine' for economic growth in an area that is otherwise marginal for agriculture. Thus, the non-arable areas of the fynbos region, which are seen by most as a burden, could represent an opportunity for economic development based on flower farming, ecotourism, farm tourism and even game ranching. If they are to take advantage of such an opportunity, communities would have to organise themselves by developing structures which can co-ordinate marketing and conservation

3 Unlike the situation for many plants, a reserve must be very large – ranging between 100 000 and 1 000 000 hectares – to conserve a minimum viable population of at least 50 breeding pairs of top predators such as black eagles or leopards. The sight of a female black eagle returning to her nest is one that is becoming increasingly rare in the fynbos region.

management. Two models provide the necessary planning principles: conservancies and biosphere reserves.

Conservancies are tracts of land where neighbouring landowners have pooled some of their resources to conserve and manage wildlife on their combined properties. They can also be used to co-ordinate tourism infrastructure such as hiking trails and overnight accommodation. Biosphere reserves are multi-purpose areas in which different forms of land use are practised by the various landowners or authorities. Established to conserve natural resources by using them on a sustainable basis, a typical biosphere reserve will have a core wilderness area which is usually a statutory reserve; a buffer zone which is usually a private reserve; an area for carrying out research; a transitional zone (normally farmland); and a settlement area (villages and developed sites). Some biosphere

reserves include rehabilitation areas where natural habitat is restored, and sites where traditional cultures may operate. Humans, rather than wildlife, are the central focus of biosphere reserves. The important issue is not so much the detail of the planning structures, but that they should emerge from within the affected communities, and that they should improve the economic wellbeing of the entire community.

The fynbos ark is still afloat, but is heading for dangerous waters. Without intervention in the lowlands hundreds of species will become extinct within a few decades, and while the conservation status of the mountains is much better, even here invasive alien plants and creeping agriculture pose a threat. We believe that the underlying cause of fynbos degradation is a lack of appreciation of its economic value, and in the rest of this chapter we

refute the myth that fynbos is an esoteric indulgence which can make little contribution to the economic growth of the southwestern Cape.

FYNBOS PRODUCTS

Food, medicine and shelter

For a quarter of a million years human beings have derived much of their food, fuel and shelter requirements from untransformed fynbos landscapes. Archaeological evidence, historical records and persistent traditions indicate that the Khoi-khoi collected a wide variety of food items including the bulbs, corms and tubers of geophytes, the berries of forest trees and the fruits of *suurvye* (sour figs) and kukumakrankas. But human beings are, after all, omnivorous animals who found the fynbos a rather meagre natural larder, and in order to supplement their vegetarian

1 De Hoop Nature Reserve is the only fynbos conservation area larger than 10 000 hectares on the coastal lowlands. It includes many lowland habitats and preserves numerous limestone and dune fynbos endemics.

2 The threatened coastal lowlands do include some private nature reserves, a few of which are well managed. One of these is Brandfontein on the Agulhas Plain where *Protea compacta* coexists with *Leucospermum truncatulum* and a variety of ericoids and restioids, including many rare and endangered species. Because of the uncertain status of private reserves, there is an urgent need to expand the formal reserve network on the lowlands.

3, 4, 5

6, 7, 8

9

Today the strongly aromatic buchus (*Agathosma* species, mainly *A. betulina* and *A. crenulata*, of the Rutaceae family) are exploited commercially for their essential oils which are used for flavouring jams and ice-creams as well as in perfumery and for medicines. More familiar to many inhabitants of the fynbos region is the use of buchu as a distinctive and pleasing ingredient in a local brandy. Besides the two agathosmas already mentioned, 256 other fynbos members of the Rutaceae contain volatile oils, and it is clear that a systematic chemical exploration of this family could yield many more species of commercial value.

Suurvye, which are the fruits of *Carpobrotus acinaciformis*, *C. deliciosus* and *C. edulis*, are extensively harvested in coastal fynbos, especially between Gansbaai and Mossel Bay. The dried fruits are used to make a deliciously unusual *konfyt*, or jam, and both the raw

diet they lived along the shores of the rich Cape seas or in the fertile inland valleys where they could hunt game.

Although fynbos has yet to yield any medicines of note, it is known that the Khoi-khoi and *trekboere* made extensive use of several hundred fynbos plants for a variety of ailments, and a research programme has been initiated to screen some of them for commercial use. For example, the Khoi-khoi used the dried leaves of buchus for stomach ailments and other aromatic plants such as *Eriocephalus* and *Salvia* species for respiratory ills, while the *trekboere* treated coughs and other chest complaints with the *bossiestroop* they made from the nectar of *Protea repens*. The Khoi-khoi had another use for the dried leaves of buchu; they mixed them with sheep fat and anointed their bodies with the concoction, perhaps as a repellent against biting insects.

3 Fynbos plants have yielded a wide array of products for human use. The waboom, or wagon tree, was widely used by the Dutch settlers at the Cape for, amongst other purposes, making felloes, the pieces of wood which form the rim of a wagon-wheel. The wood was also used to make furniture; the bark was used for tanning leather; and ink was made from the crushed leaves. Few large specimens, such as this one growing in the Cederberg, can be found today.

4 From Khoi-khoi times to the present, there is an unbroken tradition of the human use of aromatic buchu leaves. Today most buchu is no longer harvested from the veld but grown on a commercial scale. One hectare of cultivation can yield 6 tonnes of fresh buchu leaves which, when dried, have a value of between R1800 and R2500 per tonne. Buchu oil is distilled locally from the fresh leaves and stems, with about 100 tonnes of plant material yielding 1 tonne of oil.

The Khoi-khoi and *trekboere* made extensive use of fynbos plants to treat a variety of ailments. The red-flowered *Sutherlandia frutescens* (**5**) was used to treat anaemia, and the aromatic leaves of *Salvia africana-lutea* (**6**) provided relief from respiratory ailments.

Edible parts of fynbos plants which provided food for the San and Khoi-khoi include the fruits of *Carpobrotus quadrifidus* (**7**), the berries of the *skilpadbessie* (**8**), and the corms of *Watsonia humilis* (**9**).

1

2

product and the jam are available commercially. Fynbos also yields a distinctive honey which is sometimes imbued with the aromas of buchus and other members of the Rutaceae.

Of all the commercial foodstuffs derived from fynbos, rooibos tea, made from the leaves of *Aspalathus linearis*, is the most successful. It has a distinctive flavour and, being caffeine-free, is relished by health-food enthusiasts. All the original material for cultivation was collected in the Cederberg area and this is where most rooibos tea is grown today. The bushes are planted in clearings in fynbos and the leaves are harvested for three or four years before the plants die. The 15 000 hectares under cultivation yielded a crop of 3.3 million kilograms in 1993, and of this about 18 per cent was exported, generating foreign exchange earnings of R7.5 million. In the period 1988 to

1993 the local market grew by 24 per cent, while the export market more than doubled. Interestingly, attempts to grow rooibos outside its natural range have failed, possibly because foreign soils lack the particular strain of *Rhizobium*, a nitrogen-fixing bacterium, with which the plant forms a mutualistic relationship.

Another fynbos tea favoured by the health-conscious is honeybush tea, since it contains little, if any, caffeine and has a much lower tannin content than oriental teas. It is made from the leaves of at least nine of the 20 species of *Cyclopia*, a member of the pea family which is entirely restricted to the fynbos region.

For its earliest human inhabitants fynbos provided shelter as well as food. Although the Khoi-khoi were nomadic they would often spend extended periods at good grazing sites or at locations along the coast where

1 *Aspalathus linearis*, from which rooibos tea is harvested, is a relatively short-lived member of the pea family which occurs naturally in dry fynbos from Nieuwoudtville in the north, through the northern Cederberg and adjacent sandveld to Ceres and eastwards to the Caledon district. It is extensively cultivated in the Cederberg area and represents a thriving industry for domestic and export markets.

2 The leaves of species of *Cyclopia*, a fynbos genus in the pea family, are used to produce a pleasantly flavoured beverage known as honeybush tea. The species most often used are *C. intermedia* (*bergtee*), *C. sessiliflora* (Heidelberg tea) and, shown here, *C. subternata* (*vleitee*). These teas are currently harvested from the veld, mainly in the southern Cape and the Langkloof near Joubertina, and

are sold on a limited scale. Research is currently being undertaken to evaluate quality and provide guidelines for commercial plantings.

they harvested molluscs and trapped fish in shallow, rocky bays. At some of these sites they constructed rudimentary but ingenious shelters from tall, graceful restios of the genus *Thamnochortus*. The shelters, which the *trekboere* called '*kapstylhuise*', had no walls and resembled in outline modern A-frame homes. The European settlers were quick to appreciate the durability of the restios as roofing material as, depending on the climate, the roof type and the species used, fynbos thatch could last 20 years or more. Until the late 1800s it adorned the roofs of most buildings in the fynbos region, gradually being replaced by other materials which lasted longer and were less of a fire hazard.

The most important thatching reed is *dekriet* (roofing thatch), or Riversdale thatch, which may grow more than 2 metres tall and is confined to deep, sandy, limestone-derived soils along the coastal strip between Albertinia and Cape Agulhas. The plants do not live much longer than 20 years but, provided there is sufficient bare ground in the veld, some new seedlings establish every year, thus maintaining the populations. The plants are also killed by fire and the highest seedling numbers are observed after burns. However, most farmers do not use fire to manage their *dekriet* 'crops', removing instead all tall shrubs (including locally endemic proteoids such as *Leucadendron galpinii* and *Leucospermum praecox*) to create space for seedling establishment. At the height of the demand for *dekriet*, sometime during the last century, it is possible that large areas of the coastal plain were managed in this way. Old harvest sites are still recognisable today along the coast between Cape Agulhas and Albertinia by the unexpected absence of seed-regenerating shrubs as well as by the almost monospecific swards of thatch.

Other *Thamnochortus* species are also harvested for thatch, including *T. erectus*, a shorter and somewhat sprawling cousin of *dekriet* which is referred to as '*wyfieriet*' (wife-thatch) because of its inferior quality. It is occasionally harvested along the southern Cape coast where it grows in association with thicket shrubs on older and more fine-grained sands than *dekriet* does. Along the west coast, from Table Bay to Langebaan, the robust *T. spicigerus* is sometimes harvested, as is the marsh-loving *Chondropetalum tectorum* throughout the fynbos region. Should the market expand, and there is every likelihood that it will, there is great potential for the cultivation of superior strains of *dekriet*. Interestingly, although the species has a narrow habitat tolerance in the wild, it seems capable of growing on a wide range of soil types

3 In recent years there has been a resurgence in the thatching industry, as traditional forms of Cape architecture have become popular again. This renewed interest has stimulated the old Cape craft of thatching which is based mainly on *Thamnochortus insignis* or *dekriet*, a species that grows along the coast between Cape Agulhas and Albertinia. Today the industry is worth more than R10 million annually and, being labour-intensive, it provides many jobs.

4 *Dekriet* is harvested every two to five years in winter, shortly after the wind-dispersed seeds have been released. Harvesting before seed release can have a negative impact on seedling establishment since *dekriet* seeds decay fairly rapidly in the soil.

5 During the last century, when thatch was the principle roofing material for the rapidly growing towns throughout the Cape Colony, scenes such as this must have been commonplace. Evidence of old thatch-managed landscapes can be found along the coast from Cape Agulhas to the Gouritz River.

6 In addition to *dekriet*, several other restioids are harvested for thatch, including *Thamnochortus spicigerus*, a robust species which is common along the west coast. In the West Coast National Park near Langebaan it can be seen growing with the locally endemic *Agathosma thymifolia*.

and in many climatic zones. Numerous individual plants have established along roadsides and near building sites from the seeds of harvested plants.

Flowers galore

The fynbos has long been renowned for its bounty of beautiful flowers. These greatly impressed the early visitors and settlers who started a tradition of exporting fynbos genetic stock to their parent countries. Understandably, the first living specimens to appear in Europe were geophytes, since they could endure the long sea journey. The first horticultural export was *Moraea ciliata* in 1587, followed by *Agapanthus africanus* in 1629 and *Eucomis regia* in 1702. As the fynbos flora became more widely known in Europe, so did the demand grow for its plants as horticultural specialities. Proteaceae from the Cape Colony were very popular in English gardens during

the last century, and ericas too became fashionable, encouraged by Sir Joseph Banks, a well-known patron of the botanical sciences who promoted their cultivation at Kew Gardens. The export of fynbos floral diversity has continued for centuries, yet without accruing much financial gain for the local inhabitants. Only recently has it become commercialised to any extent.

The past 20 years have witnessed substantial growth in the cut- and dried-flower industries in fynbos. Altogether 36 fresh flower and 60 foliage products are airfreighted to western and central Europe, amounting to 2000 tonnes in 1992 and earning foreign exchange of about R30 million. Based mainly on Proteaceae but including foliage lines such as *Brunia*, *Erica* and *Phylica* species, the industry is still in a relatively early stage of development. Some of the crop comes from 300 hectares of Proteaceae

The fynbos has yielded many beautiful cut flowers, especially among the Proteaceae, which are known throughout the world. *Leucospermum reflexum* var. *luteum* (**1**), *L. cordifolium* 'Flamespike' (with grassbird) (**2**) and *Protea compacta* (**3**) are just some of the many popular species that are appreciated worldwide.

4 The long and graceful cone-bearing shoots of *Leucadendron coniferum* are a valuable component of the fynbos dried-flower industry. Excessive harvesting of this species and the destruction of its native habitat by alien plants and urbanisation are seriously threatening its survival.

5

orchards and 200 hectares of concentrated sowings of foliage species, but most is still harvested from the veld. And, although some progress has been made in developing local cultivars of Proteaceae, much more research and development is needed. Many other countries, including Australia, Israel, New Zealand and the United States (especially Hawaii), have made great strides in adding value to fynbos proteas, pincushions and leucadendrons. Dried flowers, too, are marketable, and this industry, based largely on an assortment of everlastings and the cones of proteas and leucadendrons, earned foreign exchange worth R18 million in 1992.

The local market for both fresh and dried flowers adds about R5 million to foreign earnings, making the value of the entire flower industry worth R53 million, at a conservative estimate. The industry also provides a livelihood for more than 20 000 people. With the appropriate scientific support, it could have a bright future, creating wealth and providing employment in an agriculturally marginal area.

Geophytes or bulbs represent another sphere of fynbos which holds great potential for economic exploitation. Compared with the work that has been done in Europe, South African horticulturists have done little to develop fynbos cultivars for local or international markets. There is certainly potential for such development: breeders in the Netherlands have created 136 forms of *Freesia* which earned R300 million at Dutch flower auctions in 1991, and cultivars of *Agapanthus*, *Gladiolus*, *Ixia* and *Nerine* have also been bred overseas. There is great demand for new lines in both Europe and Japan, and the opportunity to satisfy it – and at the same time add value to the rich genetic stock of fynbos geophytes – is too good to miss.

5 Many fynbos plants are exported for their unusual and durable foliage. At Flower Valley Farm, near Stanford, workers pack foliage of *Metalasia*, *Berzelia* and *Phylica* species.

6 The garden 'geraniums' which are cultivated across the globe are all derived from the fynbos *Pelargonium* species. This genus, with 125 species in fynbos, comes in a remarkable diversity of shapes, sizes and colours and, as the colourful *P. tricolor* shows, its horticultural potential is even greater than has been exploited to date.

Genera that show promise for cultivar development include *Babiana*, *Bulbinella*, *Cyrtanthus*, *Geissorhiza*, *Gladiolus*, *Ixia*, *Lachenalia*, *Lapeirousia*, *Nerine*, *Ornithogalum*, *Sparaxis*, *Tritonia* and *Watsonia*.

Other fynbos plants that have proved their worth as horticultural subjects include ericas, which are the basis of a thriving indoor pot-plant industry in Germany, and pelargoniums, the original form of the cultivars now grown throughout Europe under the name 'geraniums'. Local plant breeders are taking their cue from their European colleagues and have recently developed leucospermum cultivars that can be grown as pot plants. Many more species hold great promise in this respect. Indeed, the commercial value of fynbos biodiversity has barely been tapped for the production of superior cultivars for local and export markets.

Some 100 erica cultivars have been derived from only four British species of the genus *Erica*. With no fewer than 526 fynbos ericas which have a wide variety of flower shapes, the potential for horticultural development is immense. Fynbos species that lend themselves to the breeding of cultivars include *E. albens* (**1**), *E. fastigiata* (**2**), *E. mammosa* (**3**) and *E. campanularis* (**4**).

5 The Fynbos Research Unit of the Agricultural Research Council, based at Elsenburg near Stellenbosch, has made considerable progress in developing cultivars from fynbos Proteaceae. *Leucospermum* 'Vlam', for example, has been developed from *L. cordifolium*.

6 The beautiful *Adenandra marginata* holds great promise as a pot plant suitable for export to the Far East.

ECOTOURISM

Ecotourism – or tourism based on ecological resources such as flora, fauna and scenery – is one of the world's fastest growing industries. The United States alone exports about five million ecotourists to different destinations each year and their numbers are expected to increase substantially. In the developing countries, which are blessed with most of the world's biodiversity, the value of ecotourism is rising against other uses of natural habitat. In tropical forested countries such as Costa Rica, Ecuador and Thailand tourism ranks among the top five industries and generates more foreign exchange than timber sales. Closer to home, in Kenya and Zimbabwe wildlife-related tourism is a major source of export earnings.

Ideally, ecotourism should be tourism with responsibility, whereby some of the income derived from it is invested in the natural resources which attracted tourists in the first place. At the same time, the local communities living on or near these resources should benefit directly from ecotourism and the revenue it generates. Thus, by providing social and market-based incentives to conserve natural habitats and biodiversity, ecotourism can become a powerful ally of conservation.

Most ecotourists to South Africa are attracted by the landscapes, fauna and flora of the savannas that evoke for them the 'real' Africa. Although increasing numbers are coming to the southwestern Cape, there is very little promotion of the fynbos region as an ecotourist destination. There are no estimates of the contribution of ecotourism to the regional economy, so it is difficult to identify positive feedback between tourism and conservation. This is a great pity.

The fynbos region represents a sack of uncut diamonds with regard to its ecotourism potential, offering the tourist an enormous diversity of beautiful plants, an unusual fauna, spectacular scenery and a long and varied cultural history. The challenge facing planners and entrepreneurs is to develop an industry based on these raw materials, and one that will generate income in a way that is sustainable both ecologically and economically.

If ecotourism is to provide economic opportunities for local communities, training programmes are needed to educate them in the natural and cultural histories of their areas, and in fundamental aspects of the tourist trade. Once these communities benefit directly from ecological resources, they could become protagonists for conserving them. This is especially important for the embattled lowland fynbos areas which are largely privately owned.

Very little work has been done locally on developing suitable cultivars from fynbos bulbs or geophytes. The exquisite flowers of *Aristea biflora* (**7**), *Gladiolus carmineus* (**8**), *Babiana villosa* (**9**) and *Nerine humilis* (**10**) give some idea of the potential beauty that horticulturalists may achieve by breeding cultivars from species such as these.

By contributing funds for the maintenance of existing reserves and the purchase of new ones, ecotourism could plough back some of the revenue it generates into the ecological resources which attracted the tourists in the first place. At a time when state funds for conservation are shrinking, and will almost certainly shrink further, the income generated by reserves is needed for their management and expansion. This may mean that high-density tourism will have to be promoted in certain reserves in order to subsidise others. For example, the revenue of the Galapagos Islands, which receive as many as 70 000 visitors per year, pays the conservation budget for all of Ecuador. Similarly, Cape Point in the Cape of Good Hope Nature Reserve is a major drawcard in the Cape Peninsula and the income it generates can be used in the battle against alien vegetation.

A concerted effort is needed to promote the fynbos region as an ecotourist destination. After all, there is more to the southwestern Cape than Table Mountain, the winelands and the white sands of Clifton Beach. If properly managed, ecotourism can be an area where fynbos may proudly earn its keep.

COUNTING THE COSTS OF WATER

As we have indicated, there are a number of direct ways in which fynbos may realise its earning potential. Yet the most important of all – the greatest economic service provided by fynbos – is not at all obvious, even to those whose livelihood depends directly on it. That service is a steady and reliable supply of the most precious of commodities – water. In this sense, the conservation of fynbos is crucial for the economic survival of the southwestern Cape.

The fynbos region has enormous tourist potential. Just imagine the delight of a heath enthusiast nurtured on the handful of European ericas discovering, with the aid of an excellent guide book, many of the 100 or so ericas on the Cape Peninsula alone (1). The region has an excellent network of hiking trails which traverse the wilderness areas, nature reserves, catchment areas and farmlands from the Cederberg to the Suurberg, and from the coast to the highest mountains. There are places, such as De Hoop Nature Reserve (2) where it is possible to combine fynbos forays with whale-watching, birdwatching, game-viewing and the sheer exhilaration induced by the uncluttered space of wilderness landscapes.

What exactly is the link between fynbos and water? The answer is quite simple. Every year the winter rains deposit much greater volumes of moisture on the Cape mountains than on the lowlands where agricultural and industrial development is centred. The sandy, porous mountain soils act like a massive sponge, soaking up rain in the cool months and releasing it slowly throughout the dry summer – to thirsty humans and water-demanding industry, fruit trees and lawns.

Fynbos provides an ideal plant cover for ensuring a good supply of clean water from mountain catchments. Firstly, the high density of sprouting restioids and shrubs effectively bind the soil after fires, thereby reducing erosion to almost trivial levels. Secondly, fynbos uses a relatively small amount of the available moisture in the soil, even during the dry summer months. This means that

in any particular mountain catchment much of the incoming rainfall is discharged as runoff into streams and rivers. Even in the driest areas, such as the Little Karoo, the steady supply of water from the adjacent fynbos mountains permits substantial irrigation farming.

The alarming factor is that this excellent service can be disrupted so easily. When fynbos catchments are invaded by alien plants such as acacias, eucalypts, hakeas and pines, runoff can be reduced by between 30 and 70 per cent, depending on rainfall and the age of the alien vegetation. The aliens, being taller and having more extensive roots than fynbos species, extract more water from the soil. In summer, when water needs are greatest, runoff in invaded catchments may be reduced by 100 per cent, converting perennial streams to seasonal ones, with disastrous results for aquatic life. The water used by the thirsty

invaders costs the economy of the fynbos region dearly.

A shortage of water is the most important factor limiting future economic development in the fynbos region. The rapid growth in the human population throughout the area and the increasing demands of agriculture and industry have spawned proposals to secure adequate water supplies that range from desalination plants to huge dams in the mountains, including one in the Kogelberg. Yet little public attention has been given to the role of optimal catchment management (which includes clearing and preventing alien invasions) as a means of securing sustainable water supplies. Indeed, the budget for catchment management in the Boland mountains between Kogelberg and Tulbagh, which supply almost all the water for the Greater Cape Town Metropolitan Area, is 40 per cent below optimum. In vitally important areas

There are many other destinations in the fynbos region that the ecotourist is bound to find intriguing, including the fynbos, forest and wild coastline of the Tsitsikamma National Park (**3**) and, in contrast, the rocky wilderness of the Cederberg (**4**).

5 At between 35 and 55 per cent of the rainfall, runoff in fynbos catchments is amongst the highest among similar climatic areas in the world. Even in very dry areas, such as the Little Karoo, the steady supply of water from adjacent fynbos mountains permits substantial irrigation farming. Fynbos ecologists have established that more than 90 per cent of the water supply required for the Greater Cape Town Metropolitan Area is derived from the mountains

surrounding the Berg and Breede rivers. Streams such as this must be regarded not only as an integral part of the fynbos ecosystem, but also as having calculable monetary value.

such as these the battle against alien plants is being lost.

Fortunately, fynbos ecologists have not been idle, and have prepared a cost-benefit analysis of optimal catchment management for securing water supplies for the fynbos region. Their findings show that the protected mountain catchments, comprising a mere 16 per cent of the area between Clanwilliam and Port Elizabeth, yield about 60 per cent of this area's mean annual runoff – or a massive 4300 million cubic metres of water. In some parts of the region the contribution of mountain catchments is even greater: in the southwestern Cape between the Berg and Breede rivers these catchments yield two-thirds of its water requirements. This water is essential for the sustainable development of the region's economy, providing for the burgeoning populations of urban areas and enabling economic growth through industrial and agricultural development. For all economic activity, fynbos-clad catchments should be viewed as critical natural capital which ensures a water supply vital to the semi-arid and rapidly developing lowlands. It makes sound economic sense, therefore, to put a monetary value on the water service generated from fynbos ecosystems.

Water derived from mountain catchments in the fynbos region generated a gross domestic product of about R55 000 million in 1993. Hydrologists have calculated that if all mountain catchments are invaded by alien trees (as will certainly happen without optimal catchment management), at least 50 per cent of the utilisable water resources for the entire fynbos region will be lost – with disastrous consequences for the local economy. The cost of optimal catchment management is estimated, at 1993 rates, at an average of R20 per hectare per year or, based on the potential loss of runoff, at 1.3 cents per cubic metre of water. However, the cost of clearing existing dense stands of aliens would be 100 times greater than preventative management – a loud and clear warning not to reduce budgets for catchment management!

In terms of securing sustainable supplies of water, catchment management is extremely cost-effective. For example, the maintenance cost of R20 per hectare per year to prevent further alien invasion would represent a mere 0.056 per cent of gross domestic product generated for each cubic metre of water used. Catchment management is also much cheaper than any of the alternative water supply schemes mooted for the fynbos region. Optimal management of the catchments in the Boland mountains around Cape Town would be 187 times less expensive than the operating costs of a desalination

In 1993 South Africa's rapidly expanding deciduous fruit industry, 92 per cent of which is centred in the southwestern Cape, generated a gross export earning of R2105 million. What is not widely appreciated is that the growth of Cape apples, apricots, grapes, peaches, pears and plums is almost entirely dependent on the water that comes from the mountains.

plant. The capital cost for a plant capable of producing a mere 100 million cubic metres of water per year is estimated at R1268 million, or R12.68 per cubic metre of water. Similarly, the capital cost of developing new dams in the catchments around Cape Town is estimated at between R1.50 and R7.00 per cubic metre of water, whereas the capital cost of clearing dense alien stands in the same area would generate additional water supplies at the cost of only R1.20 per cubic metre. This latter value does not include the actual and potential monetary value of alien-free catchments to be derived from ecotourism, wildflower harvesting, reduced fire hazards and the conservation of genetic stock. Taking cognisance of all these figures, there can be little doubt about the cost-effectiveness of water production through the conservation of fynbos catchments in the Cape mountains.

WHITHER FYNBOS?

What is the future of fynbos? There are a number of possible scenarios. In the worst case, continued indifference and apathy regarding the threats to this special region will result in alien plants running rampant and entirely choking the lowlands and moist mountain slopes; fynbos being ploughed up for capital-intensive and specialised agriculture; huge dams being built in the Kogelberg and elsewhere to offset the loss in runoff wasted by thirsty aliens; urban sprawl consuming large areas of species-rich habitat on the fringes of major towns and cities and along the coast; uncontrollable fires periodically raging through thickets of alien plants, destroying infrastructure and threatening human life; tonnes of soil being stripped off the bare mountain slopes after fires to clog up dams with silt and cover roads and houses in a thick blanket of sand; cut-flower species being harvested to extinction without research and development being carried out into adding value to fynbos biodiversity; ecotourists shunning these pitifully degraded landscapes, and thus denying rural communities and conservation authorities a valuable source of income; and lack of funds forcing the closure of many reserves.

Eventually, this degradation of natural habitat has a negative impact on the entire economy. The cost of water becomes prohibitive for certain industries, especially agriculture; unemployment becomes a major problem in the countryside and more and more people move to the cities, which are choked with homeless and jobless people. Science fiction? Perhaps.

To offset this scenario there is a long tradition of caring for fynbos that will not simply disappear. But the battle to

Dams are considered to be one solution to the southwestern Cape's increasing demands for water, and one in the Kogelberg – the heart of the Cape Floral Kingdom – has been proposed. If this valley were to be flooded the loss to the Cape flora would be irreparable. Yet there is a simpler, and far cheaper, alternative: optimal management of the fynbos catchment areas.

conserve this precious resource will not be won on the basis of emotional and spiritual values. Fynbos must earn its keep – its material value will be its saving grace. Moreover, the money generated from the sustainable use of fynbos must be distributed among all the inhabitants of the region – everyone must be aware of, and experience, the benefits of conserving fynbos.

A brighter scenario is that a growing appreciation among the inhabitants of fynbos of its economic and cultural benefits becomes an unstoppable force for its conservation. Catchments are cleared of aliens and developed sensibly for ecotourism; the sustainable harvesting and cultivation of fynbos products provide employment and income for growing numbers of rural people; ecotourists flock to the region, stimulating economies at farm, town and city levels and providing

valuable income for conservation management; the southwestern Cape becomes home to a thriving horticultural industry, exporting value-added fynbos plants all over the world; and biological control relegates most alien plants to the 'innocuous' status. Ultimately fynbos becomes an integral part of most people's lives, and its health and welfare status is seen as a barometer of economic vibrancy and sustainability in the region.

This scenario is not a fantasy. It can be achieved, but some hard decisions have to be made which many purists may find difficult to accept. There will have to be a cost-benefit and long-term approach to problems of natural resource use; and there will have to be many trade-offs. For example, some forms of flower harvesting or cultivation may not be compatible with the conservation of the full complement of species in an area. Similarly,

some areas will have to be sacrificed to generate income for the conservation of others. Remote mountain areas will have to become more accessible to tourists, as will private nature reserves along the fynbos coastline. It will be essential to introduce more biological agents to control the spread of alien plants, and this may threaten a subsistence woodfuel industry – the only source of income for many poor people. However, fynbos-related industries based on thatch and dried flowers may provide greater opportunities for a substantial subsistence economy.

A new era is dawning, and it is one in which the value of natural habitat is no longer taken for granted. There are compelling economic reasons for conserving fynbos. Hopefully, we can look forward to the day when ordinary citizens will be able to look up at the mountains and say, 'That fynbos, it's working for me!'

Serruria florida (**1**), familiar to many as the 'blushing bride', and *Mimetes hottentoticus* (**2**) are exceptionally beautiful plants. Both species are also extremely rare, being restricted to a few populations and, therefore, vulnerable to extinction. 'But', we may ask, 'so what if they become extinct?' The truth is that we would have lost irreplaceable and unique combinations of genes that might have provided the basis for some wonder drug, foodstuff or crop to enrich the lives of

future generations. We have no right to deny our descendants opportunities not only to use fynbos, but also to enjoy its exquisite beauty. **3** We should plan now to ensure that areas such as this, on the Front Face of Table Mountain and immediately above a bustling city, remain intact for future generations. With their extraordinary biodiversity and valuable ecosystem services, these pristine landscapes are our showpieces for sustainable development. Their long-term

conservation will depend on all sectors of society showing an appreciation for the material and spiritual benefits of conserving South Africa's unique floral kingdom.

3

GLOSSARY

Some of the terms listed below have several meanings,
depending on the context in which they are used.
The definitions given relate to the use of the terms in this book.

alpha diversity: The number of species occupying a single habitat.

angiosperm: A flowering plant whose seeds are enclosed within an ovary which ripens to form a fruit. Angiosperms include all grasses and grass-like plants, as well as most shrubs and trees except conifers. Cf. **gymnosperm.**

aril: A usually fleshy and often brightly coloured outgrowth from a seed which attracts animal dispersal agents.

berg wind: A warm dry wind that occurs most often in winter and blows outward from the interior. As a result of it temperatures may rise above 36 °C, temporarily exceeding those of midsummer.

beta diversity: The amount of change in the composition of plant species along a habitat gradient, such as a mountain slope along which soil or rainfall conditions vary.

biocontrol: The use of biological agents (e.g. insects, fungi) to reduce populations of troublesome weeds.

biodiversity: The variety of organisms considered at all levels, from genetic variants belonging to the same species through species, genera, families to higher taxonomic echelons. Also includes the variety of natural communities and ecosystems.

biome: The highest category of natural communities in a particular region, defined on the basis of climate and the composition of major growth forms.

canopy: The leafy portion of a tree or shrub.

colluvium: Mixed deposits of soil material and rock fragments which have accumulated near the base of slopes as a result of gravitational action.

convergent evolution: The development, in response to similar environmental conditions, of two or more organisms or communities with strong superficial resemblances from totally unlike and unrelated ancestors or components.

dioecious: Referring to species which bear male and female flowers on separate plants.

ecosystem: The communities of organisms within particular habitats and the physical conditions (e.g. moisture and nutrient levels) in which they live.

elaiosome: An oily appendage on some seeds which attracts ants and is eaten by them.

endemic: Restricted to a given region; usually used to denote a species, genus or family which is confined to a specific area.

ericoid: Referring to plants which resemble species of the Ericaceae (i.e. small shrubs with minute, rolled-under leaves). One of the characteristic elements of fynbos vegetation. Cf. **proteoid, restioid.**

fire ephemeral: A plant which appears only in the first few years after fire, and thereafter persists as seeds stored in the soil.

fire regime: The characteristic frequency, seasonal occurrence, intensity and size of fires in a particular region.

floral kingdom: A major geographical grouping of plants, identified on the basis of floristic distinctiveness, particularly with regard to the degree of endemism at family and generic level.

fynbos: The characteristic shrubland vegetation of the southwestern and southern Cape of South Africa; it comprises proteoid, ericoid, restioid and geophyte growth forms.

gamma diversity: Diversity differences between similar habitats in widely separated geographic regions (e.g. two peaks of the same mountain range).

genotype: The genetic make-up of an organism, as opposed to its physical appearance.

geophyte: A plant with a fleshy underground structure, such as a bulb, corm, rhizome or tuber.

growth form: The term used to describe the appearance of broadly similar categories of plants such as trees, shrubs or geophytes.

gymnosperm: A plant whose seeds are exposed, as opposed to being confined in an ovary as they are in the more advanced angiosperm. Conifers and cycads, whose seeds develop in cones, are gymnosperms. Cf. **angiosperm.**

habitat: The living space of an organism or community, characterised by its physical or biological properties.

herb: A plant that does not develop woody tissue.

hysteranthy: The condition that exists in some plants (e.g. some *Haemanthus* species) whereby flowers and leaves do not appear at the same time. Cf. **synanthy.**

kwongan: The vegetation of Western Australian which is similar in appearance to fynbos.

lignotuber: The swollen axis of a plant at the base of the stem, usually just below the soil surface, which possesses numerous dormant buds capable of sprouting.

mimicry: The superficial resemblance in form, colour or behaviour of certain plants to others, resulting in some advantage to the mimic.

mycorrhiza: A mutually beneficial relationship between a fungus and a plant root that profits the former by providing shelter and a supply of carbohydrates, and the latter by providing a source of nitrogen.

myrmecochory: Seed dispersal by ants.

neoendemic: An endemic that evolved in fairly recent times and which has many close relatives. Cf. **paleoendemic.**

orographic rainfall: Rain caused by the cooling of moist air as it is forced upward by hills or mountains.

paleoendemic: An endemic that evolved in the distant past and which has few or no close relatives. Cf. **neoendemic.**

perianth: The outer whorls of a flower which protect the reproductive parts during development.

pH: The relative concentration of hydrogen ions in a solution. In a range from 0 to 14, the lower the value, the more acidic a solution, i.e. the more hydrogen ions it contains. A pH value of 7 is neutral, less than 7 is acidic, and more than 7 is alkaline.

plant community: All the plants that live in a particular habitat.

polyphenol: A group of secondary compounds found in some plants.

proteoid: Referring to plants which resemble many species of the Proteaceae (i.e. evergreen shrubs with hard, leathery leaves). One of the characteristic elements of fynbos vegetation. Cf. **ericoid, restioid.**

sclerophyllous: Referring to woody plants which have hard, leathery, evergreen leaves.

secondary compound: A chemical compound that does not function directly in the primary biochemical activities that support growth, development and reproduction, but is used instead for defence. In the case of plants it is used against herbivores.

seed bank: The accumulated store of viable seeds held either on the plant (cf. **serotiny**) or stored in the soil.

seed set: The proportion of flowers on a plant that form viable seeds.

senescence: The deterioration in physical and reproductive capacities of organisms associated with old age.

serotiny: The retention of seeds on the plant for at least a year after maturing, and sometimes until the death of the plant.

speciation: The process by which new species are formed.

stigma: The surface at the tip of the female reproductive unit that receives pollen. It often has short outgrowths or hairs on which pollen is trapped, and may produce a sticky secretion to which grains adhere.

synanthy: The condition that exists in most flowering plants whereby leaves and flowers are present at the same time. Cf. **hysteranthy.**

trekboer: A nomadic grazier moving with his flocks or herds.

vegetation type: A broad classification of vegetation, based mainly on its appearance (i.e. the predominance of certain growth forms in it) and functional characteristics.

FURTHER READING

In writing this book we referred to hundreds of scientific papers, scores of books and popular articles, and consulted many authorities in various fields. It is not possible to cite all our references here. The list that follows contains publications we think may be especially useful to those who are inspired to explore the fynbos in greater detail. In the case of botanical monographs, our choice was subjective: we have listed mainly illustrated publications that are reasonably accessible to readers with little or no botanical training. The two primary texts listed below contain references to much of the ecological research on fynbos carried out up to 1992, and a search for detailed information should start with these two publications.

FYNBOS: PRIMARY SCIENTIFIC TEXTS

Cowling, R.M. (editor). 1992. *The ecology of fynbos: nutrients, fire and diversity.* Oxford University Press, Cape Town.

Van Wilgen, B.W., Richardson, D.M., Kruger, F.J. & Van Hensbergen, H.J. (editors). 1992. *Fire in South African mountain fynbos.* Ecological Studies 93. Springer-Verlag, Berlin.

FYNBOS: POPULAR TEXTS

Fraser, M. & McMahon, L. 1994. *Between two shores: Flora and fauna of the Cape of Good Hope.* David Philip, Cape Town.

Jackson, W.P.U. 1980. *Wild flowers of the Fairest Cape.* Timmins, Cape Town.

Jackson, W.P.U. 1982. *Wild flowers of Table Mountain.* Timmins, Cape Town.

McMahon, L. & Fraser, M. 1988. *A fynbos year.* David Philip, Cape Town.

Moll, G. 1987. *Table Mountain: A natural wonder.* Wildlife Society of Southern Africa, Cape Town.

PLANTS

Balkema, B.P. 1978. *Succulents of South Africa.* Purnell, Cape Town.

Batten, A. & Bokelmann, H. 1966. *Wild flowers of the Eastern Cape Province.* Books of Africa, Cape Town.

Bayer, M.B. 1982. *The new* Haworthia *handbook.* National Botanical Gardens of South Africa, Cape Town.

Bohnen, P. 1986. *Flowering plants of the southern Cape.* Still Bay Trust, Still Bay.

Bond, P. & Goldblatt, P. 1984. Plants of the Cape flora: A descriptive catalogue. *Journal of South African Botany,* supplementary volume 13: 1-455.

Burman, L. & Bean, A. 1985. *Hottentots Holland to Hermanus.* South African Wild Flower Guide 5. Botanical Society of South Africa, Cape Town.

Coates Palgrave, K. 1977. *Trees of southern Africa.* C. Struik, Cape Town.

Court, D. 1981. *Succulent flora of southern Africa.* Balkema, Cape Town.

Duncan, G.D. 1988. *The* Lachenalia *handbook.* National Botanical Gardens, Cape Town.

Delpierre, G.R. & Du Plessis, N.M. 1973. *The winter-growing gladioli of South Africa.* Tafelberg, Cape Town.

De Vos, M. 1972. The genus *Romulea* in South Africa. *Journal of South African Botany,* supplementary volume 9: 1-307.

Du Plessis, N. & Duncan, G. 1989. *Bulbous plants of southern Africa: A guide to their cultivation and propagation.* Tafelberg, Cape Town.

Gledhill, E. 1981. *Eastern Cape veld flowers.* (2nd edition). Department of Nature and Environmental Conservation of the Cape Provincial Administration, Cape Town.

Goldblatt, P. 1986. Moraeas of southern Africa. *Annals of Kirstenbosch Botanical Garden* 14: 1-224.

Goldblatt, P. 1989. The genus *Watsonia. Annals of Kirstenbosch Botanical Garden* 19: 1-148.

Goldblatt, P. 1993. The woody Iridaceae: *Nivenia, Klattia* and *Witsenia.* Timber Press, Portland, Oregon.

Herre, H. 1971. *The genera of the Mesembryanthemaceae.* Tafelberg, Cape Town.

Jeppe, B. 1974. *South African aloes.* (2nd edition). Purnell, Cape Town.

Kidd, Mary Maytham. 1983. *Cape Peninsula.* South African Wild Flower Guide 3. Botanical Society of South Africa, Cape Town.

Le Roux, A. & Schelpe, E.A.C.L.E. 1988. *Namaqualand.* South African Wild Flower Guide 1. Botanical Society of South Africa.

Lewis, G.J. 1959. The genus *Babiana. Journal of South African Botany,* supplementary volume 3: 1-149.

Lewis, G.J., Obermeyer, A.A. & Barnard, T.T. 1972. *Gladiolus:* A revision of the South African species. *Journal of South African Botany,* supplementary volume 10: 1-316.

Low, A.B. & Scott, L.B. 1983. *Flowering plants of the Cape Flats Nature Reserve: An illustrated leaf key.* University of the Western Cape, Bellville.

Mason, H. & Du Plessis, E. 1972. *Western Cape sandveld flowers.* Struik, Cape Town.

Moll, E.J. & Scott, L. 1981. *Trees and shrubs of the Cape Peninsula.* Eco-lab Trust Fund, Botany Department, University of Cape Town.

Moriarty, A. 1982. *Outeniqua, Tsitsikamma & eastern Little Karoo.* South African Wild Flower Guide 2. Botanical Society of South Africa, Cape Town.

Rourke, J.P. 1980. *The proteas of southern Africa.* Purnell, Cape Town.

Salter, T.M. 1944. The genus *Oxalis* in South Africa: A taxonomic revision. *Journal of South African Botany,* supplementary volume 1: 1-355.

Schumann, D. & Kirsten, G. 1992. *Ericas of South Africa.* Fernwood Press, Cape Town.

Snijman, D. 1984. A revision of the genus *Haemanthus* L. (Amaryllidaceae). *Journal of South African Botany,* supplementary volume 12: 1-139.

Stewart, J., Linder, H.P., Schelpe, E.A. & Hall, A.V. 1982. *Wild orchids of southern Africa.* Macmillan, Johannesburg.

Stirton, C.H. (editor). 1978. *Plant invaders: Beautiful but dangerous.* Department of Nature and Environmental Conservation of the Cape Provincial Administration, Cape Town.

Van der Walt, J.J.A. 1977. *Pelargoniums of southern Africa.* Purnell, Cape Town.

Van der Walt, J.J.A. & Vorster, P.J. 1981. *Pelargoniums of southern Africa* (volume 2). Juta, Kenwyn.

Van der Walt, J.J.A. & Vorster, P.J. 1988. Pelargoniums of southern Africa (volume 3). *Annals of Kirstenbosch Botanical Garden* 16: 1-149.

Van Jaarsveld, E.J. 1994. *Gasterias of South Africa.* Fernwood Press, Cape Town.

Visser, J. 1981. *South African parasitic flowering plants.* Juta, Cape Town.

Vogts, M. 1982. *South Africa's Proteaceae: Know them and grow them.* Struik, Cape Town.

ANIMALS

Boycott, R.C. & Borquin, O. 1987. *The South African tortoise book.* Southern Books, Johannesburg.

Branch, B. 1988. *Field guide to the snakes and other reptiles of southern Africa.* Struik, Cape Town.

Branch, B. 1991. *Everyone's guide to snakes of southern Africa.* CNA, Johannesburg.

Frandsen, J. 1982. *Birds of the southwestern Cape.* Sable Publishers, Sloane Park.

Hockey, P.A.R., Underhill, L.G., Neatherway, M. & Ryan, P. 1989. *Atlas of the birds of the southwestern Cape.* Cape Bird Club, Cape Town.

Maclean, G.L. 1993. *Roberts birds of southern Africa.* (6th edition). John Voelcker Bird Book Fund, Cape Town.

Newman, K. 1992. *Newman's birds of southern Africa.* (4th edition). Southern Book Publishers, Halfway House.

Passmore, N.I. & Carruthers, V.C. 1979. *South African frogs.* Witwatersrand University Press, Johannesburg.

Sinclair, I., Hockey, P. & Tarboton, W. 1993. *Sasol birds of southern Africa.* Struik, Cape Town.

Skead, C.J. 1980. *Historical mammal incidence in the Cape Province: The western and northern Cape* (volume 1). Department of Nature and Environmental Conservation of the Cape Provincial Administration, Cape Town.

Skead, C.J. 1987. *Historical mammal incidence in the Cape Province: The eastern half of the Cape Province, including the Ciskei, Transkei and East Griqualand* (volume 2). Chief Directorate Nature and Environmental Conservation of the Cape Provincial Administration, Cape Town.

Skinner, J.D. & Smithers, R.H.N. 1990. *The mammals of the southern African subregion.* University of Pretoria, Pretoria.

Smithers, R.H.N. & Abbott, C. 1986. *Land mammals of southern Africa: A field guide.* Macmillan, Johannesburg.

Stuart, C. & Stuart, T. 1993. *Field guide to the mammals of southern Africa.* (2nd edition). Struik, Cape Town.

INVERTEBRATES

Dickson, C.G.C. & Kroon, D.M. 1978. *Pennington's butterflies of South Africa.* Donker, Johannesburg.

Migdoll, I. 1987. *Field guide to the butterflies of southern Africa.* Struik, Cape Town.

Scholtz, C.H. & Holm, E. 1986. *Insects of southern Africa.* Butterworths, Durban.

Skaife, S.H. 1979. *African insect life.* Struik, Cape Town.

Williams, M. 1994. *Butterflies of southern Africa: A field guide.* Southern Book Publishers, Halfway House.

PERIODICALS

Africa – Environment & Wildlife. Published by Black Eagle Publishing.

African Wildlife. Published by the Wildlife Society of Southern Africa.

Veld & Flora. Published by the Botanical Society of South Africa.

INDEX

Page numbers in italic refer to photographs.

LIST OF SUBSCRIBERS

ABC BOOKSHOP
EVELINE ABENDANON
JOY ABRAHAMS
STANLEY P. ABRAMSON
D.J.J. ACKERMANN
J.J. ACKERMANN
JOAN ACKROYD
PETER ADAMS
MR & MRS R.H. AITCHISON
IVONNE & OSWALD ALBERS
M. ALBERTS
BRIAN & MARIANNE
 ALEXANDER
W.G. ALEXANDER
GRAHAM M. ALLIN
DR PETRO ALLISON
DAVID & ANN ALSTON
H.M. ANDERSON
MRS J.D. ANDERSON
LIZ & JUMBO ANDERSON
X.G.K. ANDERSON
JOAN ANDRAG
MARY ANDREW
VINCENT ANDRIJICH
PHILLIP & DOREEN ANTROBUS
ANYSBERG NATURE RESERVE
PETER APPS
R.R. ARNDT
CHRIS & RIKKI ARNOLD
MARION ARNOLD
ELIZABETH ASHTON
PETER J. ASHTON
BRIAN ASKEW
ROELF & JILL ATTWELL
HENRY ELVEY AUSTEN
PAULINE AUSTIN

KOSTA BABICH
PAOLETTA BAKER
LINDA LOU BALDIE
MARIJKE & KEN BALL
LOUIS BANK
WINIFRED BARBER
PROF D.E. BARCLAY
NIGEL P. BARKER
ALEX A. BARRELL
DON BARRELL
SHARA & MR & MRS F.J.
 BARRELL
MR ALAN BARRETT
CHARLES RICHARD BARRETT
M. & A. BARRY
BRIAN W. BATCHELOR
DUNCAN BATES, EAGLES REST
 FARM, CAPE POINT
DAVID & CATHY BATH
AIDAN BEARD
YVONNE BECKER
EDWARD BEESLEY, ILLOVO
 BEACH
WILF & PAT BEINEKE
S.M. BELL-CROSS
BERGFLORA CC
GEORGE & JANE BERTRAM
D.J.P. BESTER
ELSA BEUKES
PROF GERHARD & ISOLDE
 BEUKES
J.C. BEVAN

JOHN R. BLACKMAN
HILTON BLAKE
PETER & JILL BLIGNAUT
ANTHONY G. BLOOMER
GUDRUN BOEMER
JEREMY BOLTON
W. BOND
PETER & BRENDA BORCHERT
PHILKE BORGELT
IN MEMORY OF CHRIS & LINDA
 BÖSENBERG
DIGBY S. BOSWELL
RUARGH & ZELDA BOTMA
C. BOUCHER
PAUL & RACHAEL BOWER
EDNA & FRANK BRADLOW
JACK BRAGG
M. BRAND
DR C.M. BRASPENNING
HARRY BRAUN
SADIE BRAUN
SIEGMAR-W. BRECKLE,
 GERMANY
ROSEMARY BRETTELL
MAIRI P. BRIMBLE
J.K. BRINCKMAN
MARIE BRINK
DAVID BRISTOW
MR GERT NICOLAAS BRITS
M. BRITS
JIM GERARD PAUL
 BROEKHUYSEN
DR C. BRUSCHI
JENNIFER BRYCE
NEVILLE & BARBARA BUCKE
E.W. BUHR
C.J. BURGERS
ROB & WENDY BURNETT
MR & MRS I.E. BUTLER

J.M. CADDICK
CALEDON FYNBOS KWEKERY
MR N.A.D. CAMPBELL
CAPE NATURE CONSERVATION
CAPE PLANT PROPAGATION
 LABORATORY (PTY) LTD
CAPRI VILLAGE
MRS S.W. CAROLINE
JOHN CARSON
MARGOT & DAWIE
 CHAMBERLAIN
WILLIE & MARY CHAMBERS
ALAN & JENNY CHANNING
HOWARD & ROS CHEETHAM
P.J. CILLIÉ
GLENDA CLEAVER
CHRISTO CLOETE
MEG COATES PALGRAVE
PETER & SALLY COBBOLD
CORA COETZEE
JOHANN & STEPH COETZEE
M.J.R. COETZEE
TERTIUS COETZEE
LOU & CHRISTA COETZER
FARREL COHEN
TREVOR COLEMAN
IVAN & CARMEN COLL
JEAN COLLIER
L. COMPTON-JAMES

LEON CONRADIE
PIETRO CORGATELLI
ALAN CORTIE
J.L. COUPER
DR GRAHAM COUPLAND
CRABTREE CONSERVATION
 INVESTMENTS
JOAN CREMEN
LLEWELLYN & NELLIEN CREWE-
 BROWN
R.B.E. CROFT
PIERRE & FRANÇOISE CUÉNOD
PATRICK CULLINAN
DONALD & ROSEMARY CURRIE
ELGIN CURRY

REINE DALTON
MR H.G. DANTU
DR S.K. DANTU
PADDY DAVEY
HERB & ELISSA DAVIES
MICHAEL DAWSON
KIRSTEN DAY
MAUREEN & RICHARD DE BEER
P.J. DE JAGER
MEJ C. DE KOCK
DR JAN DE KOCK
LINDA DE LUCA
D. DE MILANDER
MICHAEL DE NIER
M.C.C. DE ROSEMOND
F.S.E. (FAANS) DE VILLIERS
J.C. (KAY) DE VILLIERS
P.J. DE VILLIERS
DR BERNARD DE WINTER
MAYDA DE WINTER
W.R.J. DEAN
DR RAYMOND C. DEDEYNE
ANNE & GUY DEETLEFS
DEPARTMENT OF PLANT & SOIL
 SCIENCES
NOEL & MARGIE
 DESCROIZILLES
DR J. DHANSAY
LEICESTER DICEY
HENDRIK & COBA DIEDERIKS
R.F. DILLAERTS
TERRY DONNELLY
MRS M.C. DORFLING
SARAH DOUBELL
CHARL PHILIP DU PLESSIS
J.P. DU PLESSIS
MNR J.P. DU PLESSIS
KAREN & JOKO DU PLESSIS
FRANCOIS DU RANDT
CHARL DU TOIT
GYS DU TOIT
PETER R. DUCK
TREVOR N. DUCKHAM
FRIEDA DUCKITT
JOHN DUCKITT
DURBAN PARKS DEPARTMENT

TONY & SHEILA EAGLE
FRITZ G. ECKL
EDGEMEAD HIGH SCHOOL
J.C. & S.E. ELS
PROF T.S. EMSLIE
SCHALK ENGELBRECHT

MR & DR J.D. ENRAGHT-MOONY
PIETER JORDAAN ERASMUS
ROY ERNSTZEN
KAREN ESLER
MIKE & BIDDY EVANS
DIRK R.G. EVERAERT
CHARLES H.B. EVERARD
ELAINE EYRE

JOHN & JUNE FANNIN
JOHN FAURE
PROF P.K. FAURE
JOAN FEEK
J.E. FEELY
S.V. FEELY
DR DAVID FIG
DR & MRS FINKELSTEIN
JOY FINLAY
D.J. FÖLSCHER
FOREST FERNS
R.I. FORRESTER
GREG FORSYTH
MALCOLM FOSTER
ELSJE FOURIE
EUGENE & LALIE FOURIE
MARY FOURIE
MIKE FRASER & LIZ MCMAHON
RENÉE MICHELLE FREEDMAN
GEORG & HANNES FRITZ
M.R. FÜRST

CHRIS GAIGHER & FAMILY
MAUREEN GAISFORD
GAMKA MOUNTAIN NATURE
 RESERVE
THE GARDEN SHOP,
 KIRSTENBOSCH
BRETT T. GARVIE
CLAIRE GEBERS
H.W. GEBERS
KAREN GEERTHSEN
COERT J. GELDENHUYS
COMM U. GERICKE
MARIA HELENA JUDITH
 GERRITS
SARAH K. GESS
ARTHUR H. GIBSON MBE
BARRIE & PAM GIBSON
R.J. GILES
RUSSELL GILLESPIE
MRS LIZ GINN
MRS D.B. GLANVILL
PETER GOLDSCHMIDT
GOOD HOPE NURSERY
L. GORDON
NEALE GORDON
J. GORDON LENNOX
KARIN INGER GOSS
MRS M.A. GOSS
ISTVÁN GOSZTOLA
PROF HANS J. GRAMBOW
DR J.E. GRANGER
SHARON & ADIN GREAVES
M.M. GREEN
ANNE & ANDY GREENING
MARIETTE GREGOR
GRETCHEN & PETE GRENVILLE
DR J.H. GREYLING
ADV & MRS B.M. GRIESEL

MRS ANN GRIFFITHS
BEN GROEN
CAROL GROENEWALD
JULIE GROVÉ
STÉFAN GROVÉ
DR S.M.V. GUSSMANN

DAWN HAGGIE
M. & L. HAIGH
JEAN & ERIC HALL
R.S. HALL
DR JOHN HANKS
DR M.B. HARDY
PROF P.H. HARRISON
HARRY MOLTENO LIBRARY,
 KIRSTENBOSCH
E.M. HARTLEY
JUDITH HAWARDEN
C.A.S. HAYNE
GEOFFREY A. HEDGECOCK
GEOFF & FENELLA HEMM
J. HEMMES
MARTIN G.J. HENDRICKS
H.R. HEPBURN
GLYNN & ANNE HERBER
HERMANUS BOTANICAL
 SOCIETY
BASIL HERSOV
REUBEN HEYDENRYCH
DAVID HICKS
VERONICA HIEMSTRA
ALEX HITCHCOCK
HLH TIMBER PRODUCTS
G.C. HOEHN
B.A. HOFFMANN
ELIZABETH HOGAN
LINDA S. HOLLEY
BARBARA & LEX LISTON &
 JOHN HOLMES
MARŸKE HONIG
DIANA HOOD
J.R.L. HOOG
JEAN HORNE
JIM & ANNE HORTON
TIM & PAULA HOWSE
BISHOP NORMAN HUDSON
CATRIONA HUGO
B.J.E. HUMAN
G.N. HUNT
PAUL HUNT
C.R. HUNTING
L.R. HUNTING
M.S. HUNTING
IAN B. HUNTLEY
ERIKA HUNTLY
DOUG & JANE HUTSON
JOHN HUXTER
M.J. HYDE

INSTITUTE FOR PLANT
 CONSERVATION
PHILIP IVEY

HAROLD & KIKI JACKSON
ELIZABETH C. JAFF
ANTONIE JAGGA
MIMI JANSEN
DR & MRS W.I. JARDINE
D. JEFFERY

DAVID F. JENKINS
J.R. JERMAN
GEOFF JEWELL
JOHANNESBURG BOTANIC
 GARDENS
RALF JOHANNSEN
J.M. JOHNSON
PEGGY JONES
ROSE MARIE JONES
RUSSELL & ELMA JONES
W.J. JOOSTE
INEZ JORDAN
CLIFFIE & PETER JOUBERT
MARTIN JOUBERT
IVOR JOWELL
C.R. JUSTUS

RUDOLF T. KABUTZ
HILLEL MICHAEL KAHN
MR SIDNEY H. KAHN
V. KEIGHTLEY
ALIKI & CLIVE KELLY
R.E.H. KEMP
IAN KENNEDY
GRAHAM KERLEY
GISKIN KESTERTON
OWEN KINAHAN
GEOFF KING
MICHAEL W. KING
MARY KIRKER
KIRSTENBOSCH BOTANIC
 GARDEN
COLIN & LESLEY KITCHENER
KLEIN KAROO NATURE
 CONSERVATION
ALBERT & RITA KLEIN
DICK KLEIN
JEAN & LYDIA KNOTT
H.R. KOK
FRANCI & MARIAAN KRONE
MRS S.M. KRSIC
P. KRUMMECK
CHRIS & VAL KÜHN
MRS U.E. KUUN

ERIC & ISOBYL LA CROIX
GREG LABUSCHAGNE
LADY-FLORA, PROTEA FARM,
 EAST CAPE
DIRK & SANDRA LAMPRECHT
PHILLIP LATEGAN
K.A.S. LATHAM
PETER & SHIRLEY LAWRENCE
DAVID & BIDDY LE MAITRE
NIËL & MAGDA LE ROUX
REINHARD & EMMA LE ROUX
L.E. LEACH
DR HELEN LEIBEL
PROF J. LEMMER
JOHN LENNARD
JONATHAN & CINDY
 LEONTSINIS
JEAN-MARIE & ASTRI LEROY
BILLIE LESLIE
G.G. LESLIE
LETABA ARTS & CRAFTS
PROF O.A.M. LEWIS
SCHALK EN LIZA LIEBENBERG
MR P. LINDENBERG

HILTON & LOUISE LISSACK
IEUAN LLOYD
TOM & MARLENE LLOYD-EVANS
R.E.H. LOCKLEY
LYNTON & IRIS LOCKWOOD-HALL
PROF & MRS M.A. LOOS
PAT LORBER
BETTY LOUW
DAVID JOHN LOUW
PROF & MRS ROY A. LUBKE
G. LL. LUCAS

CHERRIE MACKENZIE
CORAL MACKENZIE
YAKOOB M. MAKDA
DOROTHY E. MALAN
GERHARD & ANTOINETTE
  MALAN
MR & MRS W.L. MALLEY
CHARLES MALTBY
TIAN MANS
THEO MANUEL
LOUIS J. MARAIS
DR S.J. MARAIS
SHEILA MARAIS
DR PAUL EDMOND MARCHAND
MARINA LANDSCAPING
GERHARD EN RYKIE MARITZ
OLGA & BILL MARSAY
ROLAND & ERIKA MARSHALL
CHRIS MARTIN
IAN MARTIN
LINSENT MARTIN
HEATHER K. McBURNIE
IAN McCALL
DAVE, ANNE, ROSS, BRYONY &
  CLAIRE McDONALD
PETER O. McDOUGALL
MR J.A.C. McGREGOR
GEOFF & JILL McILLERON
CANDACE E. McINTOSH
ANTON & HESTER McLACHLAN
MR & MRS R.J.W. McLOUGHLIN
DRS R. & J. McMURRAY
ADV ABRI MEIRING
DICK METCALF
PAMELA MEYER
PHIL & BERTHA MEYER
MARIJKE MIDDELMANN
ROBERT MIDDELMANN
RUTH MIDDELMANN
WALTER MIDDELMANN
DUNCAN MILLER
SUE MILTON
DR O.J. MINNIE
THULEDI NELSON MOLETO
BINGHAM MOLL
S.L. MOORCROFT
V.C. MORAN
PATRICK MORANT
DES MORGAN
ASHLEY MORLEY
MILOU MORLION
J.W. MORRIS
J.H. MORTIMER
DOUG & TERRI MORTON
NIGEL JOHN MUDGE
NIGEL WAYNE MUDGE
RENÉ & ELMARIÉ MULDER
W.O.A. MULLER
RITA MÜLLER-RABE
ELIZABETH MUNDELL

MS M.A. MUNOZ
ANDREW MULLER, ANN,
  ROLAND B.R. & BRUCE S.
  MURPHY
R.M. MURRAY
ROBERT M. MURRAY
JOHN & PENNY MUSTART
P.A. MYBURGH

DR S.A. NANA
EUNICE NAPIER
DR CON NEETHLING
J.H. NEETHLING
BRUCE & CILLA NEL
DR E. CHARLES NELSON
CHRIS & JUDY NEW
MRS L-M. NICHOLLS
D.L. NIELSEN
CHRISTO NIEUWOUDT
GERRIT NIEUWOUDT
NEIL NIGHTINGALE
MRS G.A. NIKSCHTAT
MARILYN & TIM NOAKES
NORTHRIDGE COUNTRY CLUB
DR BARBARA NORTON

M.C. O'DOWD
OAK VALLEY ESTATES (PTY) LTD
N.W. OAKES
T.B. OATLEY
DR T.G. EN MEV M.A.
  OBERHOLZER
FRANCOIS EN ESTELLE
  ODENDAL
CHARLES & JULIE OERTEL
T. OGILVIE THOMPSON
V. OGILVIE THOMPSON
DR F. OJEDA
BETH OLDFIELD
E.G.H. OLIVER
I.D. OLIVER
R.S. OLIVER
DAMION OLIVIER
SARETJIE E. OLIVIER
TONY OLIVIER
WILLIE & SANDRA OLIVIER
ONE STOP BROKERS
SANTA OOSTHUIZEN
JOCK & ROSEMARY ORFORD
  IN MEMORY OF DR NICO
  VAN DER MERWE
MAVIS ORPEN
DR & MRS P.R. OUTEN
CORA & CYRIL OVENS

ELIZABETH PARKER
ANTHONY PARLABEAN
JEFF & BEV PARSLEY
N.G. PATERSON
SEYMOUR PATERSON
MALCOLM LYNN PEARSE
JEFFRY PERLMAN
A.I. PEROLD
DAVE PERSSE
MRS K.M. PETERSEN
PETERSFIELD NURSERIES
B. PFEIL
DAVID PICKERING
KRISTO PIENAAR
ANN PISTOR
FRAN, RICHARD & KATHLEEN
  PITHOUSE

DOROTHY PITMAN
MR J.A. PITOUT
ROSEMARIE PLOGER
MR & MRS PHILIP POHL
RUIDA POOL
PORT ELIZABETH MUSEUM
MISS C.M. POTGIETER
MARK DEVON PRETORIUS
ERNEST PRINGLE
UWE PUTLITZ

YVONNE QUÉNET

PETE & GILL RAAL
DR ADRIAN W.R. RADEMEYER
CHRIS & JILL RAINER-POPE
ASOK RAJH
DAVID & ANNE RATTLE
SUZETTE M. RAYMOND
EVERARD READ
MARK READ
TONY & PAT REBELO
ROB REID
RESEARCH FACILITATION
  SERVICES
FRANÇOIS P. RETIEF
JOAN RETIEF
ANDREW G. RICHARDSON
GAYNOR RICHARDSON
H.F. RICHARDSON
STEPHEN & MARION
  RICHARDSON
CAROLE RICHTER
BERNARD RILEY
PETER & MARIAN RIMINGTON
PIERRE ROBERTS
MICHAEL & MICHÉLE
  ROBERTSON
BASIL & SUE ROBINSON
G.B. ROBINSON
JOHN D. ROBINSON
DR SUE ROBINSON
KARL & ANTOINETTE RODE
ROEDEAN SCHOOL LIBRARY
E. RÖELL, NETHERLANDS
  EMBASSY
ARIANE ROHLOFF
ROODEPOORT CITY LIBRARY
MRS INGRID ROOS
DAVE & UELAH ROSENBERG
ROBERT & PATSY ROSS
NIGEL ROSSOUW
J.P. ROURKE
NEVILLE ROWE
CORNELIUS RUITERS
DR P.S. RUSH
MR & MRS N.B. RUST

LOUW & JOAN SADIE
COLIN & CAROLE SALMON
PETER SALTER
MICHAEL J. SAMWAYS
H.L. SCHAARY
S.H.H. SCHLEMMER
ELISABETH & ERICH
  SCHMOLLGRUBER
MARJONNE CARLA H.M.
  SCHÖNEFELD
CRISPIAN & CHRISTOPHER
  SCHORR
JANINE M. SCHULZ
MICHAEL & KAROLINE SCHURR

WALTER SCHWEGLER
DR MALCOLM J. SCOBLE
DAVE & HELENE SCOTT
G.E.R. SCOTT
MIKE & ANN SCOTT
SEAGRAM SOUTH AFRICA (PTY)
  LTD
NORMAN SEGAL
FREDERICK R. SELLMAN
ROB & ANDREA SEMPLE
SETTLERS AGRICULTURAL
  HIGH SCHOOL
DR EDUARD SEVENSTER
ANDRÉ SHARE
M.T. SHAW
SYLVIA & BERNARD SHULL
WILLIAM T. SIMON
D.M. SIMONS
JANE SIMPSON
HEATHER ELAINE SIZER
DIRK & HEILWIG SKAWRAN
DR C.J. SKEAD
JILL SLINGER
ANSIE & DENNIS SLOTOW
JENNIFER V.V. SLOTOW
JURGENS & RINA SMIT,
  FLOWER VALLEY
W.S. SMIT
C.A. & E.M. SMITH
KEITH & DOROTHY SMITH
MIKE & MAVIS SMITH
DR SYDNEY N. SMITH
BUTCH SMUTS
PETER SMUTS
D.A. SNIJMAN
DR JOHN SONNENBERG
THE SOUTH AFRICAN COLLEGE
  SCHOOL
SOUTHERN CAPE HERBARIUM
MICHELLE & NATALIE
  SOUTHWOOD
I.J.J. SPANGENBERG
NEVILLE SPICER
ARCHIE J. SPROTT
JOHN I. STANSBURY
ROB & CLAIRE STARKE &
  FAMILY
ELIZABETH STEENKAMP
JAN & ANN STEKHOVEN
PETER STEYN
M.G. STRAMROOD
JOHANNES & LEONORE
  STROBOS
B.W. STROEVE
PIETER & PAM STRUIK
MARY L.D. STUBBS
T.M. SUCKLING
DAVID SUSMAN
ERIC & FIONA SUTTON
DEON SMARTENRYK
  SWANEPOEL
PROF & MRS M.B.E. SWEET
H.L.M. SWEETAM

D.H. TAYLOR
HUGH & DULCIE TAYLOR
TECHNICARE (PTY) LTD
COLIN & ANN TEDDER
PADDY TELFORD
COSTAS A. THANOS
JENNETTA TILNEY
JACK & PAT TISSIMAN

RICHARD & JUDITH TODD
M.J.H. TONKING
A.N. TOOLEY
TOWERKOP NATURE RESERVE
PROF E. TRICHAARDT
ROD & FRANCHESCA TRITTON
ALLEN & INGRID TUCKER
LAWRENCE & JOAN TUCKER
MRS JEAN TURCK
BILL & DI TURNER
JOHN & MERYN TURNER
JOE & CINDY TYRRELL

L.G. UNDERHILL
UNIVERSITY OF
  STELLENBOSCH
PROF C.J. UYS

ARCHIE VAN BILJON
ALAN LYNDON VAN COLLER
D.L. VAN COLLER
MISS DIANE VAN DEELEN
BRUCE VAN DER BYL-KNOEFEL
AAT & THEA VAN DER DUSSEN
DOUGLAS VAN DER HORST
DICK & LIZ VAN DER JAGT
M. VAN DER MARK
ANDRÉ EN BIBI VAN DER
  MERWE
JOHANN & MARIÉ VAN DER
  MERWE
HANDRÉ, ANDON, RUANN &
  TRISTAN VAN DER MERWE
MAC VAN DER MERWE
MARNA VAN DER MERWE
THEO VAN DER MERWE
MR & MRS B.I. VAN DER RIET
ANDRIES EN SARIE VAN DER
  WALT
IZAK JOHANNES VAN DER WAT
E.A. VAN DER WESTHUIZEN
H.B. VAN DYK
MADEL VAN DYK
D.H. VAN EEDEN
GERARD VAN EGMOND
ANNE & ERROL VAN GREUNEN
ANDREW VAN HASSELT
BERTY VAN HENSBERGEN
DANIE VAN NIEKERK
JOY VAN NIEUWENHUIZEN
MRS T.A.M. VAN OGTROP
PHILIP & JEAN VAN RENSBURG
M. & M.A. VAN RIJSWIJCK
C.L. VAN ROOYEN
W. VAN RŸSWŸCK
L.H. VAN SCHAIK
PAUL VAN SCHALKWYK
M.C.E. & E.C. VAN SCHOOR
LOUVAIN & JANE VAN VELDEN
A.W. VAN VLAANDEREN
F.A. VAN VUUREN
K.R. VAN VUUREN
YVETTE VAN WIJK
BRIAN & JANE VAN WILGEN
A.E. VAN WYK
DR H.J. VAN WYK
MARIUS & LENETTE VAN WYK
A.P. VAN ZYL
JOHAN VAN ZYL
LAURA VAN ZYL
MR & MRS LOUIS VAN ZYL
MARKUS & MARIA VAROLI

PETER & DIANE VEIT
KIRSTEN, DIRK & CARL VENTER
MEJ S. VERMAAK
W.J. VERMEULEN
AUDREY VILJOEN
JOSUA EN CORRIE VILJOEN
JOZUA EN ANITA VILJOEN
KOBUS & ADELINE VILJOEN
WYNAND & ELIZMA VILJOEN
HENNIE & EMPTY VIVIERS
JANNIE & ANNE LISE VLOK
MIKE & MARIE VLOK
WILLIE & JOAN VLOK
MARTIN VON FINTEL
JAMES R. VOORTMAN
DR & MRS P.J. VORSTER
WAYNE & TRELSS VOS
KEN & LENA VROOM

ERIC WAGENER
CHRISTINE WAKFER
SCHALK & ANITA WALTERS,
  KLEINMOND
NERINE WATSON
ALEX, MERYL, RYAN &
  MATTHEW WEAVER
CYNTHIA WEAVER
JOHN & SUE WEAVER
ALAN WEAVING
MRS ADRIENNE WEDEPOHL
LINDA LEE WEHRLI
ILSE & STEPHAN WENTZEL
DR C.J. WESSELS
LIEZL H. WESSELS
MEV MARIE HELÈNE WESSELS
WESSEL P. WESSELS
ROY & VALERIE WHITE
V.B. WHITEHEAD
FREDA WILKENS
DIANA WILLCOCK
HOFFIE WILLIAMS
HUW & CAROL WILLIAMS
CARLA B. WILLIS
CHRISTOPHER K. WILLIS
DERRIC H. WILSON
JEAN WILSON
JOHN & HOPE WILSON
RICKY & JULIE WILSON
ISOBEL WINDSOR
DR IRMGARD WISS
ARNE & HARALD WITT
ROB & JANET WOOD
ZOË E. WOODCOCK
G.W. WOODLAND
I.C. WOODS
GERALD & HELEN WRIGHT
MICHAEL WRIGHT
PETER & ANN WRIGHTON
DR INA WYKOWSKI
AUBREY & ELIZABETH WYNNE-
  JONES

JOHN YELD
YUKON INTERNATIONAL (PTY)
  LTD

DR C. ZIADY
E. ZILVERENTANT
DR ALLEN ZIMBLER
DR H.G. ZIMMERMAN
MAURICE & THE LATE ATHENE
  ZUNCKEL